Forever Connected

Also by
Bill Winn

The Path to Forever Together

Lessons of Love

Forever Connected:
Keeping your relationship alive after physical death

Bill Winn

Bill Winn
2018

Copyright © 2018 by Bill Winn
Cover Art by: Marnie Winn

All rights reserved. This book or any portion thereof may not be reproduced or used in any manner whatsoever without the express written permission of the publisher except for the use of brief quotations in a book review or scholarly journal.

First Printing: 2018

ISBN: 978-1-7327945-1-1

Publisher: Bill Winn
6930 Nez Perce Road
Darby, MT 59829

www.forever-connected-book.com
www.foreverconnectedbook.com

Dedication

This book is for Marnie. It is a testament to her. It is a testament to her love. It is a testament to her strength. It is a testament to the love that we built together.

For me, Marnie was the epitome of beauty, of love, of goodness, of kindness, of gentleness, of strength, of all that truly matters in this world. So I had to write this book. I had to honor her. I had to write this book as a gift of love to her. I wanted to be able to do something that would allow me to stay absolutely connected to her while bringing a sense of purpose back into my life. I wanted to bring love to the world in honor of Marnie.

I dedicate this book to my beloved. It is the love that you feel in your heart that defines your beloved…. Marnie is forever my beloved.

Table of Contents

Acknowledgement i
Preface iii
Introduction vii
Chapter 1: Death Does Not End Real Love .... - 1 -
    Marnie's Death – a Brief Introduction .... - 5 -
    My Pathway Back Home .... - 6 -
Chapter 2: Why God? .... - 11 -
Chapter 3: Marnie and me. .... - 16 -
Chapter 4: God's role in nurturing and sustaining Marnie and me. ... - 23 -
Chapter 5: God's role in our lives during Marnie's Cancer. .... - 30 -
Chapter 6: Finding my way back to God .... - 43 -
Chapter 7: My Ideas about God and the platform of reason upon which I have built my beliefs and my Faith .... - 45 -
    My Ideas about God .... - 46 -
    The Foundation .... - 47 -
    The Details .... - 52 -
    God: The Source and Substance of our Being .... - 52 -
Chapter 8: Ideas about the Soul .... - 56 -
    The Role of Our Physical Lives in Defining our Souls ...... - 56 -
    Love, the Essential Fabric of the Soul .... - 57 -
    My Personal Bond of Love .... - 58 -
    Suffering: The Unavoidable Reality of Being Human ...... - 61 -
    My Personal Testament to Marnie .... - 62 -
    This applies to you as much as it does to me .... - 64 -
Chapter 9: Ideas about Jesus .... - 67 -

God, Jesus, and Faith .... - 70 -

Chapter 10: My Journey .... - 72 -

    Journal Entries: Insights from My Journey with My Beloved - 75 -

Chapter 11: Nature Experiences as confirmation of the Living Soul - 85 -

Chapter 12: On Faith .... - 103 -

Chapter 13: On Faith and the Death of Marnie's Body – A Personal Discussion with Her .... - 110 -

    Thoughts on the Soul That Came to Me on a Morning Walk .... - 115 -

Chapter 14: On Building Faith – the Groundwork .... - 120 -

Chapter 15: On Building Faith – the Psychological Tools .... - 125 -

    Internal Dialogue and Affirmation .... - 125 -

    Physical Exercise .... - 126 -

    Rituals .... - 127 -

    Music .... - 131 -

    Reading .... - 132 -

    Sharing Your Heart .... - 132 -

    More on Affirmations .... - 134 -

    Imagination .... - 136 -

Chapter 16: A Declaration of Reality .... - 138 -

    Declaration of Reality: my Fundamental Conclusions .... - 139 -

Chapter 17: A Summary of My Keys to Building Faith .... - 145 -

Chapter 18: Grieving .... - 152 -

    My Grieving .... - 155 -

    Living Now .... - 173 -

    Overall Conclusions .... - 176 -

Chapter 19: The Struggle to Heal .... - 178 -

Chapter 20: Transitions	- 197 -
Chapter 21: A Prayer for Faith	- 202 -
A Part of my Prayer	- 202 -
Chapter 22: On Healing	- 205 -
Chapter 23: Living with the Soul of My Beloved	- 223 -
Chapter 24: How Relationship, Nature, Children, and Purpose Can Keep You Connected with Your Beloved	- 236 -
Our Relationship	- 237 -
The Role of Nature	- 239 -
Children	- 242 -
Purpose and Direction	- 244 -
Chapter 25: Dealing with Helpful Suggestions – More Thoughts on God, Faith, and the Afterlife	- 248 -
A Personal God	- 254 -
Chapter 26: On Giving to Your Beloved in the Afterlife	- 266 -
A Talk with Marnie	- 268 -
Conclusions	- 274 -
Chapter 27: Soul Mate -- My Soul's Mate	- 280 -
Chapter 28: Our Never-ending Love Stories	- 286 -
My message to Marnie	- 287 -
Chapter 29: Living now with Marnie's Soul	- 290 -
Chapter 30: A Miracle	- 300 -
Chapter 31: A Final Perspective – Looking Back	- 305 -
Chapter 32: Lessons From Beyond	- 321 -
Afterword	- 326 -

Acknowledgement

In a very real sense I'm here and writing this book because of Janelle (Nellie) Winn. A little more than a week after Marnie's body died, she wrote to me. Here are some of her words:

"I will not pretend I completely understand the pain you are experiencing right now. I will not give you words of promise that the painful thoughts of your love and your life with Marnie will go away. They never will, nor would I hope they would."

"She was amazing. She was love personified. I believe that everyone who met her could feel her joy in living and it made them feel a little lighter just for meeting her."

"Bill, Grampy, Father... I believe with all my soul, heart, mind, and strength that you will see Marnie again.... You and Marnie will always be interlinked, all through the eternities. I believe it deep enough to stake my soul and the souls of my children on it. I know you will wrap your arms around her again. I know you will laugh together again. I know you will make love with her again. I know it, Bill. With all my heart.... Marnie is smiling today and smiles every time you think of her.... Her spirit is still alive, her mind still active, her love pouring out to you, willing you to feel it. I know it. I believe it with everything there is in me."

"I know these teachings to be true: Marnie can hear you. She is watching, waiting, and still loves you. Your heavenly Father hears you too. He weeps with you, sends strength to you, and sees you for the good that you have done. Marnie does too you know. She sees only all the good you have done and continue to do. Any mistakes made are small and superficial in the eyes of someone who loves you for all that you are."   "You cannot give up. That is not who you are, and that is not who Marnie believed you to be. She gave her everything... her love, her time, her energy, even when she had none, she found some somewhere for the children…. I believe she would expect you to carry on that mission."

    Those are just some of the words that Nellie wrote to me. In a very real sense, they helped keep me alive during the first weeks after Marnie's body died. They gave me hope. They gave me direction. They provided a lifeline for me to hang on to as I moved forward into a world without Marnie's body there beside me. They helped provide the strength that made the writing of this book possible.

    I am deeply indebted to Janelle (Nellie) Winn, and will be throughout eternity. Thank you, Nellie.

Preface

Ultimately, this is a book about healing from the physical death of your beloved. Marnie was my beloved. I write about Marnie and my relationship with Marnie to make this story personal and to give examples from our life together and my thinking about her to illustrate my path to healing. I hope that sharing my heart with you will touch yours. I want to bring healing by sharing our story. That way I can feel good about what I'm doing and I can stay connected with Marnie and feel good in living our love, now.

But the truth is that I can't write about Marnie without getting lost in her. She matters more to me than anything in the universe. She is my heart and soul. So there is a chance that I write too much about Marnie. I hope you can forgive me for that if I do. I hope that you can see and understand why I get lost in her and why she matters so much to me. But I don't want that to cause you to lose sight of the message about healing.

There are three other things that I think I need to point out before you move any further through this book.

The first is that I regularly use the word "beloved" to talk about our loved ones whose bodies have died. Marnie was my beloved. She was my beloved wife. But I don't think the word beloved applies only to a spouse. You can lose your beloved mother, or your beloved father, or your beloved son, or your beloved daughter, or your beloved sister, or your beloved brother, or your beloved friend. For me the term "beloved" means someone deeply loved. I believe you are reading this book because of the loss of someone you loved deeply. I write for you and your relationship with your beloved.

The second thing I'd like you to notice is my use of the word "death" throughout this book. I avoid the words "died" or "death" except in specific instances where I think the word death is appropriate. I say instead things like, "When Marnie's _body_ died." Or, "With Marnie's _physical_ death." Or, "With the _death of Marnie's body_." And I attach the word "physically" to virtually every description of Marnie no longer being present "_physically_". I don't' say, in the past tense, "When Marnie was here with me." I say instead, "When Marnie was here with me _physically_."

The words we use shape our thinking. Death of the body, physical death, or physical presence are ultimately the more accurate descriptions and they help shape the attitudes that I hope to build. It's a specific use of words to define a specific view of the world. Our thinking creates our worlds, and our words shape our thinking. So I try to speak and think accurately.

The third thing I think I need to talk with you about is my relationship with Marnie. She meant the world to me. In my eyes, Marnie was an exceptional human being. Throughout the book I talk about how profoundly special I thought she was and our relationship was (and is).

My relationship with Marnie was for me, the most important thing in the universe. For the last 32 years before she died, Marnie was the very center of my universe. We were together 24 hours a day, 7 days a week. And because I'm trying to make my story genuine and personal, I talk from my heart about how I really felt (and feel) about Marnie. I talk in overwhelmingly glowing, positive terms. That's how I genuinely felt (and feel) about her (and us).

It is not my intent, however, to present us as _the_ model of what a relationship should be or of what your relationship should be. As you read along in this book you're going to see that I've gone to some pretty extreme measures to keep my relationship with Marnie fully alive in my heart and in my consciousness. I attempted to paint a picture of the profound depth and intensity of our relationship because I believe it was the nature of that relationship that required those extreme measures to keep our relationship alive on the spiritual level where it lives now.

I want to offer an alternative path to healing in this book. I don't want to make that path seem unapproachable or unattainable because of the way I describe Marnie and me, or because of the extremes that I personally have gone to in keeping my relationship with Marnie alive.

It's not the extremes that I hope you model. It's the thinking process and the tools for building belief that I hope you will examine closely to see if they might fit for you in your life, in your relationship, and in your road to healing. I hope that you will take the essential ideas from the book and adapt them to fit your life and your relationship.

What I hope the extremes demonstrate is that no matter how intense the relationship, you <u>can</u> keep it alive. You can heal.

My sons lost their beloved mother. I certainly don't expect them to be walking two miles every morning and every night, and another three miles at sunset. I don't expect them to exercise and affirm their connection with their mother for two hours every afternoon as I do in maintaining my connection with Marnie.

But if they choose to heal from their loss by following the path that I outline in this book, they do need to establish their own rituals. They need to establish rituals that work for them. They need to maintain the same level of communication with Marnie now that they shared with her when she was physically alive. It is the parameters of their unique relationship with Marnie that they need to nurture and keep alive to heal from the loss of their beloved mother.

That is true for each of you. It is the unique nature, the unique character of the relationship that you shared with your beloved, when your beloved was physically alive, that you need to maintain to heal from the loss of their body.

I hope you will see that if I can do it with Marnie, with all of the extreme intensity, discipline, and determination that has involved, then you can do it with your beloved too.

Introduction

Marnie's body died. After a four year battle with stage 4 breast cancer, Marnie, my wife of 43 years died in August of 2016. Marnie was my heart. She was and is my soul's mate.

Some family members, some caring friends, and books that I read on grief told me that though I had to fully grieve her loss, with time, I would heal. And to heal I would need to move on from Marnie. They told me that ultimately I would need to move her from presence into memory.

Some religious family members and friends told me that I needed to find faith in Jesus. They told me that Marnie had found her ultimate happiness with Jesus in heaven. She no longer needed me. I needed to believe in Jesus too, and move on into the rest of my life with Jesus as my lord and savior. Then eventually, when I died, I would be happy in heaven with God and with Jesus, as Marnie is. Although that feedback was given with the best of intentions, it simply did not fit for me.

Marnie and I had never quite fit into society's mold. We came together in the early 1970's when questioning society and its values was commonplace. We didn't live a straight, conventional life. We didn't always make our way in society the way we were expected to according to conventional norms. But we weren't hippies either. We didn't reject society and live totally outside its bounds. We shared a life in which we consistently tried to live _our_ beliefs and follow _our_ hearts. We always put our relationship and our family first no matter the cost. We lived _our_ life.

In living that way, we took some pretty big risks. Taking those risks resulted in what could only be called miraculous events (which I will describe in later chapters). We'd have never experienced that magic had we not followed our own road instead of living a conventional life. Some of that magic made us question whether there might be a higher power at work in our lives (which again, I will describe in later chapters). We never turned to religion, but we wondered about what Marnie called the "Great Spirit".

So with the death of Marnie's body I chose to keep following my own heart along my own path. I was not ready or willing to move Marnie into memory and move on to a new, different life. Although I knew that my life had been profoundly altered and could never return to what it was, I wanted to keep living my life with Marnie in it. For my very survival I needed to keep Marnie alive in my life. The question was, could I do that?

Could I genuinely keep Marnie alive in my life? Could I honestly and sincerely believe that she continued to be a real, conscious, living presence? Could I believe that the essence of Marnie, her soul, lived on beyond the death of her body? Could I believe in the reality of an eternal soul at all without believing in the reality of a living God?

I'm not religious. God had not played a significant role in my conscious awareness during my adult life. However, I couldn't make logical sense of an eternal, living soul, specifically Marnie's eternal living soul, without believing in God.

But how could I believe in a loving God who would allow the most loving human being I had ever known to be ravaged and killed by cancer? When nothing about the way that Marnie lived her life promoted the development or growth of cancer? How could I make peace with such a God? And if I could, if I was going to come to believe in God in spite of that, could I do so from a base of rational thought rather than a base of religion? Could I build *heart-felt* faith from a base of reason?

I was not ready, willing, or able to let go of the most precious gift I had ever been given – Marnie, my beautiful, loving wife. So I began a quest, a mental and spiritual journey to see if I could build the genuine, heart-felt belief that Marnie was indeed fully alive in every way except her physical body. It was for me a quest to build faith that I could believe with my mind and feel in my heart.

I began a search to find "God" outside the confines of religion. I deeply wanted to believe in the reality of Marnie's living, eternal soul. I didn't know if I could do that genuinely, sincerely, honestly. And even if I could, I didn't know if I could ever feel the deep joy in my life that I felt when Marnie was with me physically. I had to answer these questions:

1) Can faith in God be built from a base of reason?

2) Can faith built from reason (instead of religion) be genuine?

3) Can true healing come from reason-based faith?

4) Could I come to believe in Marnie's continued, living presence in my life through that faith?

5) Could I ever again feel deep joy and peace in my heart without Marnie's physical presence in my life?

I hope you will travel with me on the spiritual quest I've undertaken to find answers to these questions and ultimately achieve belief and healing.

Chapter 1: Death Does Not End Real Love

The theme of this book is simple: **You can heal from the physical death of your beloved by keeping your relationship with your beloved alive -- here and now**. But I have to add the caveat that with the death of your beloved, there is a dimension of sadness that can't be taken away. It may never go away completely. Perhaps it shouldn't. It gives perspective on the meaning and reality of life. It highlights the beauty and blessing of the love you shared.

In this chapter I'd like to introduce you to Marnie and me. I'd like you to feel our love. I need to share my pain with you. I want you to understand exactly why I'm writing. I hope that in sharing my heart I might touch (and perhaps heal) yours. But as I said in the dedication, I had to write this book. I write it for you, but it is also a gift to Marnie, and it is a way for me to feel a continued purpose for living in this world.

I'm writing for those of you who hurt deeply from the loss of someone you loved deeply. I am one of you. As I said in the introduction, after a four year battle with stage 4 breast cancer, Marnie, my wife of 43 years, my love for even longer, died in August of 2016. She was and is my soul's mate. Her physical death caused a fundamental transformation in the nature and focus of our interaction, but it has not ended our active relationship. I have come to believe that Marnie's death is a passageway to our ever deepening love for all eternity.

Though I have hurt profoundly since Marnie's physical death, over time I have begun to experience comfort and healing. I write in the hope that by sharing my personal journey of grieving and healing, you might come to experience comfort and healing for yourself.

I am sharing the path I have chosen to follow in coming to terms with the death of Marnie's body, and in healing from it as much as I can. I chose to go forward into unknown territory for me. I embarked on a journey of faith that I didn't know if I had, nor did I know if I had the strength to build, but I had to try.

My writings are extremely personal. I am opening my heart to you. My hope is that in being so personal, my journey will feel real to you. I hope that what I share will touch your heart. I hope it will cause you to both immerse yourself in my feelings and ultimately substitute your own personal experiences for mine in your mind and heart. If I have done so successfully, you will understand, on a feeling level, the path that I have chosen to follow. Then you will be able to decide if there is sufficient wisdom and truth in that path for you to follow it as well.

Throughout the book I will shift between different times, different places, and different perspectives as I write. I will shift from writing about Marnie to talking directly to her. I will use the flying crane that you see above, to help delineate these shifts. I hope this will help hold things together for you and prevent confusion. Sometimes I will use subheadings instead of the crane. I do so when I feel there is an important shift in substance that I want to emphasize.

If you have lost a spouse, as I have, or if you have lost a parent, or a child, or a brother or sister, or a best friend, your pain is as real as mine. Your loss is as real as mine. But your continued connection is as real as mine too. I have come to believe that there is a soul level connection that is not and cannot be severed by physical death. There are bonds that you built together and shared together which live on in the soul. Those bonds are real. They are alive. Your connection is real. Your connection is alive. Coming to understand the why, the how, and the ultimate reality of this is the focus of this book.

Nothing I can say will fully ease the pain of your physical loss, but I believe that with clear thinking, you can ease the overall pain of that loss by coming to realize that your beloved is not gone. That realization has been the cornerstone of my healing. I believe it can be for yours as well. Your bond is eternal and so is your love.

I need to tell you in advance that I am not a member of any religious denomination. I have found no religion that fully fits for me. I am not a "new age" seer or clairvoyant. I am a human being seeking meaning and healing by using my mind to heal my heart. In doing that though, I have come to the conclusion that what most religions call "God" is real.

That I am not religious will offend some people. That I talk about "God" at all will offend even more. I have found that even the name, "God", causes real problems for some people. Marnie didn't use the word "God". She spoke of the "Great Spirit."

What I've been doing is searching for a way to keep Marnie fully alive in my life after the death of her body. In the course of that search, I have come to believe that there is an infinite, loving power behind this universe that is responsible for all being. It is an infinite, personal power that is responsible for the both universe itself and for each of us who live in it.

The difficulty is in talking about that power because of the words. "God" is the word that many if not most people in our culture use. But others have real difficulty with the word "God" because of the religious connotations that go along with it. So they might use words like "Infinite Light", or "Power Behind the Universe", or "Great Spirit", or even "Om" instead of the word "God".

To me, they are all words. Nothing more. They are words that describe the infinite, conscious, loving, phenomenal power from which we all derive our lives. I need to talk about that power in this book. It has been the source of my healing. It has been my pathway back to Marnie. And Marnie has been my pathway to that power.

So I struggle with the words. I hope you won't be offended by the words I choose or close your mind to the ideas that I offer here because of them. For me, they really are just words. I don't believe that infinite power would ultimately be concerned about the words I choose. That infinite power is the source of our life, the source of our being, and the source of our ultimate fulfillment. And I believe that our fulfillment is the ultimate desire of that infinite power.

I will use the name "God" throughout the remainder of this book because it is the name most commonly used in our culture. I'm okay with it. It feels less clumsy to me than using multiple words to describe that infinite power, and it feels more real to me than using a name like "Om."

If you need to, please substitute whatever name feels more appropriate to you for the name "God". I don't want a name to cut you off from being able to examine the source of all creation, the source of all being, and the source of all healing. I hope you will travel along with me on the journey that led me to "God", Marnie's "Great Spirit". It was the journey that allowed me to connect with Marnie's soul.

I will talk about this in depth in subsequent chapters, but I suggest that if you can come to believe in "God" as the source and substance of your being, then you can also come to believe that a living connection with your beloved is real, now and forever.

Marnie's Death – a Brief Introduction

Marnie was and is my heart and soul. She was and is the center of my being. Loving and supporting her became, over the years, the focus, the purpose of my life. In doing so, I couldn't have been happier. I was bathed by her presence. I felt deep peace and contentment in her presence. Her physical death was devastating to me. I had no desire to go on living. But I promised her I would.

In the final days before she died, when Marnie's body was failing and she was suffering profoundly, I talked with her. I told her that her body was dying. I told her that it was <u>only</u> her body that was dying. I told her that she would live on. I told her it was time for her to leave her body behind. I told her it was ok to move on. I told her I would be ok. I promised her that I would live on. I promised her that I would love and take care of our grandchildren. I promised her I would love them as she would. I said, "I promise darling." I told her it was ok to die.

That was the hardest thing I have ever done in my life. I didn't know if I believed the words I said to her. I so wanted to die with her. It was only the promises that I made to Marnie that kept me alive.

My grief was overwhelming. I had to run and bike and swim for miles and miles and miles every day to escape, to survive the pain. The world for me was a hollow, empty place. I saw no beauty in it. Things that were beautiful before, when Marnie and I shared them together, were just there now. Nothing more. They held no attraction, no fascination for me. They just were. Living was a chore. Each day was endured. I would look forward to it being late enough in the day that I could feel I'd made it through one more day.

There was a hole in my life, a hole in my heart – an emptiness that I didn't think any amount of healing would ever fill. The hole is where Marnie was. I missed her. I still miss her. I miss being with her. I miss being able to put my arms around her. That's the empty place. And that's not going to go away completely until I can rejoin her in the next lifetime.

My Pathway Back Home

I'm on a spiritual journey now. It is my life-line to hope. As I've already said, caring friends, family, and books on grieving told me that I needed to leave Marnie behind -- that I would need to let go of her at some point. That I'd need to move Marnie from presence to memory. That ultimately, I'd have to move on.

I chose not to. I've done just the opposite of that. And in doing so, I am progressively finding more and more peace, greater hope, and the rebirth of joy in my life.

You see, when I believe that Marnie is still present, when I believe that her soul, her consciousness, her awareness, her self-awareness, and her awareness of me are all still fully alive, that it is only her body that has died, then life still feels worth living for me. When I don't believe those things, then all desire to keep living is gone for me.

If I am going to keep the commitments I made to Marnie before she died (and I will **not** violate those commitments) then the choice of whether or not to believe is pretty straightforward – I choose to believe.

But in my mind, believing those things about Marnie could only make sense in the context of believing in God. God hadn't played much of a role in my life for a significant portion of it. Then death came along. Marnie's body died. My heart and soul felt like they died with her. The thought of her being gone, of her simply being annihilated, gone forever – I couldn't take that. The thought of never seeing her again – I couldn't take that.

But the belief that Marnie lives on beyond physical death -- that only her body is gone, that I'll be able to see her and be with her again, that we are separated just for now, while I'm still living in this physical world -- that gives me hope. That gives me a purpose to keep living and loving. But to have that make sense in my mind required God. It required believing. It required faith.

As I told you, I don't practice any religion. As a child I grew up immersed in guilt, because of religion. As an adult, I gave up religion to achieve sanity. In doing so, I put God aside. I never stopped being a loving person, but I quit being a religious person. It took me two full years to leave behind the guilt from that choice. But it was worth it.

Now, I've embarked on a journey to find the faith that can bring me back into Marnie's arms. It's a journey to find my way back to God. I still don't consider myself religious. But I now believe that God fits. And I have begun to talk with God every day, without fail. And I talk with Marnie every day, throughout the day without fail. It is slowly transforming my life. It's been in traveling this road to faith that life has begun to feel worth living again. And now it feels not only worth living, but worth living well. I've come to believe that to earn my way back to Marnie, my path has to be one of sincere faith and committed, all-encompassing love, framed in hope.

I offer you the writings that follow as a window into my soul. They come from my heart without censorship. Sometimes, in the course of these writings, I talk directly to Marnie. Sometimes I talk about her. Sometimes I talk with my son, Ben. The thoughts and feelings that I express are not always pleasant. They are often jumbled or repetitive. But they are an honest portrayal of my journey into and through grief.

I hope you will be able to see and feel the up and down course of my daily struggle with emotions, and perhaps understand the difficulty involved for me in coming to logically, rationally, and fully believe both in Marnie's real, continued presence in my life, and in the reality and presence of a loving God.

I hope that those of you on your own journey of grief will be able to identify with what I write. Perhaps you will see that you are not alone. That you are not crazy. That you are not wrong in feeling whatever you feel.

I urge you not to accept anyone telling you that you need to move on from your beloved. Do not accept that you need to move them from presence into memory. Though well intended, this advice is neither true nor real – unless you accept it as real and define it as true in your own mind. You create your reality with your thoughts. Think clearly. Think carefully about the reality that you choose to create.

I do not claim to have **the** truth. I have only my truth. In a subject as profoundly and intensely personal as death and continued life after death, real truth must ultimately be personal. It must feel right and true in your heart. So I offer you my truth and all the intensely personal details involved in building, shaping, and defining that truth as a roadmap. Perhaps you will consider following it in finding <u>your</u> way home to your beloved. It describes the path that I travel back home to Marnie's arms.

    I write for me, and I write for you. Though my relationship with Marnie was unique, I believe that the truths we learned in living our relationship are universal. I believe the lessons I've learned and continue to learn on my journey of healing apply to your life as well as mine. Your relationship with your beloved was unique. Your grief is unique. The ache in your heart from your loss is unique. But we share the reality of grief and heart-ache. And we can share a path to healing.

    And please remember, when you love someone deeply you can't allow <u>anyone</u> else to tell you how you should be grieving, how you should be healing, or how you should be feeling. They are seeing blind. They are seeing with no conception of how you feel. You have to trust your own heart, and you have to know that if anyone understands you, it is your beloved, because your beloved shares your feelings. They can see you clearly. They understand your hurt as an outgrowth, as a reflection of your love.

    As I said to Marnie, "I never, ever conceived of myself living in a world without you physically in it with me. You are part of me. You are part of my identity. I am fundamentally connected with you in my heart and soul. I am one with you. I don't know how to live separate from you. I love you, Marnie, with all my heart, with all my soul, with all my mind, with every fiber of my being."

Only someone who shares that intensity of feeling, can possibly understand. And anyone who truly understands will never tell you how to feel or how to grieve.

I surely do miss you, Marnie. You are my heart. You are my soul's mate. Forever

Chapter 2: Why God?

Before I answer the question, "Why God?", before I talk about God and the soul, I have some fundamental beliefs that I need to share with you. They preceded the beliefs I have developed about God and the soul. These were and still are my fundamental beliefs:

Love is the heart of everything that matters. Love is our reason for being. Loving is the source of richness in living. Love is at the heart and soul of our most meaningful relationships.

Love was the heart and soul of my relationship with Marnie. My love for Marnie gave my world meaning. My love for Marnie made my world rich. My love for Marnie now, gives my life continued richness, meaning, and purpose.

Love is the reason that I have been profoundly sad since Marnie's body died. But my love for Marnie, is the reason I'm still alive. And though my world has often lacked in a feeling of richness since Marnie's physical death, the more I love, the more I can touch others with love, the more richness I bring back into my life.

If that description of basic beliefs and values fits for you too, then we're beginning our journey together into exploring God and spirituality on shared, common ground. However, because you are reading this book, I assume that you may also be non-religious. I assume that you have some of the fundamental questions about

God and spirituality, just as I have had. My purpose in writing this chapter is to introduce you to the possibility that God is real and that God can be the source for you being able to heal from the physical death of your beloved.

Turning to God for healing may be a difficult jump for you to make. It was for me. You might ask, "If I'm not religious, why do I need a pathway to God at all?" Why not just focus on love?

The answer is simple – death. Marnie's body died. Your beloved's body died. Your body is going to die. Your life in your body will end. And when it does, what will become of you? Do "you" extend beyond your body? Is there a fundamental reality to "you" that transcends your body? That lives on beyond your body?

If there isn't, then on some fundamental level, this life is pretty shallow. Then simply doing for yourself, acquiring for yourself, pleasing yourself, living exclusively for yourself might make some sense. But I have found the greatest joy, the greatest happiness, the greatest fulfillment in my life in loving – just the opposite of being "me" focused.

And when we love, when we truly love, we build feeling level bonds that extend beyond our bodies and give our lives their ultimate meaning and purpose. Love transcends the physical. The very concepts of meaning and purpose transcend the physical. It is in the non-physical, in the spiritual realm of being that life ultimately makes sense. And it is in the spiritual realm of being that we find God.

I never dreamed of writing a book that included God. God had not played a major (conscious) role in my world for most of my adult life. Then Marnie's body died, and my world was forever changed.

As I said earlier, Marnie had been the love of my life for 45 years when she died. We had been married for 43 years then, and we had lived, loved, and worked together 24 hours a day, 7 days a week for the 32 years prior to her physical death.

In the course of living together through those years we built a bond of love and oneness that was absolutely unbreakable. We "knew" that our bond, our connection, would never end in our physical lifetimes. It was for us an **absolute certainty**.

Even after her cancer diagnosis, I/we never focused on death. Though we each understood, on some level, the realistic probability that the death of her body was a likely outcome in the advanced state of Marnie's disease (stage 4 metastatic breast cancer), we never accepted it as an option for us. We did not allow that into our conscious awareness. Somehow, Marnie would beat it. Somehow, she would find a way to heal, and the beautiful life that we shared together before her cancer would be restored.

The death of Marnie's body was **the** impetus in my search to find God. If I didn't believe that God was real, then how could I possibly believe that Marnie lived on? I couldn't logically make peace with the idea that Marnie's soul (and all the dimensions that "soul" implies) could live on beyond the death of her body without coming to believe in God.

To believe in the reality of Marnie's living soul, I felt I had to come to believe in a higher power that is the creative source of that soul. I had to come to believe in a higher power that is the source of our essence as eternal, spiritual beings. I had to come to believe that we indeed are spiritual beings who temporarily inhabit a body and live on after the physical death of that body.

Physics tells us that 99.9% of matter is composed of empty space. It's the speed of the movement of the particles of the atom through that empty space that causes us to experience physical bodies as solid. Change the vibration level (the speed of movement) of the particles and you change your experience of physical reality. So from a physics perspective it could be entirely possible that physical death is nothing more than a change in the vibration level of the soul that carried its body. The soul is not dead. It is simply no longer visible on the physical plane of existence because it vibrates at a different frequency.

That would be wonderful to believe. But that belief had to be sincere for me. It had to ring true in my heart. Answering the fundamental question of whether or not there is life that lives on after physical death, whether Marnie was and is consciously alive and present after her physical death, required that I explore my fundamental beliefs about God. In my mind God and life after death are inextricably linked. For me, God and Marnie are inextricably linked.

I'd never thought much about God during my physical life with Marnie. God never seemed to hold any great relevance to us. But I believe now (in hindsight) that God was with us and actively watching over us. I believe that God's active intervention in our lives and our relationship allowed us to build the love and oneness that brought us our deepest joy and fulfillment.

And I believe that our love and oneness made us a reflection of God's love and His oneness with us. I have come to believe that love is from God. That love is God. That God is love. And I believe that because of God, through God, the bond of love and oneness between Marnie and me is eternal. Our living relationship is eternal.

I believe that all of the thinking I did about Marnie and the reality of her living soul applies directly to you. It applies to all of our loved ones and the reality of their living souls. I believe that though the story of Marnie and me is unique, its implications are not. The conclusions I've come to about God and the soul, in living our love story, are universal in their scope and application. How I arrived at those conclusions will comprise the heart of this book.

But before I focus on the pathway that I'm following in connecting with God, I think I need to share a bit more about Marnie and me. This is what I hope will make our story feel more real, more personal to you. And it was our pathway through life together that ultimately led me back to God. So here's a brief bit about Marnie and me.

Chapter 3: Marnie and me.

This chapter is personal. I write it in the hope that it will help you understand the pain that I felt and still feel with Marnie's physical death. I write it in the hope that it will begin to build a personal relationship between us, between you and me.

My relationship with Marnie was unique. I don't expect you to identify with all of it (though it would be wonderful if there are parts of it with which you do identify – experiences that we share in common). I write it to give you a better understanding of me, of Marnie and me, and hence where I'm coming from today.

I recognize that your relationship with your beloved is unique too and that the bond of love that you shared and share with your beloved is unique. Your bond is no less real than mine with Marnie. Your bond is eternal. And so is your love.

Marnie and I were doers. We did everything together. We worked together; we played together; we exercised together; we ran together; we biked together; we swam together; we hiked together; we walked under the stars together; we traveled together – we drove almost two million miles together; we talked of dreams and hopes and visions together; we envisioned the world as it should be together; we made love together – passionately and gently; we fantasized together; we wrestled together; we raised our children together; we helped raise our grandchildren together, we fought cancer together.

But we didn't need to "do". We only had to "be" together. Doing nothing, doing the menial tasks of everyday life – simply being in Marnie's presence filled me with peace and contentment. There was never anywhere I'd rather be. No one I would rather be with. We would share time with family. That was a gift we would give one another. But to just socialize, to make acquaintances, was seldom something either of us wanted to do. We kept to ourselves a lot. Simply being in Marnie's presence filled me. Anything that would divide my focus or would take me away from my awareness of Marnie, of us, of our togetherness, or of our family felt like a step down. I didn't need it or desire it. Marnie's simple presence was all I needed. Doing just made life even better.

Without Marnie's physical presence, my life suddenly felt profoundly empty. I hurt deep down inside....

I had met Marnie in the spring of 1971 at a meeting for people volunteering to help children with learning disabilities. The meeting was held in a school gymnasium. I was standing on the floor of the gym. Marnie was sitting on the edge of a stage that overlooked the gym floor.

I looked up and saw her. I was stunned. I couldn't take my eyes off of her. She looked over and gave me a brief, shy smile. I will never forget that moment. I had no idea what was in store for us over the next 45+ years, but I was utterly captivated by her, from that first moment.

My good friend, who was working on his PhD in child psychology at the University of Colorado was in charge of the learning disabilities program. I assumed that Marnie was a student at the university, volunteering as part of one of her college classes.

I had come to Colorado to fulfill my alternative service requirement as a conscientious objector. Though I didn't know it at the time, my supervisor at the Youth Service Bureau, where I was doing that alternative service, was Marnie's mother. I had graduated from Loyola University two months earlier. I was 22.

Marnie was wearing a plaid, flannel shirt and overalls. She wasn't a college student after all. She was 15.

Two months later, Marnie's mother hired me to tutor Marnie in high school algebra. She had turned 16 in the interim. We fell in love.

I have to own the fact that at 16, Marnie was more mature than I was at 22. I was her first love. I, on the other hand, had had several love relationships. None of them lasted. All of them ended whenever serious conflict arose -- whenever things were no longer "perfect" and I could no longer be the "knight in shining armor".

Though I don't remember the content of our first big argument, I vividly remember the scene and the outcome. Marnie was 17. I had turned 24. We'd been in love for almost a year without significant conflict. On this particular night though, we were having our first serious argument. We were driving along the foothills at the base of the mountains outside Boulder, Colorado. As was my dramatic style, when the argument became intense, I jerked the car over to the side of the road and screamed, "We're through!" I jumped out of the car, slammed the door, and began stomping up the side of the mountain. It was my pattern of relationship failure rising up all over again.

However, this time, Marnie jumped out of the car too. She slammed her door. She ran up the mountainside behind me, grabbed me by the shoulder, spun me around, and shouted, "Grow up! You love me and you know it!"

I smiled (which infuriated her). I knew, in that moment, that this relationship was something different; that this relationship could last through the hard times and the struggles that come with every relationship. This woman was something special.

I had no idea how special our relationship would become, but I knew in that moment that this was the one that could last. It did. Our love never ended. It goes on even today. It transcends her death. It will last as long as our souls shall live. If our souls are real, it will last through eternity.

It was neither an easy nor a typical road that we traveled together, Marnie and me. We were married when Marnie turned 18 after she graduated from high school. We wrote our own wedding ceremony and our own wedding vows. We were married among the aspen trees on the side of a mountain in Colorado with a minister merely serving as witness.

Our marriage began as an open marriage. We believed that our commitment to one another and our commitment to openness and honesty with one another was solid. We believed that our relationship could withstand the hardships and jealousies that would be involved in an open marriage. We reaffirmed our commitment to open, honest, sharing communication – no matter how scary, no matter how difficult. We made a commitment to working out any conflict that might arise no matter how difficult it might be or how long it might take to resolve it. We never violated those commitments.

Philosophically I believed that we could love more than one person. Intellectually, open marriage made sense. Marnie had had no other relationships prior to me. It seemed fair that she should be able to experience other loves, other lovers. In hindsight though, I don't believe that was the fundamental reason for the open marriage. Marnie didn't need other relationships as much as I did. I needed to have every woman I was attracted to fall in love with me. I had never truly believed that I was special or that I was good enough. Having multiple loves made me feel special.

As I said, Marnie was more mature than me. Though she did try a few relationships, it was my need that led to me having several. It was my neediness that led to me having relationships that left Marnie feeling alone and hurting -- not receiving the sufficient, consistent, ongoing love and support that she needed, especially after the birth of our first son.

It was a struggle to work through those feelings, but eventually I came to realize that I had everything I needed in Marnie. There was no one who could give me more. There was no one who gave me more in every way, on every level. I realized that our marriage and our family had to be and was my highest priority. We closed the marriage and never looked back. From that point on, our love blossomed. It grew into absolute oneness -- a love so strong, that not even physical death could end it.

Over the ensuing 37 years of our marriage (following the 5+ years of open marriage), our life together was an incredible journey. (The details of that will be the stuff of another book – "The Journey of a Lifetime Together"). It began when I quit a high paying job as director of a chemical dependency center on an Indian reservation. It was too consuming for me emotionally and timewise and hence took too much of a toll on our family. So I quit.

To survive financially, we created our own line of greeting cards and traveled the country selling them. We traveled almost two million miles together in our 45 year romance. (Marnie liked to describe us as gypsies.) We bicycled from Montana to California by way of the Olympic Peninsula with a 3 year old boy and a 100 pound German Shepard in tow.

We hitch-hiked from California to Wyoming to New Mexico, again with our 3 year old son and our German Shepard, "Bear". We worked as house parents in a facility for adolescent Native American boys who came from alcoholic families. We founded and ran our own private school. I wrote a book on relationships. And Marnie created her own puppet making business (in which I subsequently joined her) that sustained us financially for 22 years.

Throughout all of this, we were connected to nature and had magical experiences together in the wilderness. These included:

Hiking 16 miles to the top of a mountain well above timber line in Glacier National Park. We sat looking at the majestic scene in front of us and soon found ourselves literally surrounded by a herd of mountain goats.

We sat in a field in Yellowstone howling with the wolves, and had the whole pack of wolves run to us and around us (20 or 30 or more wolves) and felt totally safe, totally a part of it, totally a part of the magic.

We saw a blonde black bear run up the side of a mountain in Truchas, NM where we lived with people who, we had been told, hated white people. But they couldn't have been kinder, more generous, or more friendly to us.

We saw a mountain lion and a raccoon in a life and death struggle on our back deck, and had that same mountain lion run directly across the path not 10 feet in front of us as we went for our night walk later that evening.

We swam together with dolphins and sea lions and even the grey whales in the waters of the Pacific and the Sea of Cortez in Baja Sur, Mexico.

We sat together in a small panga (fishing boat) in the midst of a magnificent feeding frenzy in the Sea of Cortez, surrounded by a myriad of circling dolphins and sea lions, diving pelicans, sea gulls, and terns. It was a stunning spectacle.

It was a level of magic and majesty that not many people are fortunate enough to experience in a lifetime. It was a reflection of our bond with nature and our commitment to being out in nature together. (I will address our bond with nature and our special experiences in nature in greater detail in in chapter 24.) It was a product of and a reflection of our love, of our commitment to one another, and of our relationship. It was, I now believe, a gift from God.

Though we were not religious, there was a tie to God throughout everything I've described in this section on Marnie and me. I now believe that it was all possible because of God's active role in our lives (as you will see in the next chapter).

Chapter 4: God's role in nurturing and sustaining Marnie and me.

In this chapter I look in hindsight at events that occurred throughout my life with Marnie. They indicated that God was alive and active in our lives. With each occurrence, we would in fact say, "God is taking care of us." But that statement never really penetrated our consciousness. It never became a fundamental thread in the fabric of our belief system – certainly not one that shaped our lifestyle. But in hindsight, there was a clear accumulation of incidents that suggest the active intervention of a divine presence.

After reading this, I would encourage you to look back at your life and your relationship with your beloved and see if, with the wisdom of hindsight, there might have been a series of what could only be described as divine interventions in the course of your life and relationship together. I suspect that you will find some. And in finding them, the seeds of a belief in God might begin to take root.

You might be tempted, as I was, to see these things, especially in isolation, as coincidence. But coincidence, repeatedly repeated coincidence, seems more than coincidental. It is a theme that repeated itself throughout my relationship with Marnie. It's a theme that repeats itself almost daily in my life now.

I believe strongly that if you choose to maintain your relationship with your beloved following their physical death, there will be a stunning series of coincidences that will follow in your life too. Too Many coincidences for them to be merely coincidental.

I was in college during the Viet Nam war. When I graduated, I was drafted almost immediately out of my first year in graduate school. I was opposed to that war. All war seemed wrong to me. I refused induction into military service. I applied for conscientious objector status and eventually received it. This is where the coincidence began.

I wanted to do community organization work on the south side of Chicago for my 2 years of alternative service. The draft board ordered me to serve as an orderly at Denver General Hospital in Colorado. We compromised on my working for the Youth Service Bureau in Boulder, CO where my best friend from college was working as a counselor while finishing his PhD work at the University of Colorado.

The director of the Youth Service Bureau was Marnie's mother. The volunteer program run by my best friend was where I met Marnie. Marnie's mother hired me to tutor her daughter by whom I had been stunned at first sight and with whom I fell in love in a matter of months, despite our 7 year age difference.

Building our relationship together was our choice. But the circumstances that brought me to Marnie were totally beyond my control. Were they simple coincidence?

Marnie had incredible strength and maturity at age 17. Her parents were divorced. They had been dishonest with one another. They had not modeled open, honest communication with one another. They had not modeled effective conflict resolution for her. Where did Marnie's strength, maturity, and commitment to honesty, openness, and resolving conflict come from? Was that more than happenstance, more than coincidence?

There were times during our open marriage period when I thought that perhaps I should end my relationship with Marnie, that maybe I'd be better off with an older, more sophisticated, more sexually experienced woman. Whenever I even thought these things, circumstances would immediately spring up to totally block the possibility. Was that too coincidence? Or was I being carried until my maturity came closer to Marnie's level?

After we closed our marriage, when our love was truly blossoming, there were multiple times when we were carried, when we were protected, when we were literally kept alive in ways that were totally beyond our control. I will describe just three (of multiple) incidents that relate directly to events described in the chapter on "Marnie and Me" that demonstrate this.

1) In hitch-hiking from California to Wyoming to New Mexico, Marnie and I were searching for some kind of work that we could do together as a family and still make a living. When we arrived in Santa Fe, New Mexico, we were down to our last $3 – Marnie and me, our 3 year old son, Jeremy, and our 100 pound German Shepard dog, Bear. I thought I knew a short-cut to a place where we could pitch our tent and camp for the night before going to the employment office the next morning.

It started to rain. We got lost. We ended up on a street that I didn't recognize. As the four of us walked down that street in the rain, a couple in a station wagon, pulled over and asked us if we needed any help. We explained to them that we were looking for that place to camp. They said they had an extra bedroom in their house and a yard for our dog, and offered to take us home. We went with them.

Over dinner together they explained that they were house parents in a program for Native American boys from alcoholic families and that the program was looking for another set of house parents. In the morning they took us to meet the program's director.

We were hired that day and offered a place to live in the program director's guest house (with a green house and hot tub) until we could find our own place to live. The program took us as a family, 3 year old boy, dog and all – our ideal job.

We had no control whatsoever over the circumstances. We were (literally) lost, penniless, and searching for a way to make a living that would allow us to keep our family as our top priority. Everything was given to us. We could only affirm, "God is taking care of us."

2) Several years later we created our own line of greeting cards and traveled the country selling them. On the first leg of our journey, we had traveled to San Antonio, TX in our old VW van. It had an ungodly automatic transmission. We had not been selling our cards successfully along the way. In San Antonio, 1,800 miles from our home, we were literally down to our last $5 when the transmission in the VW began pouring out automatic transmission fluid. We were suddenly 3 quarts down. We pulled the van over into the parking lot of a city park and played in the park with our children (ages 2 and 7 at the time) until it was time to go to bed (in the back of the van). There was nothing more we could do.

In the morning, we walked to an auto parts store. We used our last $5 to buy transmission fluid. We put it in the VW and began driving. The transmission no longer leaked. It never leaked again on that whole trip. We sold an entire set of our cards (a dozen of each of 8 different styles) at the first store we stopped in. They paid us in cash. We were able to drive on to Austin, TX and sold 10 more entire sets of cards that same day and set up a reordering process in each of the stores where we sold our cards. We were able to drive home in a leak free van after a financially successful trip.

We had absolutely no control over the leaking transmission, the total lack of card sales, the miraculously repaired transmission, or the sudden tremendous success in card sales. It was all beyond our control, beyond our ability to control. We affirmed to ourselves again, "God is taking care of us". It became a kind of mantra for us.

3) Seven years later we were running our own private middle school in Santa Fe, NM. We traveled to Baja California Sur, Mexico to explore tide pools, swim with dolphins and sea lions, and see the grey whales – to physically experience the things our students had been studying in their marine biology classes.

We were traveling in our 15 passenger Dodge van. I'd had the brakes totally checked over and redone at a Midas shop in Santa Fe immediately before we left on the trip to be sure that we would be safe. The trip was progressing smoothly until we reached a 50 mile stretch of what at that time was a very narrow, two lane road between La Paz and Todos Santos in Baja Sur, Mexico. There were no shoulders on that road. There were rocks (boulders actually), cactuses, cliffs, and drop offs on each side of that section of road. We were driving after dark at about 50 mph.

Suddenly, in front of us, a large truck was stopped in our lane on the highway with its lights off. When I applied the brakes to slow down, they went to the floor. I pumped and pumped the brakes. There was no response. We had no brakes. At that same moment, there was a semi approaching in the other lane. I had the choice of hitting the back of a truck at 50 mph, having a head on collision with a semi at 50 mph, or whipping off the side of the road into I didn't know what. I whipped off the side of the road.

We flew... and landed on a smooth, perfectly plowed section of dirt field where we came safely to a stop. The 12 kids in the back of the van thought I had done it for fun and excitement. They had no idea what had just happened. That small section of smooth, plowed field was the only safe section where we could have landed on that entire 50 mile stretch of road. We drove on to Todos Santos at 15 mph using the emergency brake to slow us down. On the side of a mountain we met an English speaking Mexican man who had worked as a mechanic for General Motors in San Francisco and had now returned to Baja. He repaired our brakes at virtually no cost. (Midas had neglected to replace a pair of bolts in their servicing of our brakes that caused the brake failure.)

Once again, we had absolutely no control over what happened – the failed brakes, the multiple trucks, the smooth, safe landing pad, or the bilingual, talented mechanic. We could only affirm again that "God is taking care of us."

Though we affirmed that, we still never became religious. God still did not play a central role on our conscious, daily lives. We simply went on living and loving as we always had. We did regularly repeat our mantra that God is taking care of us, but we also wished on stars. Marnie would hold her breath, put her hands on the ceiling, and make a wish as we drove our car through tunnels. The spiritual world was not one of deep seated belief for us.

None the less, we continued to have special, unexplainable, magical experiences throughout our life together. Not all were as dramatic or significant and life affirming as those I've described, but all were real, unexplainable, and beyond our direct control. "God is taking care of us" remained an affirmation in our lives, and I now believe, a truth in our lives.

I would encourage you to look back closely on your relationship with your beloved. See clearly if there were events that transcend mere coincidence. And pay close attention to your life as you move forward. Especially be aware in the times you are communicating with your beloved or in the times when special memories of times together come back to your mind and heart. Notice what happens. Notice what you feel. See if there are clear signs that say, "This is real." Signs that come to you, at just the right time -- beyond the world of simple coincidence.

Just notice at first. Just pay attention. Over time, the recognition of a pattern of repeatedly repeated coincidence will begin to argue for the active intervention of a spiritual presence that transcends everyday reality.

For me now, I sometimes feel strongly that such intervention has come directly from Marnie. Sometimes I feel it as the presence of God acting in my life. Look closely at your own life and trust the insights that come to you. In doing so, you progressively strengthen your faith and deepen your sense of soul-level connection with your beloved.

We will look at all this in much greater detail in subsequent chapters. For now, just be aware.

Chapter 5: God's role in our lives during Marnie's Cancer.

"God is taking care of us." How could that be true when Marnie got cancer? How could that be true when Marnie's body died from cancer? Why did God suddenly quit taking care of us? I have asked myself those questions over and over again. How could I possibly believe in God or in His active care for us when He let Marnie suffer and physically die?

Marnie was the most loving human being I had ever met. She was the most unselfish. She was the most mature. She was the most forgiving. She was the most open to loving and receiving love. That is why it was so easy to fall in love with her. And so hard to let her go. Never have I met a more purely loving being. So how, why would a loving, caring God let her suffer and physically die? These questions have been at the core of my struggle to believe in God. But let me back up and give you some background on Marnie's cancer.

This chapter isn't essential to your understanding of the overall theme and intent of this book. I share it to make our story even more real and personal to you. Perhaps there will be parts of our story that relate to yours. I don't know. Read it only if you choose.

We felt a lump in Marnie's breast in early 2011. We discussed it in detail on Valentine's Day that year while we were camped in Myakka River State Park in Florida where we were traveling as we made our living doing art shows and selling Marnie's puppets.

I was terrified by that lump. I had an intense fear of losing her. Marnie was certain, however, that it couldn't possibly be cancer. Everything about the way she lived her life argued against it. She was an athlete -- a runner, a biker, a swimmer, a hiker, a weight lifter. She ate healthy foods. She wasn't overweight. She didn't smoke. There was no history of breast cancer in her family. She had nursed both of our children. Everything argued against cancer. But she agreed to be checked as soon as we returned home from our sales trip…

We had no health insurance at the time. We felt we couldn't afford it. We always made enough money to live on, enough money to travel as we chose, enough money to give to our children whatever they needed whenever they needed it. We believed that our fitness and our dedication to good health was our health insurance policy.

When we returned home, we went to a health care facility that was an inexpensive walk in clinic. You paid cash, and they charged less than traditional doctors who are part of the health insurance system. The care we received there seemed fine. The physician's assistant who examined Marnie was kind and considerate. He asked me to be present while he examined Marnie. He felt the lump in her breast and measured it. And he told us not to worry. He said it was not necessarily breast cancer. He referred us to our local hospital for a mammogram to determine the diagnosis.

Unfortunately, we were naïve. We simply trusted the medical system. We did not do research ahead of time, as I clearly know in hindsight that we should have done. We should have learned about what is involved in doing a mammogram. We should have learned the difference between screening and diagnostic mammograms. We had no idea there were different kinds of mammograms. We should have learned the appropriate procedure to accurately diagnose the nature of a breast lump. (A diagnostic mammogram should be followed by an ultrasound to accurately guide a biopsy of the lump.) We didn't know any of that. No one told us.

And, because we were concerned, (we had hoped to have the mammogram that same day) the PA who made the referral had us scheduled for the first date and time available to have the mammogram at our local hospital.

We had no idea that the time scheduled for Marnie's mammogram was normally reserved for screening mammograms. As I said, we didn't even know that there were different kinds of mammograms. I don't believe the radiology tech at the hospital ever even looked at the intake form on which Marnie had circled, "lump," "right breast," date of onset 2/14/11 – Valentine's Day, the day we discussed the lump and Marnie agreed to have it checked.

So they did a screening mammogram, which we know now (in hindsight) cannot diagnose a lump, particularly in a woman with dense breast tissue as Marnie had. They did a second mammogram of Marnie's left breast (a diagnostic mammogram we now know). When Marnie asked why they did a second mammogram of her left breast, the tech said, "The radiologist must have seen something there." When Marnie asked, "What about the lump in my right breast?" the tech told her, "That's just a fibrous cyst."

I had never heard of fibrous cysts, but Marnie said that her mother had fibrous cysts in her breasts. She was reassured. I accepted that. We went on with our lives as normal. When we received the bill for the mammogram, almost $600 between the charges from the hospital and the radiologist (who we never even saw or met) we thought the request to return in 6 months for a follow-up mammogram of Marnie's **left** breast (the one without the lump) was outrageous and unnecessary.

Two years later, in February of 2013, Marnie's T-12 vertebrae fractured and collapsed from tumors that had spread throughout her skeletal system from primary breast cancer. Her/our battle against **stage 4 breast cancer** began at age 57……

That battle had actually begun five months earlier. We had no idea that the battle was on, however. As I said, Marnie was an athlete. After doing an art show In Virginia Beach, Marnie water-skied with our son on the Chickahominy River in Virginia in June of 2012. At the end of July we went for a 42 mile bike ride in the mountains in Montana. Marnie wondered why she seemed more tired than usual after the ride, not realizing she was carrying a major tumor burden from her cancer.

On September 12, 2012, we rode our bikes 3 miles from our home up a steep back country mountain road to a campground where we liked to run on a trail along Boulder Creek. Before running, Marnie stretched and was doing some twisting exercises when she felt something "catch" and hurt in her back. She thought she had somehow caught and tweaked or pulled a muscle in her back. She decided to run anyway to try and work it out. We ran 3 ½ miles. It didn't get better. Marnie tried running two more times after that, but each time it was painful and we eventually quit running and only walked together.

Marnie struggled with pain repeatedly after that. Long walks were painful. We lived in the Montana back country. Cutting fire wood was essential for us. We would cut the fire wood together that heated our home in the winter. Dragging away the branches from the cut wood proved painful for Marnie that year. Carrying wood proved painful. Bicycling up hills proved painful. The pain interfered with all the physical tasks that used to be normal or even a joy for Marnie. Life became increasingly stressful, frustrating, and painful. But Marnie was determined to make it through, to find some way to heal from what she called the "muscular pain in her flank."

During that time we went to two different doctors, a chiropractor, a soft tissue healer, and two different urgent care clinics. Everyone we saw assumed Marnie had a back injury in the form of either muscle strain, disk compression, or a disk being out of place. The last doctor we saw, was a sports medicine specialist. He ordered x-rays of Marnie's lower back and pelvis areas. He did not order an MRI (that might have correctly caught and diagnosed the problem) because he knew we didn't have health insurance, and he wanted to save us any unnecessary expense. The x-rays showed no significant problems. He diagnosed the injury as "illio-psoas tendinopathy". He prescribed 3 Advil every 6 hours and physical therapy.

The prescription seemed to work. Marnie was slowly and carefully able to begin rebuilding strength without pain. She bicycled on a stationary bike at the physical therapy center, and gradually resumed biking outside on her own bike. We were able to leave on our winter art show sales trip to Florida in January of 2013.

Biking became our standard form of exercise together. As long as it wasn't too strenuous, as long as we didn't attempt steep hills, everything seemed fine. Marnie did fall on two different occasions, something she would never normally have done. Once her handle bar hit a mailbox. Once she went off the edge of the road. Both times we wrote it off to lack of concentration, never dreaming that something much more significant was going on inside of her.

But on Valentine's Day 2013, exactly two years after discussing the lump in her breast, in the same state park where we had that discussion (Myakka River State Park, Florida) we went on a back country bike ride together. In the middle of that ride Marnie said, "My God. My lower back really hurts. I've got to get back to the smooth road." The following morning, Marnie collapsed in my arms in excruciating pain.

We drove to Jupiter, Florida where I set up for the art show that we were scheduled to do. We needed the money from what was normally our best art show of the year. Marnie sat in the van in excruciating pain while I worked.

That evening we went to another urgent care clinic. The doctor there again assumed it was a muscle/disk related injury and gave Marnie an injection to ease the pain, and a prescription for pain killers and muscle relaxants. She urged Marnie to totally relax and rest her back for the next several days.

I finished doing the art show while Marnie sat and rested behind our booth. When the show was over, we drove to the Florida Keys. We stayed on Long Key where Marnie did nothing but rest in her "zero gravity" chair beside the sea watching the birds that she loved so much for two more days. However, even walking to the bathroom was now proving to be a painful chore, and taking a shower was impossible.

The third morning on Long Key, February 21, 2013, Marnie collapsed when she got up from her chair and tried to walk to our van. She was unable to get up. With the aid of a park ranger and the fire department, we were able to put Marnie on a stretcher and move her to the back of our van. We drove to the closest urgent care center where they refused to see her because she was unable to walk in under her own power. So we drove on to the closest hospital where they refused to see us (discouraged us from coming in) because we didn't have health insurance.

We drove on to Homestead, Florida where I saw a man in scrubs walking down the street. I stopped and asked him if he knew where we could go. He directed us to Homestead Hospital, a part of the Baptist Health Care system. He said they would see us as part of their treatment service mandate regardless of health insurance or our ability to pay.

Running into that nurse on the road was a coincidence over which we had no control. **Perhaps God was still taking care of us**.

In the emergency room of Homestead Hospital, Marnie was seen by a doctor who ordered a CT scan of her back. The CT scan showed the fracture and collapse of Marnie's T-12 vertebrae from tumors that the doctor suspected had spread from primary breast cancer. Marnie was immediately put on IV morphine and transferred by ambulance to South Miami Hospital (also part of the Baptist Health Care system) where they have a specialized cancer treatment unit.

We could not have been taken to a finer care facility in Florida (perhaps anywhere). It was beyond our control. **Perhaps God was still taking care of us**.

Marnie spent 9 days in South Miami Hospital. My beautiful, athletic wife could no longer even turn her head without excruciating pain. She was put on 60mg of OxyContin daily, plus intravenous Dilaudid (10 times more powerful than morphine) every 4 hours, Decadron (a steroid) plus all the other medications required to allow her body to tolerate the pain meds and steroid that had been prescribed for her. Breast cancer was officially confirmed by biopsy on February 24th. Kyphoplasty surgery restored her T-12 vertebrae to its proper size and shape and alleviated much of the pain on February 25th.

We were told that a PET scan to determine the extent of the tumors in Marnie's skeletal system, and radiation treatment on those tumors would follow later that week. However, because of our lack of health insurance, rather than incurring those costs, the hospital discharged Marnie on March 1st. A referral was made to the Montana Cancer Center in Missoula, Montana. We began our journey home and into the new world of ongoing cancer treatment that day, March 1, 2013.

Marnie received outstanding medical care at the Montana Cancer center in Missoula. Over the course of the next 3 ½ years Marnie went through 5 different hormonal treatments, 78 days of radiation treatments, and 9 different complete chemotherapy treatments, stopping each only when it failed or when the side effects become too devastating. All of that was in addition to trying various diets and alternative therapies (none of which proved effective with her stage of cancer). Marnie's tumors would shrink, and at one point they virtually disappeared. But always, they returned. We were running out of options.

Throughout our lives together we had felt like God was taking care of us. He brought us together. He kept us together when I was too immature, needy, and self-involved to be there for Marnie the way she needed me when she needed me. Yet she stayed with me as I grew up and grew into her. We built a profound love for one another. We grew into that love together. We became absolutely one with one another. Our bond became unbreakable. Our love for one another was **the** absolute certainty of our lives.

We went through life threatening circumstances. We went through situations that seemed absolutely hopeless. Yet we always came through. It felt like God always took care of us. Now, in one more state of hopelessness and fear, it felt like God was taking care of us. A distant second or third cousin that Marnie had not heard from for over 20 years emailed. She had somehow heard about Marnie's cancer and wanted us to know that her daughter earned her PhD. in breast cancer research and was working for the M.D. Anderson cancer center in Houston, TX. She encouraged us to contact her.

We did. She (Erika) encouraged us to find a program that did both genomic (the study of gene mutations related to the expression of the cancer) and proteomic (the study of over-activity in otherwise normal genes that is related to the cancer) testing of Marnie's cancer cells, and would design a treatment program specifically for Marnie based on the results of that testing. Erika gave us a list of possible programs to call that were doing that kind of testing and treatment planning. We reached out to all of them.

It felt like God was taking care of us in bringing Erika into our lives. And it felt like God was taking care of us in leading us to Dr. Brian Leyland-Jones at the Avera Cancer Institute in Sioux Falls, SD. The Avera Cancer Center accepted Marnie into their clinical trial that was based on the genomic and proteomic testing of Marnie's cancer. They would design a treatment program specifically tailored to her cancer.

We told Dr. Leyland-Jones that we had been in love for 45 years and our goal was to make it to 75 years together. He said his goal was to help us achieve our goal. No doctor had ever spoken to us in that way before. We wept with joy. We again had hope. Dr. Leyland Jones success rate in treating patients with fourth line or higher breast cancer (i.e. they had received at least 4 different kinds of chemotherapy treatments prior to coming to him {Marnie had had 7}) was 57% compared to 10% for standard chemotherapy treatment. We felt that God had brought us here.

At Avera, they surgically removed a cancerous tumor from Marnie's neck which they sent to Foundation One in Massachusetts to test for over 400 possible gene mutations that might be related to Marnie's cancer. And they took two full vials of Marnie's blood and sent them to Guardant Health in Arizona to test for circulating tumoral nucleic acid in her blood. The combination of the findings from the two testing methods would determine a treatment plan specifically designed for Marnie's genetic make-up. The blood was taken on March 30th and the surgery done on March 31, 2016. We were to return in one month to find the results of the testing and embark on the treatment program that we hoped and believed would result in the alleviation of Marnie's cancer. Our hope was restored. We believed again that God was taking care of us.

The one month interim period in waiting for the test results, however, proved to be fateful. A tumor on the back of Marnie's head grew to be intolerably painful. She could no longer sleep. So Marnie's radiation oncologist at the Montana Cancer Center immediately began a series of 10 radiation treatments on Marnie's head and spinal cord (where tumors had also been growing). The radiation treatments were completed on April 18th.

During the period of time that she was receiving the radiation, I became increasingly concerned about Marnie's developing confusion, forgetfulness, and lack of coordination. I expressed these concerns to her medical oncologist, Dr. Linda Ries. Dr. Ries immediately scheduled a CT scan of Marnie's neck and thorax, and an MRI of her brain for the following day. The tests showed that Marnie's cancer had spread dramatically. There were 11 new tumors in her brain, and tumors now in her liver, kidneys, and lungs. Full brain radiation treatments began April 22, 2016 and continued through May 4, 2016.

On May 9th, we returned to the Avera Cancer Institute to get the results of Marnie's genetic testing. The results showed 6 different genetic pathways into Marnie's cancer, including the "PD-1, PDL-1 pathway" which is normally found in only 20% of breast cancer patients. That was exciting. With the PD-1 pathway active, the cancer is able to bond with and shut down the immune system's normal response to invaders, allowing the cancer to grow, unchecked. That seemed to be exactly what was happening to Marnie. The immunotherapy drug, Keytruda (pembrolizumab) had been shown with other cancers (including Jimmy Carter's) to shut off that PD-1 pathway and allow the immune system to begin recognizing and killing the cancer. Once again, we felt like God was taking care of us.

Dr. Leyland Jones' treatment recommendations included the chemotherapy drugs Afinitor (5mg three times per week) and Xeloda (2000mg daily for one week on followed by one week off.

(He felt it vital that Marnie go back on the Xeloda, which she had tried before, because it crosses the blood brain barrier and thereby protects the brain from developing further tumors.) And he prescribed an IV infusion of Keytruda every three weeks. Finally he recommended the initiation of Ibrance treatment at a future date when the combined effects and side effects of the first 3 drugs could be assessed. We had our plan for healing.

It didn't work out. In hindsight, things had probably progressed too far. Maybe we should have continued the treatments with the chemotherapy drug, Doxil (that Marnie had begun two weeks earlier) to significantly reduce the tumor burden before beginning on this new 4 pronged treatment plan. Maybe the Doxil wouldn't have worked either. The problem again was side effects. Maybe the side effects would have mounted with the Doxil as well. We will never know. It is with profound sadness that I question the wisdom of our choices (in hindsight).

Marnie began the 4 pronged treatment program with Afinitor on May 13, 2016. The events and happenings over the next 2 ½ months are complex and complicated. Rather than spell out every drug taken every step along the way, it is probably simpler to say that Marnie began an unrelenting period of extreme digestive distress. It began with extreme gas and bloating. It progressed to virtually daily vomiting. Combinations of various drugs would relieve the vomiting for a day or two, but it always returned. It grew progressively more intense. It grew to the point that Marnie vomited 16 times in 3 days in late June. Marnie had begun Xeloda again on June 11th. After successfully fighting for approval of the Keytruda (it had not been FDA approved for breast cancer), Marnie received her first infusion of Keytruda on June 23, 2016.

The treatment program was in full swing. Unfortunately, so was the vomiting. The drug that seemed most effective in preventing the vomiting (promethazine) also seemed to bring about significant mental confusion. The Afinitor seemed to be significantly reducing Marnie's blood counts. She no longer had the energy to go for even the short walk down our driveway to the mailbox. She began receiving weekly blood transfusions to bring her blood counts back up. Throughout all of this though, Marnie remained positive and confident that she would make it through.

My concern during this period when a myriad of drugs (each with their own set of side-effects) were being taken to counteract the side-effects of the drugs being taken to fight the cancer, was that mental confusion, forgetfulness, lack of coordination, clumsiness, vomiting, and upper abdominal pain – all in this once beautiful, athletic woman, were the same symptoms Marnie had when the tumors in her brain and liver were growing.

The symptoms could have come from the combination and interaction of all the various drugs Marnie was taking. Dr. Menendez, Marnie's radiation oncologist, said it could take a full 12 weeks or more for Marnie's brain to recover from the full brain radiation, so that the after effects of the full brain radiation could be a cause. The Keytruda could be causing significant inflammation at the tumor sights where the immune system was now directly battling the tumors. There were simply too many possibilities for us to know for sure what the exact cause might have been.

Dr. Ries, Marnie's medical oncologist believed that the Xeloda was a significant cause of Marnie's vomiting. So she discontinued the Xeloda treatment. There was some improvement, but then the vomiting resumed. While Dr. Ries was away at a medical conference, Dr. Linford, her substitute believed the Afinitor was another cause of Marnie's vomiting (as well as the lowering of her blood counts). So he discontinued the Afinitor.

Our treatment program was falling apart. By the second full week of July, Marnie was sleeping 12+ hours per day. On July 16th, she woke, weeping, not knowing who or where she was, or who I was. We felt we had to abandon the treatment program for the time being and go back to the infusions of Doxil. We met with Dr. Ries on July 20, 2016 and asked to do precisely that. Dr. Ries said that in good conscience, she could not do it. At this point, it would do Marnie more harm than good. There was nothing more that could be done medically.

All hope seemed gone. We could now only pray for a miracle. Marnie's body died two weeks later. I lost my heart and my soul's mate. I could only turn to God to find them again, but it felt like God had abandoned us, that God was no longer taking care of us. I feared that my faith in God had been fantasy. I feared that I would never be able to find or fill my heart again in this lifetime.

That's my personal story, the story of Marnie and me. That has led to the creation of this book. Your story, I'm sure, is quite different. But our stories share loss. Our stories share pain. And I believe our stories will share continued connection and ultimate rejoining.

In spite of Marnie's cancer, suffering, and physical death I suggest that God is the pathway to both that connection and the rejoining. Let's look at how and why I came to that conclusion.

Chapter 6: Finding my way back to God

The pain, the grief that I felt following Marnie's physical death was excruciating, unrelenting, and at times utterly overwhelming. I would sob, howl, scream, and beat the floor until I collapsed in exhaustion. Massive amounts of exercise were my primary survival mechanism. In the first 4 weeks after the death of Marnie's body I biked over 700 miles, ran another 100 miles, and swam across the lake where she loved to swim 8 times (despite my being a poor, fearful swimmer). I simply had to lose myself in physical effort in trying to keep the pain at bay – at a level that I could survive.

I could not leave Marnie behind. I could not live or even conceive of living without her continued presence in my life. She was my heart. She was my wife, my lover, my best friend.

Virtually all religions believe in the reality of an immortal soul. I had not given that any serious thought my entire adult life. But I realized with Marnie's physical death, that If I could come to believe in the soul, if I could believe that the soul is our fundamental essence as human beings – if I could believe that our consciousness, our awareness, our self-awareness, our intelligence, and our love all reside in a soul which is eternal and lives on beyond the death of the body, then my relationship with Marnie would not be over with her physical death. I would have a reason to keep living. My heart and soul would still be alive. So I began my quest to come to fully believe in the reality of our souls. Because of it, I began my journey to find God.

That journey has involved a combination of trying to think clearly and in depth about God and the soul, and experiencing a series of profoundly moving occurrences in the natural world that have seemed to confirm my thinking. I will begin by sharing my reasoning. I ask you to examine it closely and see if it fits for you as it does for me.

Chapter 7: My Ideas about God and the platform of reason upon which I have built my beliefs and my Faith

If like me, you are not religious or at least not solidly grounded in a religion, then this chapter may prove difficult for you. But I ask you to look at it closely. I ask you to examine it in detail. I ask you to ask yourself if there is any other explanation for life and the meaning of being that makes greater sense to you than the ideas that I present in this chapter. I ask myself that question repeatedly. The answer is the key to my faith. The answer could be the key to your faith. So consider what follows closely and carefully.

In writing about God I've had to keep asking myself, "Am I absolutely genuine in what I am saying? Do I fundamentally believe what I am writing? I question myself every day. But it is clear to me that what I write here is what makes sense to me. There is no other explanation for reality, for the meaning of life and death that makes more sense to me. I can come up with no other more reasonable way to account for the meaning of being than what I write in the following ideas about God.

As I have said, I do not write as a member of any religion. No religion fully fits for me. Each seems filled with its own set of stories that we are expected to accept as truth. I can't do that. I am writing for those of you who also question religion. I have come to believe that you can build faith in God without religion. God makes sense to me. Faith makes sense to me.

Faith is at the heart of my connection to Marnie. Faith is at the heart of my connection to God. God is at the heart of my connection to and the source of my belief in Marnie's continued, conscious, living presence. Living in faith is now the only thing that makes life make sense to me. It is the cornerstone, the foundation for my feeling a continued purpose for living on this earth.

So I work on deepening and strengthening my faith every day. I do so in prayer. I do so by repeatedly affirming the beliefs that make sense to me. I do so in sharing my heart and soul with Marnie, out loud, every day. I do so using all the psychological tools I have at my disposal. I will describe all of this in detail in subsequent chapters. But I believe that my reasoned thoughts about God are the foundation upon which my healing is built. I hope that sharing those thoughts about God with you will allow you to decide whether or not the path to healing that I have chosen to follow is a path that fits for you as well.

Keep in mind though, that to accept the wisdom of my thoughts about God and the meaning of being, you will ultimately have to make a fundamental leap of faith. So examine these thoughts carefully to determine if that leap makes sense for you. Only you can make that determination. It is with that in mind that I offer you the process of thinking that led to my belief in the reality of an eternal, loving God.

My Ideas about God

I worked and continue to work every day at strengthening a fundamental, deep-seated belief in God. I began building that belief from what I hoped was a base of reasoned, logical, and scientific thinking. I tried to build that belief in a way that made sense to me rationally. And I continue to affirm and work at strengthening what I believe to be a belief that bridges the gap between the physical world that I live in now and a spiritual world that transcends it.

Doing so has required walking a bridge of faith that I hope has been built upon pillars of reason. It is the bridge that allows me to believe that Marnie, the essence of Marnie, is still fully alive -- that I can still have an active relationship with her (albeit purely mental and emotional for now). Through that belief I can trust that I will rejoin Marnie again (fully) when my body dies. Believing this, trusting in this, pulling this belief deep down into my core, makes life still feel worth living for me.

The Foundation

Marnie's continued, conscious, living presence makes sense to me in a world with an eternal, loving God as its source and its foundation. To arrive at this belief, I start from the fundamental premise that **something cannot come from nothing**.

Even the universe itself could not simply spring forth from nothingness. It had to have a beginning – no matter how many billions of years ago. Prior to the "big bang" there had to be something, a source for the seed from which the universe could spring, and from which all of physical creation could evolve. There had to be something that preceded physical existence.

From a quantum physics perspective, that "something" can be described as a combination of energy and information. All reality as we know it is a combination of energy and information. We could not exist, there could be no physical reality without energy and information. Energy can be transformed into matter creating physical reality through a shift in its vibration level according to the information programming or directing it. But that energy and information had to exist prior to the creation of physical reality. There could be no universe without energy being present before its birth and without the information needed to program its creation, its level of vibration, and its evolution.

So what is the source of that energy and information? Since something cannot come from nothing, the source must of necessity be eternal. If it were not, there would have to be a source for the source. Ultimately, **an eternal source is the only possible explanation for all of creation**. And since prior to the birth of the universe there was no physical reality, the source of all being had to transcend the physical. It had to precede the physical. It had to be what we call "spiritual".

An eternal, spiritual source of all being is essentially the definition of "God". Without God (the eternal, spiritual source of being), the universe itself would not be. Without God, we could not be.

And I further suggest that not only is God the ultimate source of physical reality, but God is the source of consciousness and all of the other dimensions of spiritual reality (of mind) as well.

Physical evolution, particularly in the context of billions of years, makes sense to me. It can account for the diversity of life on this earth, in this universe. But I return again to the fundamental logical premise that something cannot come from nothing. Awareness, consciousness, awareness of self – these things are not physical. Though they co-exist with the body, they transcend it. They are fundamentally different. They are dimensions of "mind", not body.

I am not my body. I am aware of my body. I direct my body. But the "I" is not my body. The "I" is a quality of mind, of awareness, of self-awareness. It exists in a non-physical, spiritual realm. You cannot see or touch or hear or smell or taste mind as you can physical reality. But the awareness, consciousness, and self-awareness that are the fundamental dimensions of mind are no less real. We experience them through our physical bodies while on this earth, but they are fundamentally different forms or levels of reality. They could no more suddenly spring forth from the physical than dog could spontaneously spring forth from cat. Their natures are fundamentally different. The non-physical cannot suddenly spring forth from the physical.

There are some who might argue that the brain is the source of our consciousness. I disagree. "I" direct my brain through my consciousness. The brain is an incredibly powerful super-computer, but as with any other computer, it requires an operator to turn it on, to set it into motion. It requires a programmer to give it direction. The "I" does that. The "I" lives separately from the computer. The "I" transcends the computer.

What we call the "soul" is the essence of the "I". My soul is fundamentally who "I" am. My soul is the operating force behind my brain through the conscious awareness that resides in my soul. The soul directs the brain from a level of being that is separate from it and transcends it.

The brain dies with the body. The death of the brain is the very definition of the death of the body. But the "I", the soul-level, conscious awareness that directs the brain does not die with the body because it exists separately from it. It transcends it, even in the brain's death.

But, as with physical reality, the soul could not spring forth from nothingness. There had to be a source from which the soul could be derived. That source of necessity had to possess mind, awareness, consciousness, and self-awareness to give birth to those things in the soul. And of necessity, that source had to be eternal. Otherwise mind (something) would have to spring from nothing – that logical impossibility. The eternal, the infinite, God has to be not only real, but conscious, aware, and self-aware to bring these things forth in the soul.

To take this a step further, we can see from direct observation that there is a level of organization in the seemingly infinite complexity of nature and the universe. There is an organized, interdependent flow and cycling of energy and relationships throughout both. Such complexity and organization couldn't randomly come into being and stay in place. It argues for an underlying intelligent design to nature and the universe.

Even seemingly random, spontaneous, coincidental events that occur in the process of evolution or seemingly totally unrelated events as described by chaos theory do not destroy the balance. They move it forward. They enhance it.

All of this argues for an intelligent design underlying even the process of evolution. This in turn argues for an intelligent designer as the source of the blueprint that set the process of evolution into motion. Nature and the universe argue for an intelligent designer – an intelligent designer who could chart their precise course to a lasting, infinitely complex, balanced flow of energy and interdependent relationships.

That designer had to precede nature and the universe in order to create and shape them. And such a designer would have to possess infinite intelligence and creativity to create the blueprint for evolution. Such an infinite designer could only be God.

God, therefore, is intelligent and creative as well as conscious, aware, and self-aware. All of this is inherently required for the design and creation of the organized, infinitely complex universe and the interdependent natural world in which we live.

And to go one final step, I believe that **God has to be and is loving**. This is the central tenant that underlies all that I have come to believe. God gave us life. He gave us the ability to be self-aware in living that life. And God created us as beings capable of loving and feeling love. He created us as beings capable of building profound, unbreakable bonds of love. As our source, God created us from His essence, as individualized expressions of His essential being. He could not create us from something that He is not. He is by definition infinite and there can be nothing beyond the infinite.

Loving beings, therefore, could only come from a <u>loving</u> God, capable of giving, knowing, and feeling love.

I personally believe that the essence of God is love because of the profound experience of love that I was able to share with Marnie in my lifetime. I experienced that love in my body, but it absolutely transcended my body. It became woven into the very fabric of my being.

For me, there is no question that the love that we felt for one another transcended the physical. As an example, in the weeks before her death, Marnie and I could no longer physically make love. But the intensity of the love that we felt for one another increased exponentially rather than being diminished. In looking into Marnie's eyes, I had a profound feeling that I was seeing something far deeper than her body. I was seeing something beyond her body. I was seeing into the real essence of Marnie. I now believe I was looking into her soul.

And I say, because of my personal experience, that love is the most profound, meaningful, fulfilling experience we can have on this earth. It is the central fiber that defines who we are as human beings. And more than anything else, our love defines who we are as unique individuals. Love gives us our fundamental, unique, personal identity.

I restate, something cannot come from nothing. Something cannot come from what it is not. Our ability to love (and ultimately the loves we build in our lives) had to come from a source of love. That is God. God created us as unique, individual manifestations of himself, as an act of love. He gave us love in our lives as a gift of love. By creating us from His essence as unique loving beings, as unique, individualized dimensions of Himself, God further defined the infinite scope and complexity of His love.

The Details

I'm going to risk overkill here, because I believe that my thoughts about God and the creation and shaping of our eternal souls are <u>the keys to the whole healing process</u>. I will to restate some of my thoughts from a slightly different perspective, in slightly different words to hopefully make them crystal clear.

God: The Source and Substance of our Being

We are creations of God. We are reflections of God. We are individualizations of God. It can be said that we are the children of God. God is the ultimate source and substance of both our physical being and our spiritual being. In the short term perspective, our physical bodies came from the DNA of our parents. Our physical bodies can die. All physical bodies die, even the magnificent trees that can live to be a thousand years old or more, eventually die. There is no escaping physical death.

But our spiritual bodies were created from the "stuff," from the "DNA", from the combination of unlimited energy and information that comprise the essential being of God. It could be no other way. God is infinite. His essence must be the source and substance of ours. And yet, ironically, we give individualized expression to that essence through the choices we make in the course of living out our physical lives while remaining literal "children of God."

As God is conscious, aware, self-aware, intelligent, creative, and loving, we, as individualized dimensions of God, must also be conscious, aware, self-aware, intelligent, creative, and loving beings. And most importantly (from a healing perspective), because our fundamental nature is derived from the eternal, spiritual nature of God, our fundamental essence must also be eternal and spiritual.

There can be no destruction of God's spiritual energy. God had to exist for all eternity in order to be the source of all creation. Eternity (by definition) extends in all directions simultaneously. Therefore, God, and the spiritual energy that comes from God, cannot be destroyed. They will continue to exist for all eternity. So we, as creations from and of the essence of God, will continue to exist for all eternity as well. In our living souls, we transcend physical death. We are **eternal.**

This same reality can be seen from a quantum physics perspective. According to the first law of thermodynamics, the total amount of energy in a closed system can neither be created nor destroyed. It can only be transformed from one form to another to maintain overall balance within the system.

The death of Marnie's body, therefore, was not destruction, but rather transformation. When a body dies, a transformation into a higher level of spiritual information and energy must occur to balance the loss of the physical energy. At death, physical energy is transformed into spiritual energy. Marnie's physical death would bring her soul to a higher level of energy. She would possess a stronger energy presence without the limits of her physical body, while maintaining full consciousness and awareness because they don't die with the body since they are not physical.

From a spiritual perspective Marnie's soul would now possess a greater, stronger connection with God. Love and the loving energy of the soul are enhanced by, are moved to a higher level by, and are magnified and intensified by the death of the physical body tied to that soul. So for us, our connection, our oneness in the love that we shared and share would now become even stronger for Marnie.

For each of us, our intelligence, our awareness, our self-awareness, our consciousness, our consciousness of self, our love, and the bonds of love that we build in our physical lifetimes are heightened in the life of the soul that is freed from the ties to its physical body at the time of physical death. They do not die.

In the course of living together, Marnie and I built a bond of oneness and love that we felt was absolutely unbreakable. We grew certain, we "knew" that our connection would never end. **It was for us, an absolute certainty**.

In the transition that occurred at her physical death, Marnie, moved out of her body to a higher, spiritual level of vibration. That didn't change our oneness. Our oneness was and is still there. We are still connected. We are one now. We will be one for all eternity. I have come to view that as true from both a physics perspective and a spiritual perspective.

It has been through defining my ideas about God and the fundamental reality of the soul that I have begun to heal. Through this foundation of belief, Marnie's continued, living presence makes sense to me. And it is in feeling Marnie's continued, living presence and hence in the reality of our continued living relationship that I have begun to heal.

I hope you will look closely again at my thinking thus far and see if it fits for you. If it does, then the reality of the living presence of your beloved and the living, ongoing relationship between you and your beloved can begin to bring you healing as well.

The key is God. You have to think clearly about whether it makes sense to you, on the most basic level, that a loving God is real. If a real, living, and loving God makes sense to you, then the soul and life itself will make sense in the context of God's reality. And, if you come to see God as the source and substance of your being, of all being, then you can and will come to feel the ongoing reality of your <u>eternal</u> connection with the one you love.

    I hope that by looking even more closely at the soul (in the next chapter) you and I will be able to travel even further down the path of healing together.

Chapter 8: Ideas about the Soul

As I explained in the previous chapter, to begin to heal from the death of Marnie's body, I had to first come to a fundamental belief in the reality of a living God. In and through this belief I came to believe in the reality of an eternal soul as the essence of our being.

In this chapter I want to look closely at the dimensions, the intricacies, and the implications of an eternal, living soul. In it I believe we find the key to healing and the rebirth of joy in our lives.

The Role of Our Physical Lives in Defining our Souls

We are physical beings as well as spiritual beings. We were born physically into life on this earth for a reason -- to allow each of us to develop the unique personality, the unique character, the unique identity of the individual soul that we will carry with us throughout eternity.

Each of us has an absolutely unique set of experiences. Each of us makes an absolutely unique set of choices. It is from those experiences and choices that we each become the unique person with the unique self-concept that defines the identity of our soul.

While we become unique individuals living in the physical world, we remain fundamentally bound in oneness with the God as dimensions of and extensions of Him. We are, therefore, simultaneously human and divine. We are individual human beings who are simultaneously connected in divine oneness with God.

Love, the Essential Fabric of the Soul

Love is inherent in God. It could be said that love is the essence of God. The love that we build, the love that we give, and the love that we share in our physical lifetimes, therefore, are what connect us with and put us most fully in harmony with God. And that love, our love, becomes **the** essential dimension of our personal, soul-level identity.

Love transcends the physical. It is fundamentally spiritual. It can't be bound in or contained in some part of a physical body. It exists beyond the body and it fills the body in such a way as to create intense feelings that further and fundamentally define the identity of each of us. And since the spiritual level cannot be destroyed, at physical death, we carry our love with us and we carry our soul-level identity with us throughout eternity.

Our love and the loving energy of our souls are enhanced by, are moved to a higher level by, and are magnified and intensified by the death of our physical bodies. Again, this is a direct expression of the first law of thermodynamics. Because death ends physical existence, the life of the soul that is bound to that physical body is moved to a higher level of energy to maintain the balance (the homeostasis) inherent in all of being. Our intelligence, our consciousness, our awareness, our self-awareness, our love, the bonds of love that we built in our physical lifetimes – those qualities that fundamentally define our souls are all heightened by the death of our bodies. They do not die. They are magnified.

All of those qualities are fundamentally Godly and eternal. Though the choices we make on this earth while living in our physical bodies can limit us (or even cut us off) from the perfect expression of that Godliness, they cannot change the fundamental reality of the Godliness that is our essence. Our souls are fundamentally Godly and eternal.

In the maturation of our souls, through the loving choices we make in our human lifetimes, we gradually become more and more fully realized, dimensions of God. That is ultimate truth, ultimate destiny for each of us. It must be so. In the context of eternity, we will each (all) at some point, come into harmony with and live that reality.

Living love now is the key to realizing and participating in our divine essence now. The physical death of a loved one is a passageway, a profound stimulus to a greater, more fulfilled understanding of who and what we really are – divine, eternal beings. The physical death of one deeply loved can be a passageway, a stimulus to feeling and living love absolutely, and hence a passageway to full harmony with our fundamental, divine, spiritual essence.

Though we became unique individuals living in the physical world, we remained fundamentally bound in oneness with God because He created us as unique dimensions of and extensions of himself. All being was created by and is contained within God. God permeates everything. We are each an extension of God – a uniquely individualized dimension of God, each of us. We are inseparably one with and in God.

My Personal Bond of Love

With all that being said, I restate: the love that we build, the love that we create, the love that we share in our physical lifetimes becomes the essential core of our identity. And love is not physical. It can't be bound in or contained in some part of a physical body. Love is fundamentally spiritual. The spiritual level cannot be destroyed. It is by definition eternal.

For me, therefore, Marnie is alive. Her soul is alive. It was shaped by and through our life and love together. Who Marnie was, who she still is, and who she will always be was shaped by our life and love together. A significant part of her spiritual reality was and is her love for me. That cannot die. And combined with her living awareness, she still sees me. She still hears me. She still feels me. She still knows me. She still loves me. Now. In the form of the spiritual reality, the pure "soul" that she has become.

I can't pretend to know all of the dimensions, all of the subtleties, all of the possibilities that are there for Marnie now in her spiritual state. But I can know that she is here. That she is real. That our bond of love is real and absolutely undying. She left this earth absolutely loving me in the best way that any human being could have ever loved. And if I maintain my love for her, my commitment to her, my bond of marriage with her, then we as a couple will have a shared identity, a shared spiritual reality that will last forever.

It is profoundly painful missing Marnie's physical presence, but I love her more than anything in the universe. I always will. I will never stop. Our commitment is forever. The depth and meaning of our commitment has grown exponentially since our profession of it in our wedding vows. I actually love Marnie now, more than I ever have. I love her with a greater depth and intensity than I ever knew was possible. The death of her physical body heightened and magnified my love for Marnie on a spiritual level just as it did hers.

Perhaps that had to be so. Our souls became bonded as one in love during our lifetime together. And they are bonded as one in and through God as well. So with the death of Marnie's physical body and the resulting heightening of her spiritual energy, I experienced a concurrent heightening of spiritual energy through our bond of oneness. Though we are separate, unique individuals, we are simultaneously one in love and one in God.

On a human level, Marnie is my forever wife. I am her forever husband. We are one in love. On a divine level we are each one with God as direct, unique dimensions of Him, and therefore, we are one together with Him, in Him, and through Him. We are husband and wife, one in love. We are one together with and in God.

Eric Fromm said that real love means, "I, in you, me. I, in me, you". I now carry that forward to include, "Us in God. God in us". In real love, a oneness is created that can never be destroyed.

We are simultaneously human and divine. We are individual human beings who are simultaneously connected in divine oneness with God.

Perhaps my soul and Marnie's soul chose one another in the very beginning. Perhaps it was God's plan that our souls find Him through our love and oneness with one another. Perhaps we brought that plan to fruition in this physical lifetime through the choices we made in building our love together. I don't know.

But I do know that our oneness is real. And I believe that it is in finding and creating a lifetime that is absolutely defined by love that we get to move on beyond the limits of our physical lives. Marnie and I became absolutely defined by our love for and with one another. Now, when my body dies, the possibilities for our future together become unlimited.

Perhaps God has a plan for each of us that we will each ultimately live out, which will bring each of us divine fulfillment. It's just that for some, that fulfillment may take multiple lifetimes to accomplish. Marnie and I were fortunate enough to build loving, divine oneness now, in this lifetime. And it has been in Marnie's dying, in the loss of her physical body, that I have come to experience the profound depth and intensity of the reality of our divine, loving oneness.

I wish there could have been another way of getting there. I miss Marnie's physical presence profoundly. I so look forward to rejoining her in the next chapter of eternity together. In that chapter, I hope to live love fully and perfectly together – in love and loving together.

Suffering: The Unavoidable Reality of Being Human

The reality of our spiritual, Godly essence does not negate the reality of the mortal nature of our bodies. That mortal nature of necessity involves sadness, loss, and suffering. We cannot have a physical body without death. We cannot love someone deeply and experience their physical death without a feeling of profound loss and hence sadness and suffering. Suffering, pain, and loss seem an integral, essential, unavoidable part of the experience of being human.

Perhaps they are required for perspective. It is in the profound hurt, the profound sense of loss that I have experienced with the death of Marnie's body that I have come to fully appreciate the astounding blessings we were given in our life together. I treasure now what was so easy to take for granted when Marnie was physically alive, when I never considered not having her in my life. I wish now, in hindsight, that I had shown her every day how profoundly I treasure and treasured her.

From a religious perspective, Jesus is the model given by the bible for how to live. Christians define him as simultaneously a human being and the son of God. Yet even Jesus suffered. He suffered deeply. He experienced sadness and grief. He did not want to die. He asked to be able to avoid the pain if it was at all possible. But he accepted it as the will of his Father. He accepted it as the reality of being a human being. He accepted it as his role in living love in his lifetime. Because of his humanity, he could not avoid the pain and suffering of physical death. In that, he was an exquisite model for all of us (whether we are Christians and believe in the bible or not). And, according to the bible, Jesus rose from the dead. Jesus transcended death. He is the model that teaches that we too transcend death.

From a logical (non-religious, non-biblical) perspective, mind, soul, spirit, consciousness, awareness, self-awareness, and love are not physical. They are spiritual. Because of that, they do not and cannot die with physical death. They are our birthright. They are our gift from God. They are our essence. They are what make us unique individualizations of God.

God is eternal. Our souls are eternal. As individualizations of God, our souls rise above physical death. Love resides in and defines our unique souls. Our love rises above physical death. Our love joins us in inseparable oneness with God and God's love.

And I know from my personal experience that it was in love, and only in love, that I found real, lasting joy. That was a fundamental truth in my life. I believe it is true for each of us. Therefore, in transcending the death of the body, as we carry with us our love, we will also carry with us joy – for all eternity.

My Personal Testament to Marnie

All this stuff just makes sense to me logically. I can make no logical sense out of existence and awareness in any other way. Therefore, my beloved Marnie is still fully alive and aware in every dimension except her physical body.

She is now living on higher level of spiritual energy with a greater, stronger connection with God. She now possesses a stronger energy presence without the limits of her physical body, while maintaining full consciousness and awareness. Our connection, our oneness in the love that we shared (and still share) is now even stronger for Marnie (and, as I have learned, for me).

The death of Marnie's body severed our physical connection. It did not and cannot sever our spiritual connection. It did not and cannot sever our oneness on the level of the soul. Marnie and I became one in love. We truly became **one**. The death of Marnie's body could not end that. Death cannot sever oneness. They (death and oneness) exist on different planes of reality – on different levels of vibration. The oneness that Marnie and I built together became part of the fundamental essence of our spiritual, soul-level being – untouchable by physical death.

While we were physically living together, Marnie and I "<u>knew</u>" that our connection would never end for as long as we lived. We knew that our connection was absolutely unbreakable. <u>That was for us an absolute certainty.</u>

The death of Marnie's body hasn't changed that. Since Marnie carries her mind, her consciousness, and her love with her beyond the limits of her physical body, she is fully aware of me. On some level (that is beyond my full comprehension because I have not experienced physical death) she watches over me; she hears me; she sees me; she feels me; she feels my profound love for her; she feels and knows my profound commitment to her; she feels and knows my absolute desire to live every remaining moment of my physical life on this earth as an instrument of her love and as a testament of my love for her.

We are still connected. We are still one. Now. Marnie is with me. Now. We are joined as one for all eternity. We are one in love and one in God. And what is joined in God cannot be torn asunder. It's infinite. It's eternal. Our oneness is forever.

I carry Marnie in my heart and soul constantly. I have chosen to actively and consciously nurture our love every day for the rest of my physical life until I can be rejoined with her at the death of my body in absolute oneness, in full, conscious awareness of one another and in the full expression of our love for one another, forever.

Every day, I affirm, as I speak with Marnie, "Our souls are one in love, sweet darling. Our souls are forever one." Physical death cannot sever our oneness. Living on different planes of being does not sever our oneness. We are one in love and one in God.

The death of Marnie's body has been the most painful thing I have ever experienced or could ever imagine experiencing. But it may have been the necessary source for my being able to make the transition into eternity, into the world of spirit, soul, and supernatural reality successfully. Marnie brought me to God.

Marnie's arms are and always will be my home. That's where I need to go to come home. And ultimately, I need to come home.

This applies to you as much as it does to me

If you have lost a spouse as I have, or if you have lost your mother or your father, or your son or your daughter, or your brother or your sister, or a dearly beloved friend, your pain is real. Your loss is real.

And your continued connection with your beloved is real. There is a soul level connection that is not severed. It cannot be broken by the death of the body. There are bonds that you built together and shared in your physical lives together which live on in the soul.

Those bonds are alive. Those bonds are real. Your continued connection is alive. Your continued connection is real, just as mine is with Marnie. The nature of your relationship is different from mine. The unique personality of your relationship is different from mine. But the potential for your living an active, loving relationship with your beloved here and now is every bit as real.

There is nothing I can say to ease the pain of your physical loss. No matter how much they love and care for me, no one's words have eased the pain of my physical loss.

But I believe that with clear thinking you can ease the overall pain of your heart's loss by coming to realize that your beloved is not gone. Your beloved is not gone from your life now. Your relationship with your beloved is not over. It has undergone a transformation, a fundamental transformation that will ultimately bring you even greater fulfillment in the context of eternity. Your bond is eternal, and so is your love for one another. You will always be together on the most profound level.

We all have to face physical death. We all have to come to grips with the question of whether we have a soul that will live on beyond our physical bodies. In facing that reality, all of the thinking that I have outlined in my search for understanding the spiritual nature of being, in my search for finding God, in my struggle to keep my relationship with Marnie fully alive in my heart and in my consciousness, applies directly to you. It applies directly to your life, and to your relationship with your beloved.

I call my bond with Marnie a bond of oneness. Your bond is real and personal. You will define it as it fits for you. Your bond is absolutely unique. But it is a real bond of love nonetheless. And bonds of love cannot be severed by the death of the body. They are inherently eternal. The bonds of love that we establish with those we love deeply are enhanced by the death of the body. They are strengthened by it. Physical death is a passageway to deeper love, not an event that terminates it. Believing this flows directly from the belief that God is real and loving.

And God is eternal. God is the source and substance of your soul. God is the source and substance of your essential being, and the essential being of your beloved, who now and always will continue to love you. In that reality, your beloved is conscious, aware, loving, and perhaps most importantly for your healing, eternally present. Your task is to come to understand that reality, to pull it down deep inside of you, and translate it into an active, present, ongoing relationship on your end. That, ultimately, will bring about your healing.

As you come to experience that healing there will be a fundamental change in both the physical and the metaphysical vibration level of your being. You will be transformed just as your relationship was transformed by the physical death of your beloved. You will come to feel a greater responsibility to live love now with everyone else in your life as a part of your focus on nurturing the loving connection between you and your beloved. In doing that, your relationship with the soul of your beloved will be deepened and intensified through the combination of your active focus on loving them, and in the loving that you do in your life.

In finding healing and comfort in God, in maintaining a soul level, loving eternal connection with your beloved, you tap into the divine. You become more Godly. The physical death of your beloved becomes a gift, not a curse.

> You don't have a soul.
> You are a Soul.
> You have a body.

Chapter 9: Ideas about Jesus

The majority of people in our (American) culture are Christians. So I felt it important to write a chapter addressing Jesus. I am not a Christian. I try to live Christian values as I understand them, but I don't go to church or follow the teachings of any specific Christian denomination. I don't in any way intend to be disparaging of Jesus or those who identify themselves as Christian. I believe there is wisdom in the Christian religion (and in all religions) that we can adopt and carry inside us that will enrich our lives. In this chapter, I hope to identify what that wisdom is (for me), and how it can be applied to each of our lives regardless of our religious beliefs.

Christians have told me that I must turn my life over to Jesus to truly heal from Marnie's physical death. They have told me that Jesus is the only true pathway to God. They have told me that Jesus' crucifixion and death atoned for all of our sins and suffering, and that his resurrection earned for us our resurrection to eternal happiness in heaven. They have told me that it is only in believing in and turning myself over to Jesus as the Son of God and my lord and savior that I will find ultimate peace and healing.

I personally cannot accept all of this. I am not finding my way to God through Jesus. I am finding my way to God through Marnie, through my love for her and my bond with her.

But the essence of what Jesus stood for makes sense to me. However, my understanding of Jesus varies from what my Christian friends believe. Again, I don't claim to have **the** truth – only my truth. But based on what I have learned from the bible and from other writings about Jesus, what I see him being more than anything else is a model of love. If the writings about Jesus are true, he may very well have been an almost perfect model of love. My Christian friends believe that he was absolutely perfect. He would have to be as the perfect Son of God that they profess him to be.

But this is what I see. Jesus lived love. He taught love. He modeled generosity and forgiveness. His words, such as, "Feed the hungry. Give drink to the thirsty. Clothe the naked.... Blessed are the poor in spirit....Forgive them Father for they know not what they do." All of these were loving and forgiving messages. His actions – healing the sick, comforting the suffering, mingling with and forgiving those who were considered sinners – were loving and forgiving.

Even though he saw himself as the son of God, even though he saw himself as the savior of all mankind, he knew he was going to suffer and die. Yet he chose to go ahead and do it as an act of love (and still modeled forgiveness in the midst of his suffering both in his capture and while hanging on the cross).

And, perhaps most importantly, he is said to have risen from the dead to conquer death for all of us, to demonstrate to all of us that our real nature is spiritual and everlasting.

Perfect love. Absolute love. Eternal love. If the writings about Jesus are true, then these were the most profound, fundamental realities of Jesus that really matter to me.

Unfortunately, for me, there are also messages about sin, the devil, eternal damnation, and a vengeful, angry God throughout the bible. Dimensions of those messages are woven into the stories about Jesus as well. Those messages simply don't fit for me. I cannot accept them as truth. And, therefore, I cannot unconditionally accept Jesus as my lord and savior. However, I can accept the positive dimensions of Jesus as a model of love.

So for me, if Jesus is the only true pathway to God what that really means (to me) is that **love is the only true pathway to God**.

It is in loving that we find ultimate meaning in life. It is in loving that we find our atonement. It is in loving that we find our way to God. It is in our essential loving, spiritual nature and in God's love for us that resurrection is achieved. It is in loving that we live on in an eternal, spiritual state of being, with full consciousness, awareness, joy, peace, and understanding as a gift from and in God – God, the source, the substance, the essence of our being.

Much is made of sin and the forgiveness of sin in Christian religions. Sin is not relevant or real to me. Jesus forgave people. He forgave their "sins". An all-knowing, all-understanding, and all-loving God would certainly understand all of my shortcomings and be absolutely forgiving. Sin (to me) simply means being imperfect. It means needing to continue to grow into being a more perfectly loving being – which is my ultimate essence as a child of God.

It all comes back to love. Saying Jesus is the only, the ultimate pathway to God is in essence saying that love is the only pathway to the all-loving being that we call God. We were created in love. We were created by love. We were created of love (and awareness, consciousness, intelligence, and an eternal spiritual essence). Therefore, it is in loving that we ultimately find our way back to that source of love, the source of our very being.

When Jesus says, "I am the way, the truth, and the light," I read "love is the way, the truth, and the light". When Jesus says, "No one comes to the Father except through me," I read, "No one comes to the Father except through love". When Jesus asks us to eat the bread and drink the wine of his flesh and blood, I read, "let love be your real sustenance". When Jesus asks us to be baptized, to be "born again of the spirit" that doesn't mean to me that I must be immersed in water. It does mean that I must be baptized through immersion in love.

Those who know love -- be they Buddhist, Hindu, native tribal people, or atheists – know the essence of Jesus, even if they have never heard of him by name. If they know and live love, then they know the real pathway to God.

Marnie was not a practicing Christian. Marnie did not worship Jesus as the son of God. But Marnie was the most unselfish human being I have ever met. She was the most forgiving. She was the most open to loving and receiving love. Marnie was (and is) a living reflection of the essence of a loving God. If anyone was ready to make the transition from mortal, physical reality to eternal spiritual reality in the presence of God, joined with God, it was Marnie. So ultimately, Marnie knew Jesus, because she knew and lived love. And I believe that if Jesus is both a real person and the son of God, then Jesus would be proud of Marnie and love her deeply, with absolutely no resentment of her not knowing him or believing in him personally as the son of God.

For me, God is love. Jesus is love. Loving is following the path of Jesus. Loving is the path to eternal being, happiness, and fulfillment. If we love, both Jesus and God will be pleased with us and joyfully share eternity with us. Nothing more is required.

God, Jesus, and Faith

In these last three chapters I have offered you my fundamental ideas about God, Jesus, and our immortal souls. I think about these ideas repeatedly, virtually every day. I read my own words about God over and over again. I affirm them as truth over and over again. I confirm logically in my own mind that no other explanation for our life, for our being, makes more sense. I actively work each day at building and strengthening my faith. Faith is the basis for everything in my life now. But it must be both real and sincere for me to feel right about how I am choosing to live my life. It must become absolute, certain, fundamental to my very being for me to feel a genuine sense of peace in continuing to live my life.

If you are going to choose to follow a pathway to healing similar to mine, you too need to think clearly about God. You too need to think clearly about the soul. You too need to think clearly about the ultimate meaning of being and what makes the most sense to you. You can use my thinking as a guideline, or you can follow your own path of reason. But ultimately, I can think of no other pathway that makes more sense than the one that leads to God. And it is in God that I believe you will find the pathway to healing.

God leads to the soul. And "soul" defines the eternal essence of your beloved. And eternal means being alive now and always. And being alive means being conscious and aware and loving. And the living, loving presence of the soul makes the potential for an active, loving, sharing relationship with your beloved real. Now. And it is in living that relationship with your beloved that healing and comfort are found.

It all flows from God. It all flows from the essence of God which is love.

Chapter 10: My Journey

I hope that to this point I've successfully shared enough with you that you've to come to know Marnie and me and what our relationship meant and continues to mean to me on a feeling level. I hope that I've done so with enough clarity and intensity that you understand my profound grief and my need for healing.

And I hope that I've shared both the process and the content of my thinking about God and the soul with sufficient clarity that you've come to have a thorough understanding of those beliefs. For me, those beliefs are the foundation of my road to healing.

In the remainder of this book I hope you will travel along with me to the road's ultimate destination – full healing and rejoining. There have been multiple twists and turns and bumps that I've encountered along that road to healing, but I hope that in sharing my experience maybe, just maybe, you can avoid some of these.

I will share the tools I used in building my healing road and the process I used to build it. I hope and believe that in traveling along that road together, we will both move closer to the full healing that will come when we rejoin our beloved in the afterlife.

I set out on my journey of healing by setting out on a physical journey. A bit more than three months after the death of Marnie's body, I left on a trip. (I want to remind you that I try to consistently say "the death of Marnie's body", instead of Marnie's death, because it is the more accurate description, and the words we use directly influence how we think and ultimately what we believe.)

Marnie was an artist. We spent the last 22 years of our physical lives together traveling to various art shows around the country. In my grieving I decided that I needed to get away and spend some time alone with my thoughts and my feelings. I had to see if I could find some way to heal.

I knew I wanted to be in Florida for Christmas to bring my son, Ben, my daughter, Nellie and my grandchildren there. That was Marnie's dream. She wanted to fly them to Florida (and to all of our special places). She wanted them to fly. She wanted them to see the ocean. She wanted them to experience the magical ecosystems that we have shared together that they had never encountered. She didn't get to do that in her physical life. I decided to do that for her to fulfill her dream.

That's what the trip was for me in the beginning – fulfilling **Marnie's** dream. It became much more than that. It was the beginning of my road to healing.

I traveled to many of the places that were special to Marnie and me. Being in each of those places brought back so many memories. We did so very much together. We discovered so very much together. Our relationship, our life together was a truly magical journey. With each stop I would vividly remember everything we did in that place. I remembered every trail we ran and walked. I remembered everything we saw and discovered. In my mind's eye I could see it. I could feel it.

In each special place, I would talk with Marnie about it. I would grieve the loss of not being there together physically – of my not being able to be there with Marnie ever again physically in this lifetime. I would weep and weep and weep.

But it was transformative for me. In talking with Marnie about it all, in believing that her presence was there in these special places with me, I began to see and feel the beauty in it again.

I would describe to her what I saw and what I heard. I asked her what she was seeing and hearing. I ran for miles on the trails that we ran together. I felt her presence with me in strength that seemed to flow into me. I thought of her floating over the trails with me, not hurting anymore. I thought of me being the one to tire, not her. In doing so I began to feel a sense of strength and peace that I had not known before on these trails, or any trails.

Though I grieved the loss of Marnie's body intensely in each of these special places, I began to regain a sense of beauty in the world as I shared my experience of those places with her.

I'd like to share with you some of my journal entries from that trip. I hope they demonstrate clearly to you the way in which I talk with Marnie every day to keep my relationship with her fully alive in the present.

Talking with Marnie is absolutely crucial to my healing. It is *the* most important thing that I do. I suggest that the same will be true for you. **Regular communication with your beloved is, in my view, the primary key to keeping your relationship with one another alive, and in that, the key to healing.**

Your beloved's body has died. You can no longer share with them physically in this lifetime. But it is in keeping your mental and emotional relationship (your spiritual relationship) with your beloved alive, in the present, that you will find mental and emotional healing. You are tapping into the true nature, the ultimate reality of being.

The frequency and intensity of your communication with your beloved will reflect the frequency and intensity of the communication that you shared when they were physically alive.

To say it in slightly different words, your relationship with your beloved is not over. It has been transformed. Though gone from your life physically, your beloved is still present mentally and emotionally on a soul level. By maintaining your relationship with their soul you not only ease your grief and promote your healing, but you bring them joy.

I have come to trust and believe in that. I hope these journal entries will illustrate clearly my experience in going about maintaining my connection with Marnie's eternal soul. But I must warn you, I'm madly in love with Marnie. That is the nature of our unique relationship. Your relationship is different from mine. Your communication will be different from mine. Communicate genuinely from your heart in your way. That's what these journal entries are for me – genuine communication from my heart. If they seem to drag on too much, skip ahead to the next chapter. ☺

Journal Entries: Insights from My Journey with My Beloved

From a Night Walk in Myakka River

"When I do what we did together, I feel the magic, I see the beauty. The world becomes beautiful for me. When I only remember what we did, I grieve. I weep. I miss you profoundly. I know I have to go through the grief to get back to feeling our connection in the present. For now I need both. I look forward to feeling the magic with you every day without having to grieve first. But I'm willing to go through the pain to be with you now, darling.

I love you. We would always keep going on the trail on our runs in the wilderness, no matter how hard it got. We would keep going together until we found beauty. And we always found beauty together, Marnie. Life with you was beautiful magic. I want life to be beautiful magic for our children and our grandchildren. And I have to teach them that it isn't always easy. So I will keep going, for both of us."

A Testament to Marnie

"Sitting with you at sunset Marnie is the best part of my day. I will do it every day that I can for the rest of my life. Talking to you, feeling you, feeling with you – it gives direction to my life. And I kiss you, I kiss you, I kiss you. I kiss you in my heart as the sun sets, as we did with our lips while you were here in your body. As we will again when I join you after my body's death. I will live strong for you. I will live strong with you in me. You are my heart. You are my soul's mate. I will wear our rings, our bracelets, and your lockets as long as I live. I love you forever, and that's just beginning, so I need to stay patient."

Highlands Reflections

"I don't understand Marnie. I don't understand the complexity of the feelings I have. How can I feel your presence and miss you so much simultaneously? I go from being full to empty. Back and forth. I'm out here on the trail feeling so sad, missing you, remembering you.

I have such tremendous respect for you. You walked here with your cancer and all of its side effects. You never complained. You had to hurt. You just kept going. You never said anything about it. You just went on, and we had magical experiences. You are my model. You are my inspiration.

But I feel so sad remembering. And then I'll feel like I'm here with you and it's beautiful and I'll pass it on to our grandchildren and I feel good again. And then I get back to the start of the trail and I feel empty all over again and I want to cry. I miss you so very much.

When I felt the stuff about passing it on – passing on the beauty, passing on the magic, a barred owl hooted in the middle of the day, in the sunshine. They don't do that. And I haven't heard one since. So it had to be your influence. You have to be here. So how can I be sad? If you're here, how can I feel happy and sad at the same time?

I hope you feel my love for you (right now). I hope it makes your life richer. I hope you see through my eyes and it makes your life richer. I hope you feel what I feel and it makes your life richer. I hope you hear what I hear (out here) and it makes your life richer. I want to fill you. You carry me. You are my strength. You are what allows me to keep going. I love you darling. I love you."

Ancient Hammock reflections

"There was magnificence in the ancient forest that I walked through with you today, Marnie. Magnificence and profound stillness. I felt the presence of God there. I hope you felt it along with me. I grew deeply sad in the dark wilderness, missing you, missing having you there right beside me, even though I was talking to you. But after telling you how much I missed you (and weeping) a sense of peace came back over me and of course the owl immediately hooted. The magnificence came again. Thank you for helping.

It's humbling here sweetheart – magnificence and magic, humbling in the presence of God. I never would or could have been here without you. I never would have discovered this without you. I love you, Marnie. You are beauty. You carry beauty. You reflect beauty. You inspire beauty. I love you, my beautiful wife. Thank you for the gift of beauty in my life. With you, with your help, I will pass it on."

Orange trail reflections

"My task on this trip is to transform my hope that your presence is real and alive into belief. And to transform that belief into knowledge. And to pull that knowledge deep down into my core and transform it into unflinching conviction that I carry with me always and absolutely.

When I came to this realization and stopped to sit down and record it, I looked up and I was right beside the giant oak that we discovered together here last year. It's beautiful and it's magic. And it is confirmation of my task. Once I've completed that task, then I can move on to the next phase of my life. Thank you my darling. I love you."

"When I **know** deep down in my core that you will always be with me when I need you, then I can work. Then I can move forward with living. Then I can continue to discover beauty and share it with you, and share it with the children. Thank you.

I don't know if I talked enough when you were alive. I don't know if I told you often enough how much I like you, how much I liked being with you, how much I liked doing with you, how much I liked just being in your presence. You made the world special for me. Not only did I love you, I really liked you.

Now that I'm here, seeing everything that I see, feeling everything that I feel, you're still making the world special for me, and I want to be making the world special for you by talking to you, by seeing for you, by sharing with you. When these thoughts came to me I was directly beside our next giant oak. It's another confirmation. This is one of my missions in this world – to experience beauty and magic, to thank you for it, and to give it back to you with love and joy and magic."

Lawrence reflections

"I realized yesterday that I'm on a farewell tour. I'm remembering everything we shared in these places that I'm traveling to. I may never come back to them again. I know I won't ever physically share those experiences with you again in this lifetime. I don't know if there will be more lifetimes. So being here now is bittersweet.

I miss you so much, Marnie. My tears fall like the rain. We did so very much together. I was stunned to remember how much we did in this unspectacular place. Damn we were good together."

A Talk with Marnie

"I won't be able to hug you again in this lifetime. That's probably the hardest thing for me to deal with. I won't be able to physically do with you all those special things we did together (and we did so very much). But I will be able to hug. I will be able to do those things. I will be able to love as you in me -- me loving as you would love. Me growing more fully into the kind of human being that you were -- me being a person of kindness, understanding, and forgiveness.

And I want and need to believe that you are with me now in that loving. I want you to see me loving. I want you to hear me talking to you and talking for us. I want you to feel my profound love for you in both my actions and in my suffering and sadness and loneliness. I want to share all those experiences with you in consciousness and awareness as long as you can see my pain as an expression of my profound love for you – as long as you can experience it with joy, knowing that so much more joy is coming for us together in the future beyond my physical death. If only I could see in my body now what you can see living beyond yours.

Feeling your presence in me and around me helps me to move forward with purpose rather than staying lost in the past, in memories alone. Feeling your presence here and now allows me to use my memories of us and all that we did as a guide to build on, as directional signposts for how to move forward into the future. Feeling your presence with me in that process makes everything feel worthwhile.

Surrounding myself with photos of you keeps my awareness of you totally, keenly alive. Talking with you as I am doing now keeps my connection with you, my best friend, alive. We always talked together to sort out even our most difficult feelings and fears. Doing so now, doing so still, allows me to keep my thinking clear and positive. I love you so very much…… Please send me your love and strength to help me deal with the fear and doubts and criticisms that I know are coming my way on this journey into faith."

The book, "Experiencing Grief" says healing involves "changing the relationship with your loved one from one of presence to one of memory. And saying good bye is part of the concluding process."

"I do not accept this. Physical presence is gone. Shared physical experiences are gone. But your continued life presence gives emotional meaning to my world. Feeling your love and your awareness of me gives my life stronger direction and purpose. I live and love as 'us' in my choices and actions. I affirm our continued oneness each day in each action I take. That enhances my sense of internal peace as I move through this physical world toward our full reunion in the spiritual world.

I need to feel the presence of your soul, of your consciousness, of your awareness, deeply embedded in my heart and mind. I need to feel your 'spiritual presence' wrapped around me, even as I grieve the loss of your body and all that that entails."

At Gold Branch Head

"Our oneness is a manifestation of God, Marnie. In that, it can never end. You are the center of my universe. You are my heart. We are forever one. I share this love with you here, now, as I did when you were here physically. I will not stop. I will believe. I will rejoice in this world because I'm sharing it with you. And I will pass it on to our grandchildren because of you. Thank you."

Myakka Trail run

"I love you so much darling. I feel like everything that's beautiful in my world is a gift from you. Everything that's good in my life is because of you. You are my heart. You fill my soul. I love you. I love you. Thank you for the gifts of goodness and beauty that I could have never known without you.

I'm out on the trail that we ran on together, Marnie. I remember this trail. It was kind of scary. It felt like we were lost. It felt like we were going the wrong direction and we were afraid. It was getting late and we were way out in the back country. But we kept going, and we got home.

And I feel like that's how it is in my life now without your physical presence. I'm kinda lost and I'm afraid. It's scary and I'm afraid I'm going the wrong direction, but I've got to keep going. I've got to keep going. And if I can keep going, I'll find my way back to you. You are my home. I love you sweetheart. I miss you (sobbing). I will keep going. I love you."

Hillsborough River Reflections

"I'm standing alone on the suspension bridge overlooking the Hillsborough River. I'm seeing the beauty, feeling the magnificence, and watching the fish in the water. I remember being here and sharing this with you. I miss you so much, darling. I weep and I weep out of the sadness of wishing you were here with me now physically.

And I weep thinking maybe you are here with me now. That you are seeing all this with me, not having to carry your cancer body, being able to walk this far again with me without pain and seeing the beauty through my eyes. I hope it fills you. I hope it fills you to overflowing. I love you."

Leaving Hillsborough River

"It's so beautiful here, but so empty without you, sweetie. That's how the world ahead of me feels, beautiful, but empty without you, Marnie.

I need you sweetheart. I need you to wrap me in your love. I need you to wrap me in your presence. I need you to fill me with your presence. I need to carry you with me everywhere, to have the world no longer be empty for me.

Oh Marnie, be with me darling. Make my world not only beautiful, but full and rich. Help me find my way forward. I love you."

Manatee Springs Reflections

"Everywhere I go, my task is to find magic. And my task is to share the magic I discover. As my faith grows stronger, I will give credit to you and to God. I will testify on your behalf.

I think my task, as I continue to heal, is to think about you less, and to feel you more -- to feel your presence with me and to carry you in my heart as I move forward in the world. We are together now, you and I. I affirm that, repeatedly, every day. We are together, you and I, now. I love you girl. I carry you with me. I'm not carrying your memory. I'm carrying your living presence, now.

Everything is coming in pairs today – a pair of turtles, a pair of pileated wood peckers, a pair of crows, a pair of cormorants, a pair of grebes – it's a good sign for us. I carry you with me my darling. Thank you for blessing me."

St. Joseph's Peninsula Reflections

"Sometimes, Marnie, I feel blessed and ripped off simultaneously. I feel like God really blessed me by bringing you into my life. And I feel like He really ripped me off (both of us really) by allowing you to have cancer and taking you out of my life far too soon.

It's only when I can see things from the perspective of eternity that the blessing totally overshadows the feeling of being ripped off. Then losing you gives me a profound sense of perspective. Then I feel a far greater recognition of the depth of the blessing I was given in having your love and the joy that you brought to my life.

My difficulty is in seeing eternity. I wish I could feel eternity as an understandable reality. That's still a tough one for me. But it's in eternity, and in sharing it with you, that I will find heaven."

That's a small sampling of some of my journal entries. I will be sharing many more with you throughout the rest of the book. But I wanted to introduce you to how I communicate with Marnie. I treat her as my forever wife and my best friend. She is both. I say everything I possibly can to make her feel absolutely loved and treasured. And I talk to her soul now as I would talk to Marnie when she was physically present. It keeps us real and alive in my mind and heart, and in what I believe is ultimate spiritual reality.

The way you communicate with your beloved will certainly be different from the way I talk with Marnie. But that you do it is what truly matters. Talk to your beloved in your way. In maintaining your communication with your beloved, you will keep your relationship alive. In that, I believe, you will find ultimate healing.

I can't over-state the importance of continuing to talk with your beloved. It is an absolutely essential part of the process of healing as a non-religious, spiritual person. You are working at building feeling level confidence in the reality of continued, genuine two way communication. To do that you have to keep talking. You have to keep sharing your heart in the way you would have if your beloved was present physically. Doing so affirms them and it affirms your belief in your reasoned, stated beliefs about God and the reality of the soul.

Deep-seated confidence that you are talking to a real soul that is really hearing you will progressively increase as your faith increases. You have to build faith. Faith is the ultimate key to healing.

I have had to work at building faith and confidence every day. I have been building it on the foundation of my reasoned beliefs about the true nature of our being. But beliefs are something I think in my mind. Faith is something I feel in my heart. From this point forward we'll focus on how to build heart-felt faith. We'll look at the tools that I have been using for doing that. Hopefully, many of those tools will fit for you too. But for any of them to work, you have to keep communicating with your beloved. That in itself brings joy and healing.

Chapter 11: Nature Experiences as confirmation of the Living Soul

The essential key to healing for me has come from developing faith in a loving God who is the source of Marnie's conscious, living, eternal soul. Faith, and the tools that I have used to build that faith will be the focus of much of the rest of this book. But faith can be built from multiple sources. We've looked at the reasoned basis for belief. But reason is only one of the tools for building faith.

On the trip that I began describing in the last chapter I experienced a series of occurrences in the natural world that seemed to repeatedly confirm the reality of my thoughts, beliefs, and insights about Marnie's continued, living presence. I continue to have those kinds of experiences to this day.

In isolation, each could be seen as a coincidence. But the repeated frequency, nature, and timing of these coincidences seems far too coincidental to be coincidence. It seems to me that nature is a tool that Marnie has available to her to give me tangible evidence of her real presence and to confirm the validity of my thoughts and my faith.

Even these incidents of "tangible" evidence must ultimately be taken in faith. But the accumulation of that evidence gives it more weight. The accumulation of incidents becomes increasingly harder to ignore or explain away as mere coincidence. I will share with you some of these incidents from the first year of my grieving, beginning on my trip, and continuing after my return home. I hope that in reading about them you too might question if there is more than coincidence at work here.

I present these experiences to you in the hope that they offer another level of confirmation that the soul lives on after death.

Though these experiences are totally personal, they argue for a level of being, a level of reality that truly does transcend the "normal" physical world.

As part of this description I should explain that Marnie loved birds. Her father was a birding expert and he shared with her his love for birds. And Marnie shared her love for birds with me. Since her physical death, birds have played a powerful role in confirming Marnie's presence. For various reasons the most significant birds in my life since Marnie's physical death have been the pileated woodpecker, the red shouldered hawk, the barred owl, the king fisher, and the robin. Other birds, grackles, bald eagles, herons, crows, dippers, pelicans, and blue jays have played significant roles in our interaction as well. A red shouldered hawk (who I had not heard for many hours) began calling the moment I began writing these words. Here are some of my experiences.

1) When I first arrived in Florida, as I went out to do my morning walk and talk with Marnie, within the first 10 steps, a red shouldered hawk flew over my head calling and calling. Red shouldered hawks were special to us. We discovered them together in Florida. A half mile further on, as I was wondering if Marnie's presence was <u>really</u> real, I heard a pileated wood pecker pecking in the trees. I know the unique sound of their pecking because Marnie introduced it to me. Though it was a dense woods, I was able to look up and find him immediately.

After another mile of walking and many tears and much talking, I began telling Marnie how much I love her. I told her that I choose her and re-choose her again forever without hesitation or reservation, I said to her, "We are forever one. Our oneness is a manifestation of God." Those words, that thought just came to me. I wept. I stopped and looked up. The red shouldered hawk was in the tree directly above me, looking down at me. He did not stir, he did not leave as long as I stayed. Perhaps that was no accident.

    2) During my prayer walk (I'll explain my prayer walk in chapter 15) in my second stop in Florida, I was deeply melancholy. I missed Marnie so very, very much. My sadness was deep. I thanked God for bringing Marnie into my life, for keeping her with me, and for giving us the space to build our love and oneness. But eventually I just shared my sadness and asked for the joining in oneness with Marnie that I pray for so fervently every night.

    I finished my prayer kneeling on a dock at the end of a board walk, out over the Suwannee River. I got up and moved to a bench where I sat and just listened. I felt at peace again. I sat for a long time in that magnificent wilderness. Except for the occasional sound of a vulture's wing as it shifted position in the trees, or the sound of a fish jumping, or the sound of a turtle breaking the surface of the water, there was total stillness.

    When I asked Marnie if she was with me, if she was listening to this magnificent silence with its special sounds, a breeze came up and blew over me. Then all was quiet and still again. I continued to sit in silence for what seemed a long time. Then I wondered aloud if God was present. Immediately a breeze stirred and blew over me again, and then was gone. Those were the <u>only</u> breezes of the night.

    3) When I arrived at my third stop in Florida, Myakka River, there were a pair of crows at the ranger station. One was feeding the other. It felt like a reflection of us. When I arrived at my campsite, there was a pileated wood pecker pecking in the tree directly behind our trailer. A barred owl called in the middle of the day. They felt like messages that Marnie was here with me. Then a group of crows came over the trailer, landed in the trees above it and called and called and called. It felt like they were calling me outside to say, "Get going on your bike ride."

I went on that bike ride. When I did, I came upon a pair of cranes, just as Marnie and I had on our first trip here together. A bit further down the road I came upon a raccoon who just stood there in the middle of the road complaining at me. I heard another pileated wood pecker in the trees. When I looked up to find him I saw two baby raccoons in the tree waiting for their mother, who I had met on the road.

It seems there was sign after sign that said, "I'm here. I'm with you."

4) On my walk and talk with Marnie the following morning. I realized how much happier, how much more at peace I feel when we are talking. As I was wondering how I can trust the reality of her presence, a pileated woodpecker flew by. Exactly then. I wondered aloud, is this the only way you can really show me your presence? Are you demonstrating it to me repeatedly in nature? That's the avenue you have available to you, and that's where we lived so fully together – out in nature. It was such a vital, essential, beautiful part of our magic together. And we were magic together.

A few minutes later, when I reached the secluded beach that was my destination, there were a pair of black vultures standing together, their necks intertwined, wrapped around one another, grooming each other – just as we would wrap around one another in the mornings, intertwined, and kissing. I have never seen that behavior in vultures before. It came with my wondering about Marnie's presence, and how it can be demonstrated in an understandable, believable way, here, now.

5) On my morning "Marnie walk" in Hillsborough River, I said to her, "The transition of your dying, Marnie, of moving from your body to the next level of being doesn't change our oneness. Our oneness is still real. We are still connected. We are one now. You are with me now. We will be one for all eternity". The moment I said these words, a pileated woodpecker flew over me, landed

above me, and called out constantly – Marnie's absolute confirmation of the truth of my words.

    I said, "You're not just watching over me as some say. You are joined together with me. We are still joined together and we will be for all eternity. Oh God! Thank you! I love that! That is my deepest prayer! That soothes my heart profoundly."

    Suddenly there were birds everywhere. I said, "It's as if they are rejoicing in recognition of our marriage, our commitment, our bond, our oneness. Thank you God. Thank you Marnie. Thank you birds."

    The birds kept coming and coming. I said, "I've never experienced this before, Marnie. Birds are everywhere. They are over me. They are around me. They fly by me. They are singing for me. I've never experienced this here (in Hillsborough River) before. This is magic. This is a confirmation – I LOVE YOU!"

    That was intense magic. It felt divine. When I decided to walk on, as soon as I moved further down the trail, everything grew immediately silent. Everything became stillness and quiet except for the call of a red shouldered hawk. I couldn't have had a more clear confirmation.

    6) On my last morning walk in Hillsborough River I came to what I call "our tree". I have a special photo of Marnie crouching inside an opening in the trunk of that tree. I had to be with "our tree" one last time. I went to kiss it, and there, inside, was a huge, beautiful, perfect feather. Weeping, I said, "This couldn't be just an accident. It couldn't be just coincidence. I carried the feather with me. And as I walked on and said, "This can't be just an accident," above me in the top of the tree, the red shouldered hawk called.

I said, "Oh Marnie, be with me darling. Make my world not only beautiful, but full and rich. Help me find my way forward. I love you."

I begged. I sobbed, "Please hear me darling. Please hear me. Please hear me. Please hear me darling. I'm asking for peace. I'm asking to feel your presence as peace in my heart." And when I stopped begging and sobbing, a pileated wood pecker pecked on the top of the tree directly above me, as loud as a drum. And I smiled.

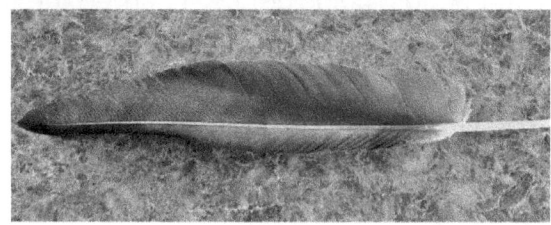

7) At my next stop on the trip I went out for a walk and run in the woods. I said to Marnie, "It's funny how the pileated woodpecker just seems to appear when I need to feel your presence. I was just talking about how important it is for me to talk to you, because you're my best friend, and wondering, 'Do you really hear me? Or am I just talking?' And a pileated woodpecker appeared. Seems like an answer, doesn't it?"

A little further on, I stood in somewhat of a daze, catching my breath. I was remembering a fantasy that I'd had about Marnie and me making love in an open sided thatched roof hut that was a short distance off the trail back in the woods. I'd been running, and trying to talk with Marnie. I was laughing, talking about the fantasy, and saying, "I hope you hear me darling. I hope you liked the fantasy."

Without realizing it I had gotten close to that fantasy spot. But precisely then a pileated woodpecker swooped over me calling and flew directly down the trail in front of me. He turned, flew off into the woods to the right, and landed above the hut where I had fantasized us making love. He called and called and called until I came there, following his voice. I was stunned.

It really couldn't have been a much clearer message that you're really here, that you're really hearing me, that you're reaching out to me darling. (And maybe you liked the fantasy.) I said, "I thank you. I love you, forever."

That same evening after watching the sunset and kissing Marnie in my mind and heart (as I always do at sunset) I leaned over the dock and looked into the water. A manatee swam up directly underneath me. I saw him more clearly than I've ever seen a manatee at any time in my life. The sunset, our sunset, was magnificent.

These repeated coincidences begin to accumulate to such an extent, that they argue against coincidence. The pileated woodpecker, flying to our fantasy spot; the manatee swimming directly under me after sunset -- immediately after talking with you and kissing you (in my mind and heart). And as I began walking back down the boardwalk from this magical sunset, I thought of you and wondered about your presence. Just then, precisely then, a barred owl flew above me and called. They just keep coming (the coincidences). They come repeatedly. They come at the most important times – an accumulation of coincidences that argue against it being coincidence.

8) I was walking the back trails at Ochlockonee State Park, feeling like it was a pretty plain place, feeling like there wasn't much magic to be seen here. I was talking to Marnie about that when I realized that she had died exactly 6 months ago to the day. I felt so sad. I started to weep. At that moment, a pileated woodpecker called, and shortly thereafter, a beautiful fox ran by directly across my path. I said, "There is indeed magic here and there is presence in my loneliness and sadness. Thank you sweetheart."

A bit later I met an old couple on the trail. They said they were out "birding". I told them I'd heard the pileated woodpecker. They were quite excited. Even though they walk here regularly, they had never before seen or heard a pileated woodpecker out here. And I told them about the fox. I described the fox to them (he had a reddish head and a grayish, multi-colored body). They told me that he was a silver fox, and that they too are extremely rare here.

Again, it was too miraculous to be coincidence.

9) On Valentine's Day in Fontainebleau State Park I was sitting paralyzed in our trailer, feeling sad, and missing Marnie deeply. I keep thinking I'm getting better, but then the pain all comes rushing back and washes over me and I feel so deeply lost.

I decided I had to force myself to get up and go out on my morning Marnie walk. As I began walking through the campground, I took a short cut across a field and a dry streambed, and realized that I was coming directly to the campsite that Marnie and I had first stayed in together here.

I said, "This is our spot, Marnie. This is <u>our</u> spot." And from the tree above that spot came a beautiful sound, a melodious single note. There were four birds in the tree, each making that single melodious note as if they were singing in a chorus.

I looked up and I tried to figure out what kind of birds they were. I could only see them from underneath. They kept singing for me. It looked as if they were blue jays. But they weren't making the screeching sound that blue jays make. Since I could only see them from underneath, I couldn't see the blue on their backs to be sure. But they were crested like a blue jay and they had black stripes including one around their neck like a blue jay. They seemed like that kind of a bird. But their song was so different, so unique, and so melodious.

Some people began to walk towards me and I decided to ask them if they knew the bird sounds here. As soon as I asked, the birds were gone. I didn't know where they had flown to. All was silent.

So I continued on with my walk. I cried a lot thinking about Marnie, missing her. Eventually (a half mile further along) I came to a beautiful bench that was dedicated to the memory of the man who was the superintendent of this park for some 24 years until he died in 2013. They put that bench directly in front of one of the big, beautiful, moss covered, spreading oak trees. I went behind the bench and took a picture of the bench and the tree it overlooked.

Suddenly there were multiple butterflies all swirling together in pairs as if they were doing a mating dance in front of me. And in the oak tree, above me, came that song again, that beautiful, melodious, single note sounding from bird to bird. As I sat to write about all this, a woodpecker landed in the tree above and began pecking as I wrote.

It felt like magic. It felt like a testament of Marnie's love and Marnie's presence on this very difficult day. It felt like her Valentine's gift to me. "Thank you my darling. Thank you. I love you."

10) The next morning, as I was out walking on the trail, I expressed my profound appreciation for Marnie. I expressed my wish that I had said more and shown more and given more and let her know more, in every way, how very special I thought she was while she was physically alive. As I told her how I wish I had just wrapped her in feelings of beauty and goodness, I was surrounded, almost instantaneously by a plethora of birds.

All of them were special to us for various reasons. Robins were everywhere. (Robins were special because Marnie had said to her father as a child, "They're "just robins.")". Grackles (that we discovered together in San Antonio on what was a magical "trip of courage" for us) filled the trees and called constantly. A pileated woodpecker flew in front of me and landed on the tree directly beside me. And the blue jays sat high above me in the trees, calling in those single melodious notes. The birds were everywhere. And they were _our_ birds. It felt like a gift from Marnie, saying "Thank you for recognizing me and sending me your love now."

I thought aloud, "I guess it's better to send love late than never. This is the same thing that had happened at Hillsborough River. It's exactly the same."

I started walking down the trail, feeling a bit stunned, feeling like, "We're really having an interaction. I say my words and they are intense, and they are loving, and they're about you and your goodness and how special you are to me, and then all of a sudden I'm given this magic experience".

I stopped and questioned, "Can this really be real? Is this really happening? Is this really more than just my imagination?" And as I stood there, the birds flew. They flew directly over me and around me. They just kept flying and flying and flying. All of them, dozens and dozens and dozens of them. And then the forest was silent. The message seemed so clear. It seemed so magical. Maybe it's because I'm out here so much. You have to put yourself out in nature to feel the magic. But it is so powerful, so clearly tied together with us.

At the end of that walk, as I came off of the trail, back out in a clearing before reaching the parking lot, structures, and people, I stopped and said, "You brought me to all this, Marnie. You brought me to nature. This is your gift to me."

I looked to my right. The field was covered with robins. A whole flock of grackles flew in. And blue jays landed in the tree across from the clearing calling in their single melodious notes (not their screeching cries). Just one more confirmation of the magic between us. As I walked away from the field, I looked back. The robins were gone. The grackles were gone. There was traffic on the road and the blue jays screeched.

When I stopped and sat on that special bench a little further on along the trail to record all this, the birds came and sat and called in the trees above me. Our interaction, our relationship is still fully alive. "Thank you. Thank you Marnie. Thank you God. I don't know how all these things can be orchestrated, but they seems so much more than coincidence."

11) As I walked that evening I said aloud to Marnie, "It happens so repeatedly whenever I'm thinking something about you, Marnie. When I express something I feel really deeply about you, or when I express something really intensely to you, Marnie, things happen!"

Just then, as I was talking, a red shouldered hawk that I hadn't seen or heard previously anywhere here in this park landed in the tree directly above me.

As I walked further down the trail, talking to Marnie and intensely feeling my love for her, I heard the sound of a great horned owl. When I looked up, there in the tree, was a pair of great horned owls -- a pair, literally snuggled together.

Then, in bed that night, talking to Marnie, almost like calling out to her from my soul, I heard the call of a barred owl, loud and clear, from right behind our trailer. I'd seen no barred owls. I'd heard no barred owls at any other time in this park.

I said to Marnie, "It's like they are clear signs that come to me in a way that's almost a conversational response -- in the best way that you can give it when we're separated by the boundaries between life and the afterlife. We really are interacting still. No matter how few believe it, no matter how many experts say I need to be moving on, this is a pathway to greater depth, to eternal love. Thank you. I love you."

12) The following night I added a new part to my evening prayer. For the first time, not being absolutely sure I could say it, I thanked God out loud for the death of Marnie's body. I thanked Him for releasing her from her suffering. I thanked Him for the

awareness that Marnie has risen above death. I thanked Him that Marnie is still fully alive, fully conscious, fully present, and fully loving. I thanked Him that her physical death has brought our love to a whole new level of reality and awareness. I thanked Him that our love transcends the death of the body (which everyone must face). I thanked Him that our love transcends the boundary between the physical and the spiritual.

As I said all that, a light in the distance began moving towards me. It was a clear light. It came closer and closer until it was directly in front of me. It came so close that I could have reached out and touched it. It was a lightening bug – the first and only one that I have seen this year. It came directly to me, right with this new part of my prayer, and then went on its way. I could see it nowhere. I saw no more lightening bugs. I saw no more lightning bugs on the rest of my trip.

It felt like a clear sign. I sang, "Let the light guide your way. Hold every memory as you go. And every road you take will always lead you home." And when I finished singing, the barred owl called again – the barred owl who hasn't been here, who only called once, that night when I was calling out to Marnie. His call came again as the song completed my prayer. Perhaps both God and Marnie are giving me pretty clear signs.

13) The next morning, when I neared the end of my morning walk, I sat again on the special bench at Fontainebleau. I just watched and listened, I said, "I'm looking at everything really closely, Marnie. I'm listening really carefully, so you can see through my eyes and hear with my ears." When I said that, a mocking bird who had been serenading landed in the field directly in front of me. And a red headed woodpecker came and landed beside him. And a blue jay flew to the tree above of me and began calling in his single note. And a breeze came up and the wind chimes behind me sounded.

"I don't know if I have a vivid imagination, but it sure seems like you're telling me that you're here, my darling. I appreciate that. I love you."

14) Sometimes I feel a shiver. And it really feels like it's a shiver of Marnie's presence. That means so much to me. It requires faith to believe in the shiver, and at the same time, the shiver confirms the faith. It's one of those ironies.

After my return home from my healing trip, I was pulling knapweed on my morning walk back in Montana. Marnie would pull knapweed. It meant a lot to her to try and keep the knapweed under control, to keep it from spreading. So I was pulling the knapweed for Marnie. And the thought came to me that I wasn't just honoring her memory, my memory of her doing that. I was doing it as a gift for her because I think she's watching over me and would appreciate that. And when I said that out loud, I felt a shiver go down and through my whole body. Thank you for the shiver sweetheart."

15) I was having a particularly hard day, a sad day. I was missing Marnie profoundly. I think she was sending me every sign she could to help me get through. I looked out the window to see our yard filled with at least 50 elk -- mothers with babies nursing and a massive 14 point bull elk. When I went outside a great blue heron flew directly over me calling and calling and landed on the very top of the tallest pine tree on our land, over our pond. I walked down the road and saw wild turkeys. I biked down the road and saw a moose for the first time in over a year. Signs kept appearing over and over again – from robins to king fishers to a perfect sunset.

Marnie's presence is not something blatant, not something I can reach out and touch. I still miss her body so very much. I miss looking into her eyes. I miss her profoundly. But the subtle signs are there, and they are there to soothe me. So I have to keep moving forward in faith. And my faith in God and my faith in Marnie are both deepening by the day.

    16) As I sat watching the sunset with Marnie (as I do every day when I'm alone with her and there is a sunset to watch) I remembered doing push-ups together on the beach one night during our travels. We were totally alone on the beach. It was hot and humid, and Marnie took her shirt off and did pushups in her bra. I found that to be tremendously sexy.

    I was thinking to myself that I do a tremendous amount of biking and running, but I haven't been doing much strength training. I thought that I should do push-ups more regularly. I smiled and asked Marnie if I should do my pushups with my shirt off. I asked her if she would find that to be sexy as I did with her. Immediately after I asked, a robin flew in and landed on a post not ten feet from me. He literally bobbed his head up and down and up and down, repeatedly, as if clearly shaking his head yes. I've never seen a robin do that before or since.

    I did push-ups with my shirt off that night, and have done so ever since.

    17) I was out walking and talking with Marnie. I said to her, "Maybe in the afterlife, in eternity, we can create and live multiple lifetimes together, while retaining our consciousness and retaining our awareness of one another. We will always recognize one another's souls. We are bound together in loving oneness in our souls. We can continue to grow, together. We need not lose track of one another, of us, of ourselves, and of our bond as we move in and out of future lifetimes."

    "I love the idea of really relishing each moment, every second of the new lifetimes that we create together. Relishing each and every moment is a gift that has come out of feeling our separation now, and realizing how precious every moment was that we had together before your physical death."

"I feel like these are new insights. I feel like you send them to me as a gift to give me hope, to help me keep going through my sadness."

The moment I said all this, I saw a feather, a big, beautiful feather, lying all by itself on the side of the road -- like the feather in our tree at Hillsborough River after the insight that I had there. Like a feather that floated directly in front of me in the water at Manatee Springs after I had a special insight there. And now this magnificent feather, just there, on the side of the road after this insight. It felt like a gift from her saying "Yes! Yes!" you are on track. We are going to share eternity together".

18) On my morning walk the following day, I made a declaration of choice. I thought clearly about the option of moving Marnie into memory and moving on to a new lover, a new relationship in this physical lifetime – a new love, a new dimension of my life. And I said out loud, "I'm not doing that. I choose you, Marnie. I choose the life that I am living now. I take full responsibility for it."

"I say to you, Marnie, You are my heart. You are my soul's mate. You are my forever wife. You are my forever love. You are my forever lover. You are my forever best friend. I choose this life that I am living. I choose to maintain my connection with you. I'm at peace with this life. I'm happy with it. I want no other life."

At that very moment, a feather came floating down out of the sky right into my outstretched hand. It seemed like an absolute confirmation.

    This is a small sampling of the experiences I have had and continue to have in nature to this day. Coincidences. Coincidences? Too many coincidences to be coincidental. They bring me confirmation of Marnie's continued living presence.

    I don't know if you will have similar experiences. But you have to be open to what I call magical experiences. They may not be nature experiences for you. They will fit your life style and your values. They will flow from what fits most naturally into your life. They will of necessity come from the tools that your beloved has available and can influence. They may be subtle experiences. They may seem at first like coincidence. But if you open yourself to repeated coincidence, you will find confirmation of a new level of reality, a new level of connection between you and your beloved.

    After having written the bulk of this chapter, I said to Marnie on my walk the next morning, "I will keep living until you and God decide that it is time for me to come home". And I said, "You do understand that you are my home." And the moment I said this a pileated woodpecker flew directly over me and landed on the tree trunk behind me. And another came in on the tree beside it. And they are here with me as I speak my awareness.

    "You are with me, Marnie. I will stay here and keep loving until I can come home.

After I reread and revised this chapter I said to Marnie, "I don't understand what you are or how you are as a soul. I don't even know what you look like now. But all that matters to me is that 'you are'". And when I said those words I looked up and there was a great blue heron perched in the tree in front of me. And I looked down the river, and there was a bald eagle on the top of a tree. It's just too coincidental. It is you telling me that you really "are". Thank you.

Finally I said, "My whole life is now grounded in faith. If any couple is ready to make the transition to the next life, to the next level of being, it is you and me, Marnie Winn. Thank you. I love you."

With this that declaration, a pair of kingfishers flew out over the river in front of me. A whole flock of small birds flew over me and around me and called out. A dipper flew in and landed on the water in front of me. A whole group of nutcrackers flew into the tops of the trees. A pileated woodpecker called, and I felt a shiver run through me.

"Life just keeps getting better. Thank you, Marnie. You permeate everything that matters to me." That is absolutely true.

Chapter 12: On Faith

I'd like to shift now beyond looking at the impact that my travels, my talks with Marnie, and our experiences together in nature have had on my faith and on my belief in Marnie's living presence. I'd like to focus on building feeling-level faith directly.

I'm trying to build a genuine faith in God outside the confines of religion. I'm trying to build spiritual faith through clear thinking. I'm building my belief in God and the spiritual nature of being in a way that makes sense to me. I'm building a system of beliefs that makes it possible for me to believe that we really can bridge the gap between the physical world that we live in now and a spiritual world that transcends it. In doing so, I can make sense of believing that Marnie, the essence of Marnie, is still fully alive. I can still have an active relationship with her, albeit purely mental and emotional for now. And I can believe that I will rejoin her again fully when I die. Believing this, pulling this belief deep down into my core, makes life still feel worth living for me.

I cannot and will not move on from Marnie. I cannot and will not move her into memory. I cannot and will not remarry. I choose not to. I choose to affirm my commitment to and my marriage with Marnie as eternal choices. We all have to die. There has to be more to life than this physical journey on this earth. Our intelligence, our awareness, our consciousness, our self-awareness, our ability to love and be loved, they all argue for there being more to ultimate reality than just the physical body.

Marnie, my love for Marnie, is bringing me to God. My love for her has pushed me in a whole new direction. The spiritual world is now central to my consciousness, to all my thinking. I still battle within myself. When I am outside, in the wilderness, engaged in an active relationship with Marnie, talking to her and feeling her presence, I feel really good. Or at night when I'm walking and talking to God and talking with Marnie as well, I feel really, really good. I feel determined to go forward and love in the world in a truly positive way. I ask both God and Marnie for support, direction, and wisdom in helping me walk the path forward that will fulfill God's will and Marnie's desires for me. Everything is ok.

But the rest of the time, living on faith alone, without physical touch or interaction is profoundly difficult and sometimes, profoundly painful. I weep every day, some days much more intensely than others, but every day. Choosing to live your life based on faith, when that faith has not been an integral part of your fundamental being since childhood, is one of the hardest things I can imagine doing. But I'm choosing to do it. The alternative in my mind would be dismal.

Faith is the key to my healing. Living in faith is the only way that I have been able to begin to find peace in my heart. In this chapter I hope to share more with you about what faith means to me and to share again the basic thinking I've been using to build it. But I'm building my faith in the ashes of grieving, so it will be clear, I think, that building faith is not a simple or painless process for me.

Believing in Marnie's real, continued, living, loving presence is an act of faith. I can't physically hold her hand, or look into her eyes, or feel her head rest on my shoulder. Many times the intensity of missing those things is still so overwhelming that I feel sick inside from the emptiness. I feel a crushing emptiness in my chest. I feel as if my heart has been ripped out of my body. I don't want to keep living.

That is real. That is intense. Marnie's physical presence, which was at the very center of my life, is gone. It won't be back for me in this lifetime. I have to accept that as real. And all I have to counter-balance that emptiness is faith – the belief that Marnie's spiritual presence is real, the faith that Marnie's spiritual presence is ultimate reality, the faith that Marnie's spiritual presence is in fact eternal reality.

When I can feel those things, really feel them, not just think them, then life is still feels worth living. Then I can think about rejoining Marnie in the next chapter of our never-ending love story together. Our physical life together here on this earth was chapter one of that story. It was both a beautiful and a bittersweet chapter. But it was only the first chapter. If spiritual reality is our ultimate reality, then our story has barely begun. That is exciting. But for now, in chapter two, our story must be totally grounded in faith.

Logical thought is the ground for my faith. But it has not brought me immediate, absolute, feeling level faith or conviction. I have to keep going back to the idea that there is not a better explanation for the reality of our being.

If you have read the book or seen the movie "<u>The Life of Pi</u>" you might remember the scene in which Pi asks the interviewer, "Which is the better story? The story with the tiger? Or the story without the tiger?" And the interviewer replies, "The story with the tiger." To which Pi replies, "And so it is with God."

And so it is with Marnie and me. It is only with God in the story that our story makes ultimate sense. I feel that way. My faith may not yet be absolute on a feeling level, but there is for me a story with God and Marnie's living soul in it, or there isn't. And the story with God and Marnie's living soul is a much better story. That's the story I'm basing my life on now. And that's the story I look forward to completing with Marnie in eternity.

Without God, being itself makes no sense.

Faith in God and belief in the eternal reality of our souls have not been ultimate, unquestioned reality, fully engrained in my very being since childhood as they have been for many. Choosing to build faith as an adult is (I believe) a far more difficult process than growing up with faith – "knowing" in your heart and soul that God is real and active in your life. For me, I so profoundly want that to be true that I often question if what I experience is really Marnie and God acting in my life, or if is it just that my desire that it be true is so strong that it colors my interpretation of my experiences and kindles my imagination.

Though less frequent, that questioning continues in my life to this day. But I know that when I believe, when I "walk the bridge of faith," life feels worth living. When I doubt, I sink so low that it is only the promises I made to Marnie before her death that keep me alive.

I am building my faith from the ground up. My ground is reason. To repeat once more (as I do to myself every day) my fundamental belief, the fundamental truth for me is that **SOMETHING CANNOT COME FROM NOTHING**.

An eternal, spiritual source for all that is – God, is the only logical, sensible explanation for the reality of being. The reality of being cannot be denied. Nor can its source -- no matter how incomprehensible the reality of an eternal, infinite source of being may be.

In my physical life, I am finite. My physical body was born and it will die. Infinity itself is a concept that requires faith to believe. I have no direct experience with infinity. Believing in an all-knowing, all-loving, all-powerful, eternal, infinite, spiritual source to all being is a step way beyond that. Such concepts are honestly beyond my capability to fully grasp. But since I can think of no better explanation for the reality of being, I must ultimately accept those concepts. To accept them in this lifetime requires faith.

Everything keeps coming back to faith. When Marnie was physically alive and sharing this world with me, I could ignore faith. I did. Ultimately, love was all that mattered to me. Now that Marnie's physical body has died, though love is still what matters most, continuing to love Marnie, who is at the core, the very heart and soul of my being, requires faith. Faith is something I can no longer ignore. Faith is at the very center of my world every day.

Unfortunately, I don't have faith just because I want it. It hasn't become fundamental conviction for me simply because I need it to be. So I am building it. And I believe it can be built. Faith is my pathway to God and my pathway back into Marnie's arms – my true home.

Every day I explain to myself again (sometimes briefly, sometimes in elaborate detail) that God makes sense. The reality of being makes sense with God as its ultimate, creative source. And if God is real, God who is eternal, intelligent, creative, aware, self-aware, conscious, and loving, then we who are his children and his reflection are eternal, intelligent, creative, aware, self-aware, conscious, and loving beings. We were created by God. We were created of God. God is both our source and our substance. There could be no other substantive source for the spiritual dimensions of our being. And those are indeed <u>spiritual</u> qualities of our being. They are not physical. They did not evolve from a chemical, physical source. They can be experienced within the context of a physical body, but they transcend the physical. The physical does not contain or create spiritual qualities. Spiritual transcends physical.

I fundamentally know now that love does not require the physical body. My love for Marnie is more intense, more profound, and more real for me now than it has ever been even though she has left her physical body. That is a reality that I fundamentally know. I feel it every day. I feel it throughout each and every day.

I saw Marnie's body die. I saw her stop breathing. I was massaging her back with lotion when her body died. Her body was a broken, empty shell. It was no longer reflective of who or how she was in any way. But her spirit did not die. As her body failed, her spirit remained strong and loving. It never diminished. It did not weaken as her body weakened. It had a life of its own, separate from her physical reality. I experienced that directly. She never once complained.

God had always taken care of us. I can say now that perhaps even in Marnie's death, God was taking care of us. Marnie exchanged her physical body for a significantly higher level of consciousness, a higher level of awareness. She traded pain for a joyous reconnection with all those who had gone before her. She traded in her pain for fulfillment. Yet that is still so hard to believe on a **feeling** level for me. I was left behind.

Every day I have to affirm to myself that Marnie is alive. That her soul is alive, conscious, and aware. That she loves me. Now. Believing those things is the only thing that makes life still make sense to me and makes life still feel worth living for me. So I pray. I talk to God. I keep working on building faith. And sometimes I have to just keep surviving another day.

If you are choosing to embark on a journey of faith similar to the one I have described, know ahead of time that it will be a process. It is an ongoing journey that will only be fully completed upon your physical death. There will be times when that journey will feel joyful and fulfilling. There will be times when it feels like you are making no progress whatsoever in coming to truly *feel* your beliefs. There will be times when you will feel like you have fallen backwards and have lost all faith – times when you feel like curling up and giving up. But if your love for your beloved is real, you will not give up. Your love and commitment <u>will</u> carry you through.

There are tools that I have been using and that I believe you too can use to help carry you through the difficult process of building non-religious, spiritual faith in God and faith in the continued living relationship between you and your beloved. We will look at those in detail in the chapters that follow. But know that it can be done. You can do it.

Chapter 13: On Faith and the Death of Marnie's Body – A Personal Discussion with Her

Before moving on to a description of the specific tools that I've been using to build my faith, I want to share with you a personal discussion I had with Marnie about the death of her body and living with her now in faith. I think that it was in this discussion that I clarified my thinking. It was through this discussion that I came to feel and understand the essential role of faith in healing, and for me, in choosing to continue to live. Here is that discussion:

"There have been times when I have wondered if I'm delusional in what I'm thinking and what I am trying to do in maintaining this ongoing relationship with you after the death of your body, Marnie. I've wondered if I'm trying to make myself feel better about not having loved you well enough while you were physically alive by professing my love for you now.

I have had to face those questions in myself. I've had to take them deep down inside, and see what I find in my true heart. I have done so. They do not fit. I know that I loved you the very best that I knew how while you were physically alive. Our love, the beauty and magic that we shared was real. It dwarfs the regrets that I carry.

But here's the thing for me Marnie, if I view you as being gone, then for me, the best of life is over, and there's very little reason for me to go on any further. I can. I will. I will be as kind and loving as I know how to be, but everything will be pretty much a hollow, empty shell for me, tinged with sadness all the time. I will lack any desire to be in the world let alone rejoice in it.

On the other hand, if I believe that you have left your body behind, but that your soul, your awareness, and your consciousness are still with me, that you travel with me, you see with me, you hear with me, you feel with me, and you love me, then life is still rich. Then I still have a whole world to discover and share with you, my beloved, and to pass on joyfully to everyone that I touch, especially our grandchildren.

It's a pretty stark contrast emotionally between the two. The third option is to just not be sure and to vacillate back and forth and back and forth between those options, which begins to feel like a swirling whirlpool of defeated depression.

For me, there is only one positive option, and that's to choose you. I choose to believe in you and to believe that we continue on together here in this lifetime. In that, I can offer each new experience in this lifetime as a gift to you. I can love each person I touch in this lifetime as deeply as I possibly can as a gift to you. I can love them as us. I will continue loving as us as long as I live, until I can rejoin you fully, once again in the next lifetime. That is my choice. No other way to continue living life makes any sense.

I am creating feeling level reality for myself. I am actively sustaining that feeling level reality. But it is not a fantasy level fairy tale. Being physically alive in my finite body, I can't know, on an experiential level that I can absolutely confirm with my eyes or with my hands, that you, Marnie, are real, present, and alive. That kind of knowledge is beyond my current capability. I may very well never have that kind of absolute knowledge during my physical lifetime. I wish I did. I don't. But I can think. I can think clearly. I can look clearly at alternatives. And when I do so, the only explanation of life that makes sense to me is that you, Marnie, are a spiritual being who, for a limited time, possessed a physical body.

You possessed your body. The essence of you, that which is fundamentally "Marnie" was not your body. Your body was the vehicle through which you grew into and defined your identity. Your body allowed you to develop the personality, the identity of your soul that made you a unique, individualized dimension of the God that created you, who was and is the source and substance of your being.

God is the source and substance of every being. But we would not have individual consciousness, individual self-awareness, or individual identity as unique beings without the experience of living and making choices while inhabiting our physical bodies. God gave us the opportunity to develop our unique identity by giving us those physical bodies. Once our identity is fully established, there is no longer a need for our souls to continue carrying our bodies. We can move on from them.

Your loving identity was fully established, Marnie. It was profoundly established. Your physical body had failed, and it was indeed time for you to move on beyond its limits.

That left me alone in this physical world. I hurt profoundly. I continue to hurt every day. I miss seeing you. I miss touching you. I miss hearing your voice. I miss holding your hand. I miss feeling your head resting on my chest. I miss you. And the missing you can be so intense that it drowns out your spiritual presence. It makes it profoundly hard to feel your spiritual presence. It makes it profoundly hard to continue believing in your spiritual presence. It makes me question everything. It makes it profoundly hard to live in faith.

But I keep going back to the reality that living in faith, believing in your real, living, conscious, aware, loving spiritual presence is the only explanation of life that ultimately makes sense. And I go back to God. I go back to the fundamental explanation that God is (and only God could be) the source and substance of our very being. And with God as our source, our substance, and our very essence, then we are, we can only be, eternal spiritual beings.

God must be for being to exist. And we must be so as individualized dimensions of God's essence.

It all makes sense. I can find no better explanation for life itself. But since I cannot absolutely confirm this while I am physically alive in a mortal body, I can only believe this in faith. Faith is my source of hope. Faith is the fundamental ground for the very meaning of my being. Ultimately, for me, faith is the basis for my continuing, ongoing choice to keep living. Faith is my lifeline to you.

So I affirm that you are real and alive now, Marnie. You are conscious and aware of me. You love me. Your soul is real and alive. My soul is real and alive. (This is perhaps the hardest thing for me to believe right now because my body is still real and alive. I can't yet conceive of myself actually dying. If I can't even conceive of my physical death, how can I possibly conceive of my life after death? I know your body died, Marnie. I witnessed it. I know that I will die. It just isn't yet real to me on a feeling level.)

There is a part of me that wishes I could die. I want to rejoin you right now more than anything. But I believe I still have work to do on this earth. I believe I still have loving to do. I think I won't be ready to die and rejoin you until that work is complete. I believe I need to finish that work in order to earn the right to rejoin you, Marnie. My suffering here, my missing you so profoundly, is my cross to bear. It is my atonement for the hurt I caused you and others in this lifetime. So I choose to stay. I fully accept the hurt, the suffering. I welcome it (though I hate it) as my ticket back into your arms. It is there, in your arms that I will truly be home again.

Facing death requires faith. Again it comes back to faith. For physically living beings, the ultimate meaning of being has to be grounded in faith. Everything that matters requires faith. I can tell myself that. I can tell myself exactly why faith makes sense. I can explain and re-explain all the logical reasons for believing that I have already explained and re-explained. Unfortunately, that doesn't immediately translate into <u>feeling-level belief.</u> And without feeling-level belief, I can still doubt and question.

But without some miraculous, dramatic, direct intervention from God absolutely confirming the reality of the beliefs I've outlined, faith is the only positive pathway into the future for me. So I have to have faith. I have to live in faith. I have to affirm and re-affirm the reality of the beliefs that are the core of my faith. I have to work at building the feeling-level foundation of my faith.

As I said earlier, you, Marnie, were the most unselfish human being I have ever known. You were the most mature. You were the most forgiving. You were the most open to loving and receiving love. That is why it was so easy to fall in love with you. And so hard to let you go. Never have I met a more purely loving being.

You were and are a living reflection of the essence of a loving God. If anyone was ready to make the transition from mortal, physical reality to eternal spiritual reality in the presence of God, joined with God, it was you, Marnie.

My task is to go forward on a loving path in this lifetime that will allow me to become an equal partner, deserving to share eternity with you as one.

I truly hope that these words have totally embarrassed you and have filled you with absolute love, joy, and pride. I want to fill you to overflowing, now and forever.

I'm loving more deeply, more profoundly, more consistently than I have ever loved, Marnie. I'm loving at a higher level of vibration. Your body died. Everything for you (in your soul) now vibrates at a higher level. Your love is stronger. My love is tied to you because we are one. Our souls became one in love. Because of that, I'm loving at a higher level of vibration as well. We are one, Marnie. The heightened level of intensity and quality of my love proves it.

My love for you is the source of ultimate meaning and purpose in my life. My love for you has led me to God. My love for you has led me to the recognition of the Godliness that is our essence. My love for you is both human and divine. You have transformed my world. "**I love you**," is the heart and soul of my life. "I love you," is the most profound truth in my life. My task now is to live out that love in my everyday life – translating my love for you into loving in this world until I have completed the tasks that you and God and I have set out for me.

This is a real journey that I am undertaking – this journey of faith through my life. It's an act of faith. It's an act of courage. I can't have absolute certainty. But I believe there are others who have traveled this path. And my love and commitment to you are so strong, that I'm willing to undertake this journey of faith, no matter how difficult or painful it is sometimes. I do miss you, you know."

Thoughts on the Soul That Came to Me on a Morning Walk

"My soul chose you, Marnie, in the very beginning. Your soul chose me. We truly are soul mates. There are desires – hunger, thirst, sexual desire -- that are primarily physical. But the choices that we make that are more profound, that are spiritual in nature come from our souls. Our consciousness lives in our souls. Our consciousness directs our brains. Our consciousness precedes our brains. That which is really important, the decisions that shape the unique identity of our souls come from our souls. They come from a divine source.

On some fundamental level, our souls knew in the very beginning that we would grow into oneness with one another – that our souls were meant to be bonded as one in love for all eternity.

> "Important encounters are planned by the souls long before the bodies see each other."
> -Paulo Coelho

It is in finding and creating a lifetime that is absolutely defined by love that we get to move on. The identity that we built together, Marnie, was absolutely defined by love -- by our love for and with one another. Now, when my body dies, the possibilities for our future together become unlimited. You are my heart, Marnie. You are my soul's mate."

That was my personal discussion with Marnie. It provided for me the feeling level purpose for my faith. I believe that you too can and should have a personal discussion with your beloved. It will be different from mine, but I absolutely encourage you to have it. It may involve much sadness and many tears, but it will be liberating and uplifting. It will ground you in your faith.

Every day I speak with Marnie. And it seems like every day I think of things I wish I had said to her or things I wish I had done with her when she was with me physically on this earth. And whenever I think of those things, I express them to her out loud. I'm expressing regret, but with belief in the continued reality of Marnie's living soul, I am expressing love. I am expressing my desire for what I want to give to her in my heart now, and how I want to live with her upon our soul-level rejoining when my body dies. Faith in Marnie's living soul is my lifeline to hope.

I see more clearly now. I love with greater purity and intensity now. So of course I see the past with greater clarity and a whole new perspective that I lacked when I was caught up in the demands of the material world. So ultimately, my regrets become sign posts, guidelines for what I will do and share in the next chapter of our life together. In the context of the living soul, regrets can be transformed into gifts to be shared now in faith and in the future of ultimate spiritual reality together. In faith you see the preview of the next chapter of your never-ending love story.

"Marnie, I now have a profound appreciation of how deeply I was blessed in having our relationship. I wish that I could have lived with the perspective that I have gained from the loss of your body and treasured every moment of our exquisite life together, of your exquisite love for me.

I hope I can help others recognize and understand how important it is to treasure each moment and not get lost in the demands of the material world and the physical demands of life – the financial pressures, the day to day struggles. They are ultimately so insignificant. They pale in comparison to the reality of our love.

There's an appreciation of life that comes with death that is so significant, I can't overstate it. I wish I could teach it to people. I wish I could share it. I sure as hell hope I will have the chance to live life with you carrying the perspective that has come to me with the death of your body. I love you Marnie.

I hope I am absolutely filling you with love right now, Marnie. In the recognition of how much you mattered. In the recognition of how intensely I love you. In the expression of my love for you now. I want to do that now. I want to do that forever. I look forward to eternity with you. You are my heart."

"Immediately after the death of your body, Marnie, it was so easy to look at all my regrets. But now, I feel such a depth and intensity of love for you that I find it almost overwhelming. In recognizing the reality of your eternal, living soul and in affirming the reality of our ongoing connection and the reality of our coming rejoining I am beginning to find both peace and excitement. I will get to be with you again. And I will carry with me the sense of perspective that I gained from losing you. And I will carry that profound depth and intensity of love. That makes me smile and that makes me cry. I so look forward to it, Marnie.

It is in the joining, in the rejoining of our souls that absolute fulfillment will be achieved. The death of your body was a gift, as long as I know that your soul is real. You are my heart."

As a human being, in looking back at your life and your love for your beloved, you too will find reason to regret. Expressing that regret out loud is a gift of love. It is a direct expression of who and how you are in your true heart. Your beloved will hear it. Your beloved will receive it that way -- joyfully and gratefully. It will be the prescription for how you will live and love together in your next life when you too leave this earth.

Regret, owned and expressed is transformed into a gift of love and beauty. It is a picture of what can be, born from faith.

Chapter 14: On Building Faith – the Groundwork

I learned a set of tools through my counseling and teaching training and experience that I know work for self-concept building, developing effective attitudes, and achieving success in sports and business. I've had to question, can I legitimately use these tools to build a real, unshakeable, fundamental faith in God and the reality of Marnie's living soul? If I do so will the faith that I build be genuine? Will the faith that I build be more than a product of my desired fantasy?

My answer to these questions is, "Yes." I'm not trying to build some artificial belief system. I have thought through my beliefs as fully and clearly as I possibly can. They are real. They make sense to me. My task now is to attach a feeling level dimension to those beliefs so that I can find peace in my heart and in my life. This is an absolutely reasonable, appropriate, honest, and genuine reason for using the psychological tools that I have at my disposal. To choose to not build peace in my heart when I have the knowledge and ability to do so would be self-defeating and irresponsible.

This is true for each of you as well. If you look clearly and honestly into your own hearts, and determine what makes sense to you on the deepest, most profound levels and have developed your own fundamental set of beliefs, then using psychological tools to attach a feeling level dimension to those beliefs is both sensible and appropriate.

For both of us then, the tool we must begin with is thinking.

"Nothing is but thinking makes it so"
                                                            Shakespeare

A basic lesson that I learned about thinking is that what we dwell upon repeatedly, continually, will eventually grow into reality. If we repeat a thought often enough, with enough intensity, we create belief. And our deeply held beliefs create our feelings. Over time, feeling-level beliefs create our view of reality. Our beliefs become our reality.

When I think clearly about the source of being, I come to God. And when I think about the profound love and joy I was able to experience in my life with Marnie, I conclude that God, as the source of our being, is loving and generous. And I conclude by logical extension that God will continue to be loving and generous, always. For Him to not be so would be random and capricious. That would in no way fit with the intelligent design of the universe. It would in no way fit with the whole series of events that demonstrated God's active presence throughout Marnie and my lives together. I conclude that God intended our lives to be filled with love and the joy that comes from that love.

As I see it, God creates each of us as a spiritual being who is a dimension of and an extension of himself. That spiritual being begins as a perfect, blank slate. We fill in the details on that slate through the choices we make during our physical lifetimes. Those choices shape the unique personality, the unique individual identity of our spiritual being. We complete the process of defining the unique character of our spiritual being through the bonds of love that we build in our physical lifetimes. Our initial Godly essence becomes fully defined as our unique, personal, eternal soul.

A loving God would only intend our success in this process. A loving God would only intend ultimate joy and fulfillment for us, His (literal) children. A loving God would give His children all the tools they need to ensure their success. And that loving God gave us our most important tool in the form of our brains.

Remember, we transcend our brains. We control and focus the thinking of our brains by means of a conscious mind that is a central dimension of our souls. The mind directs the brain on the course we want it to follow. And the brain has the virtually limitless, God-given power to translate that direction into reality.

Unfortunately, many of us don't fully tap into our God-given brain power. But that power is there. It is at our disposal. All we need to do is tap into it. And the source for tapping into that power is our reasoned, conscious thought. We have the power to inundate our brains with the thoughts that we hold most dear. And I repeat, when we do this repeatedly and relentlessly, those thoughts become beliefs. And those beliefs create feelings. And ultimately our intensely felt beliefs create and become our reality. We are tapping into a divine source of power that cannot be denied.

Tapping in to that power can bring success in virtually any field of endeavor in this lifetime. It's a psychological programming tool used by the most successful people to achieve material and physical level success. It's a tool used by professional and Olympic athletes. But I believe it can go beyond that. It is a tool given to us by a loving God that can bring us back to faith in that loving God. And it is a tool that can bring about a feeling level recognition of our true essence as eternal spiritual beings with unique, eternally living souls.

To achieve faith, I had to do the thinking first. I had to do honest self-reflection. With that being done, my task became doing the consistent, daily, mental work needed to bring my heart into alignment with my mind.

I was raised by a conservative, religious mother. I grew up riddled with guilt. I believed from a very early age that I was going to hell. When I was 20 years old, I finally decided that I was not an evil person and that I did not deserve to be consumed by guilt every day. I decided that I had to choose between religion and sanity. I chose sanity. I quit religion. I quit believing in hell. I made logical choices based on reason. I thought through what made sense to me, and made decisions based on that thought. What I did totally made sense to me. But it was still a process. It took me two full years to leave all the feelings of guilt behind.

Now, I'm choosing to believe again. When I actively worked to cut loose of the fundamental belief system in which I was raised, it was a daunting task. I'm finding that my task now in building a new belief system is even more daunting. But my thinking is clear. My thought process has been rigorous. I can find no other belief system that in any way comes close to explaining the meaning of being to me. My task, therefore, is to build the feelings that go with those beliefs.

Not feeling those feelings raises doubt. It raises questions. Is this real? Am I maintaining a real relationship with my beloved? Or am I simply fantasizing? Is this all simply an outgrowth of profound loneliness? Is this all simply a product of missing Marnie so very much and wanting her back again when I know I can't have her again in this lifetime? The doubt can be consuming. The doubt can be devastating. But the doubt is not based on reason. Nothing has changed in my logical thinking about creation, life, death, physical reality, or spiritual reality. The only thing that shifts are feelings. And the feelings shift with fears. And then it comes down to a fundamental question – do I want to live my life based in fear? Or do I want to live a life based in reasoned hope and belief – a life based in faith?

The only reasonable answer for me is the latter. So I work.

I believe that the only reasonable answer for any of us, if we want to maintain an active, living, feeling-level, connection with our beloved, is to put in the work required to build the feeling. In the next chapter, we will look in detail at how to do that.

> LET YOUR FAITH BE BIGGER THAN YOUR FEARS.

Chapter 15: On Building Faith – the Psychological Tools

In this chapter I will share the psychological tools I have been using to build my feeling level beliefs. I will talk about "my" tools, "my" actions, "my" beliefs. These are not "my" tools. I have borrowed them from multiple sources. They work. Don't let the word "my" get in the way of what works for you.

I believe that these tools will work for you too. You have to choose which of these tools is appropriate for you personally. They may very well not all fit for you or your lifestyle. But whichever ones you do choose, apply them with determination, discipline, consistency, and commitment. If you do, over time, they will work.

Internal Dialogue and Affirmation

The first tool for building faith is managing internal dialogue. To become a fundamental, feeling-level belief, the ideas that comprise that belief must come to dominate your thinking. We talk to ourselves almost constantly often quite unconsciously, throughout the day. Now, in choosing to shape and take control of my feeling-level belief, I am working at taking full control of that internal dialogue in myself.

I talk with Marnie out loud every day. I talk with her the way I talked with her when she was here with me in her physical body. I share real **conversations** with her. I do so with such frequency that I find myself continuing those same kinds of conversations in my mind, in my internal dialogue.

And I have developed a series of **affirmations** about God (about His living, loving reality) and about Marnie. I affirm our love for and with one another. I affirm Marnie's continued real, living presence. I affirm the reality of our souls and their oneness through our bond of love.

I say those affirmations both out loud and in my mind over and over and over again every day. I say them repeatedly. I say them relentlessly. I say them especially when I exercise. I say them out loud when I bike. I say them sometimes out loud and sometimes in my mind as I run. I say them in my mind with each and every breath when I swim. I'll say them with such frequency and intensity that often I will notice that even when I haven't been consciously thinking, those are the thoughts that fill my head.

The combination of my conversations with Marnie and my affirmations now comprise the overwhelming bulk of my internal dialogue.

Physical Exercise

Physical exercise in general is crucial to me overall as well as in developing my feeling level beliefs. It is so easy for me to get lost in loneliness, in the sadness of missing Marnie's physical presence. By hiking, running, biking, and swimming, I can transform my brain biochemistry and move back into positive feeling. My mood is uplifted by the endorphin release brought about by the exercise itself. When that is combined with positive affirmations about God and about Marnie's real, living presence and our real, continued love, then those thoughts are imbued with even more intense positive feeling, strengthening their reality for me. I try to exercise for about two hours every day.

You do not need to go to the extreme of exercising for two hours each day. You may not be into running specifically, or swimming or biking, but I strongly recommend that you do some form of repetitive physical exercise that you can maintain for 30 minutes at a minimum. It will allow you to transform your brain biochemistry and affirm your desired beliefs simultaneously.

For me, **swimming** has become an increasingly important tool for developing feeling level belief. Not only do I affirm my love for Marnie and the reality of our loving connection with every breath I take (and I breath with every stroke) but I'm removed from normal, everyday reality. I'm living in a water reality. I swim with a mask and snorkel and do the breast stroke so I can stay fully immersed under the water throughout my swim. I can visualize Marnie swimming in front of me. (She was an excellent swimmer – far better than me.)

And as I'm living in this different medium (a water medium), Marnie is living on a different plane of reality, a different level of vibration. So me living in a different medium, makes the reality of Marnie's continued living presence in a different medium (on a different plane of reality) more tangibly plausible, more understandably believable on a feeling level. Combining that level of connection with relentless statements of love and oneness has a powerful effect on me. I feel our connection much more strongly for a significant period of time after the swim.

Rituals

Rituals (combined as always with positive affirmations) are perhaps my most important tools for developing my faith and belief. I walk for two miles every morning and two miles every night virtually without fail. And I talk. I talk with Marnie and I talk with God. These are disciplined rituals. I do them every day. The words I speak on these walks can often be the same when I am praying or affirming. Certainly they are the same in their meaning and intent.

I define God as real, as actively loving, and alive. I define God as the source and substance of Marnie's living soul. I affirm that Marnie's soul is real and alive. I affirm that her conscious presence is real and alive. I affirm that her love for me is real and alive. My love for her is unquestionably real and alive. And I pray. I pray for deeper, stronger, feeling-level faith every day. I ask God for certainty in my faith and beliefs. And I affirm those beliefs as reality, over and over again.

I follow a similar process at sunset. I either walk or ride my bike to a place where I can see the sun set. And I talk. I talk with Marnie. In our travels together, Marnie and I would watch the sunset whenever and wherever we could. And we'd kiss, just as the sun was sinking below the horizon. Now, every day at sunset, I tell Marnie how much she means to me. I tell her how profoundly I love her. I express the depth and intensity of my love for her in specific, elaborate detail. Then I describe each of the special places where we kissed at sunset. And I close my eyes and kiss her again just as the sun sets below the horizon. I commit myself to kissing her over and over again, every day of my life in my mind and heart, until I can rejoin her again on her plane of being and kiss her again in physical reality.

I said these words to Marnie as I sat and watched the sunset at Myakka River, "Sitting with you at sunset Marnie is the best part of my day. I will do it every day that I can for the rest of my life. Talking to you, feeling you, feeling with you – it gives continued meaning to my life. And I kiss you, I kiss you, I kiss you, I kiss you. I kiss you in my heart as the sun sets, as we did with our lips while you were here in your body. As we will again when I join you after the death of my body. I love you forever, Marnie, and that's just beginning, so I need to stay patient."

I do these rituals no matter what. Sometimes I don't feel like going out. Sometimes it's really hard to get started. Sometimes at night I'm so tired that I drift off into sleep for a while. But I have made a commitment to myself and to Marnie to do our walks. So I get up. I go. And they are transformative. Though I may be lost in random thoughts or simply empty and lost and virtually without any meaningful thought as I begin my walk, by the time the walk is completed my world and my emotions have been transformed.

Walking is a ritual for me because it works for me. I find that when I sit, I can easily get lost in my mind. My mind wanders and I lose focus. When I'm tired (and being emotionally drained from grieving often leaves me tired) I can easily fall asleep. But when I go outside for my walk, I have a clear purpose in mind. I am committed to that purpose. I want to connect with Marnie. There is nothing more important to me. I want to feel my connection. And, especially at night, I want to talk to God about my faith and about my connection with Him. I want to talk with Him about my love for Marnie and my profound desire to be rejoined with her. I want to thank him for our love. Walking outside is the tool that works best for me in accomplishing my purposes.

Walking need not be your ritual. But you need to develop your own special rituals that you will do without fail, every day, regardless of how you feel. It is transformative. Having a ritual that you follow without fail defines and declares the importance of your beloved to you and to them.

Our loved ones (whose bodies have died) have a special place in our hearts. We still love them deeply. We have a special, unique bond with them. We need to establish a special ritual that confirms that bond. It's in living out those rituals and talking with your beloved every day that strengthens the bond and makes its living reality a heart-felt belief.

　　　Sometimes it's the conversations that I have with Marnie that bring about a transformation in me emotionally. I can get lost in my conversations with her. Then I suddenly realize that I'm having those conversations. They are real. They <u>feel</u> real. I am speaking from my heart to my best friend. There is depth to those conversations. They feel genuinely real – not simply a product of my imagination. I may share problems I'm facing in dealing with family and family issues. I may share worries and concerns about how to make a living financially in a way that doesn't interfere with me actively living my values and living out what I see as God's will and Marnie's wishes for me.

　　　Then a flash of insight will come to me. Ideas about what to do and how to do it will appear in my mind. I believe Marnie or God sends me those insights. They come after I ask for help. They come after I ask Marnie to wrap me in her love. They come after I ask Marnie to help me feel her presence. And it feels as if they come <u>to</u> me – not <u>from</u> me. And my faith, my belief is strengthened.

　　　It is in your conversations with your beloved that at some point you will experience a magical connection. You will experience a transformation. But you have to have those conversations daily, without fail. You have to stay committed to them no matter what. Some days the conversation will feel empty, lacking in depth. Some days you will feel lost and not know what to say at all. But isn't that how it was in physical life too? It certainly was for me. If you maintain the discipline of doing the rituals and having the conversations, magic will happen.

Sometimes it is the process of affirming over and over and over again that transforms my feelings. Sometimes the affirmations lead to songs whose words blend with the message of the affirmations. And I sing those songs to Marnie aloud. I feel the words profoundly in my heart, and my heart is filled with love for her. That leads me back to the beautiful life that we shared together. That leads me back to gratitude to God for bringing Marnie into my life, for keeping us together through the difficulties we endured (through my selfishness and self-centeredness in the early stages of our relationship), and for actively taking care of us and protecting us as our love blossomed and grew into absolute love and oneness.

It is in being grateful for these gifts, in seeing how we were taken care of repeatedly in ways that were clearly beyond our control that God feels real. Divine intervention in our lives is the only plausible explanation for a whole series of miraculous events in our lives (as I described in chapter 4). When I see that, when I remember that, then God begins to feel more real again, here and now. And with God's reality comes the feeling level reality of Marnie's living soul. God leads me to Marnie. Marnie leads me to God. I come back transformed (for a while).

Music

Music can be a part of your daily rituals. For me it is the lyrics that carry me to Marnie. For you it may be the music itself. Marnie was a classical flutist. The music itself uplifted her soul. Trust your experience. But go with it consistently. Don't let it slip away if you don't want your relationship to slip away.

When Marnie was alive, I would play the guitar and sing for her. I still do. I sing to her every day. Sometimes I sing while I walk.

I sing the songs whose lyrics match my thoughts and my mood for that moment. In the evenings and times during the day when I don't feel rushed or pressured by the need to "accomplish" something, I play the guitar and sing special songs of love to her.

Reading

Reading can be a part of your daily rituals. Marnie and I would read to one another. She would read to me on long drives. We would read to one another at night before sleep. I continue to read aloud to her at night before sleep (when I'm not too tired) as a gift of ongoing love. It feels like an act of sharing that keeps her alive for me. I don't know how much it matters to her or if she listens to the stories in her level of being, but I know she feels it as an act of love.

Sharing Your Heart

In spite of using all the tools I've outlined above, I still have times when I fall back into doubt and fear. I'm living a life based on faith. I'm choosing that life. But it is a life grounded solely in faith. I don't have absolute, tangible, physical proof that what I believe is real beyond any possible doubt. I won't ever have that proof in this physical lifetime. And I carry the sadness of the loss of Marnie's physical presence. I have said this over and over and over again -- I can't hold her. I can't look into her eyes. I can't kiss her. I can't feel her head resting on my chest. I miss her physical presence profoundly. I always will. My sadness is real. But sadness can be a breeding ground for doubt and fear if I allow myself to dwell in it.

So I give voice to my sadness. It is real. It is at times intense. I express my sadness out loud. I share it out loud with Marnie. I weep with it, sometimes intensely. The sadness comes from memory. It comes from remembering and feeling the beauty and magic of what we shared together in the past and can no longer share in this physical lifetime. There are so many little, seemingly insignificant memories that pop up into my mind. But they carry with them so much feeling. I can suddenly be drenched in sadness. But sharing my sadness and my tears with Marnie brings me closer to her again. We always shared our fears, our sadness, and our doubts with one another when Marnie was physically alive. So doing so still, only makes sense. She was and is my best friend. It is the real, feeling level continuation of our loving relationship.

And I find that when I allow myself to fully feel and express my sadness, when I allow myself to weep, to sob with it, it is released. A feeling of peace returns. I don't know if Marnie actively wraps me in her love to lift me back up, or if I can only do so much crying before the sadness is temporarily drained out of me, or if it's both. But a feeling of peace returns to me and I can talk with Marnie again and genuinely feel her presence.

It is a level of grieving that we each go through, each in our own way. It is, I believe, unavoidable. But it is only in going through it that I have found I can release it (for a while).

After releasing the sadness, I actively work to move back into the present and the future. The key is to not dwell in the sadness. I shift my focus back to the loving that I can do now to fulfill Marnie's wishes and to fulfill what I believe to be God's will for me. I focus on the specific tasks that I can do today to achieve that loving purpose. I discuss them with Marnie and I ask for her help, insight, and direction in achieving that purpose effectively today.

I ask her to wrap me in her love. And insights come – not always, but sometimes. Sometimes I'll feel a shiver run through my body and an insight will come to me about what to say or what to do or what to write. It's an insight that comes _to_ me. It's not an extension of a thought I had been thinking. It genuinely feels like it comes to me. I feel it as Marnie's or God's response to me. And I _feel_ the reality of Marnie's presence then. The two way nature of our conversation feels confirmed, and our relationship feels real.

More on Affirmations

Then I shift my focus to feeling my profound love for Marnie. I describe the reality and the intensity of the love that I feel for her in detail. Often I will weep.

Always I will say, "I love you darling. You are my heart. You are my soul's mate. You are my forever wife. You are my forever love. You are my forever ideal lover. You are my forever perfect partner. You are my forever ideal playmate. You are my forever best friend. You are my inspiration and my motivation. You are my reason for living. You are my reason for loving. You are my pathway to God. Our souls are one in love sweet darling. Our souls are forever one."

I say that affirmation with intense emotion, multiple times every day. There is nothing that I say with greater feeling or intensity. I have a whole series of affirmations like it that I draw from and repeat as they come to me. They are a fundamental part of me now. Every day I affirm that God is real, loving, alive, and active in my life. And linked to this, I affirm that Marnie's soul is real and alive, that Marnie is real and alive, and that our love is real and alive. I affirm that Marnie sees me, she hears me, and she feels me, and in that she feels and is deeply touched by the profound love that I have for her.

And I affirm that she sees with me, and hears with me, and feels with me. In that, I can still actively give to her every day. I affirm, "All the people I touch in this world (especially our children and grandchildren) all the people I love, I love for and with you sweet darling, as a gift of love for you. And all the beauty and magic and majesty and mystery that I see and experience in this natural world, I offer as a gift of love to you as well. I hope I enrich your world. Everything I do is a gift of love for you, sweet darling. And I will keep on loving you while God helps me build my faith."

The affirmations I shared above are totally personal. I speak them from my heart. The words are absolutely genuine. Your affirmations will be totally different, totally unique, and totally personal. But I cannot overemphasize the importance of you developing your own set of affirmations. They define your world. They define your relationship. They define your reality. They are transformative. For me, combined with prayer, there is no more important tool in building my faith, in maintaining my relationship with Marnie than speaking my affirmations aloud to Marnie every single day. I suggest that the same will be true for you.

    And as I speak my affirmations I know that I am also building my faith. It grows stronger by the day. I believe that my faith will gradually overwhelm my fear and doubt and will unleash all the power of my unconscious mind. As that occurs, I believe that joy will come to dominate sadness as I continue on my pathway back home into Marnie's arms on the plane of her soul's living reality. I will arrive there upon my physical death. When I do, I will finally have absolute confirmation of the reality of our living souls.

    Living in faith is the only way of living that ultimately makes sense to me. It is a choice. But since the only ultimate confirmation of the reality of life after death can come after one's own physical death, why would you choose any other way of living? There are real forces that will always try to move us in a negative direction. Old, negative programming can do that. The news about the pain and suffering in the world can do that. Well intentioned friends who want us to be "realistic" about our situation can do that.

But thought is creative. What we think, how we interpret what happens to us, creates our feeling level perception of the world. It is not what happens to us, it is what we think about what happens to us, what we tell ourselves about what happens to us, that ultimately creates our personal world. Therefore, living in faith with a positive attitude is realistic. We can live in hope and belief, or we can live in fear and doubt. Both are choices. We must choose. To not choose is to choose to live in a state of ongoing consternation, confusion, and doubt. That too is a choice.

To choose to believe in love, to choose to believe in life, to choose to believe in God, to choose to believe in the conscious reality of the living soul, to choose to believe that God loves us and that life ultimately does have meaning and purpose, and (for me) to choose to believe in Marnie's continued conscious, living, loving presence is the only reasonable, responsible choice I can make.

Imagination

Once you have made such a choice, then commitment, determination, and persistence come into play. That choice is ultimately grounded in and is based solely on faith. It can be no other way. And living in faith without tangible confirmation is profoundly difficult. A key for me to be able to emotionally handle this has been to think with my imagination as the director of my thoughts, not my memory. I imagine what life can be and what I want it to be for Marnie and me in the next chapter of what I call our never-ending love story together. Thought is creative in this lifetime. There is no reason to believe that thought will not be creative in the next.

So I talk to Marnie about what I want to share with her in our next lifetime together, in the next chapter of our never-ending story. I take every regret about what I didn't do or how I didn't act as I wish I had in this lifetime, and translate it into a statement about who and how I am now and into a vision of how I and we will be together in the next chapter of our never-ending love story together.

I try to paint a verbal picture of the beautiful adventures that I hope we can share. I add to that picture whenever I can. When they are vivid, intensely heart-felt pictures for me, I repeat them day after day. I want them to feel real in my heart. I know that I have no understanding of the next lifetime. I don't really know what is and isn't possible. But in the expressing of these visions, I'm expressing my love.

We shared our dreams and hopes together in this physical lifetime. I'm keeping that pattern of interaction alive in our soul-level connection. They are real, sincere, hope filled visions. And as thought is creative, perhaps the process of sharing them with emotional intensity will lead to their coming true. At the very least, they are new, unique ways that I can express my love to Marnie.

When your relationship is alive, there are always possibilities. When your relationship is alive, it can always grow. Your soul level connection with your beloved is alive now. So are the possibilities. There is potential for growth. I am suggesting that you not let death (of the physical body) halt or block your thinking about the continued, ongoing possibilities in your relationship with your beloved. The world around you may suggest that this is crazy. I suggest that it is not. With and in God, the possibilities are limitless.

Live your life based in hope and faith. It doesn't make sense not to. Hope and faith make much more sense than living in loss and despair. Trust in God. Trust in your beloved. Hope. Pray. Believe. Affirm. Every day.

Chapter 16: A Declaration of Reality

On my "journey of healing" last year I wrote these words to Marnie: "I think my task, as I continue to heal, is to <u>remember</u> you less, and to <u>feel</u> you more -- to feel your presence with me, to carry you in my heart as I move forward in the world. We are together now, you and I. I affirm that, repeatedly, every day. We are together, you and I. Now. I love you. I carry you with me. I'm not just carrying your memory. I'm carrying your living presence. Now."

But I had trouble hanging on to that affirmation. I had not yet been able to move it down into my heart, to the level of heart-felt belief, to a level of certainty and conviction. In spite of using the tools for building faith that I outlined in the previous chapter, I would slip from hope and confidence (hence happiness) back into doubt and fear, over and over and over again.

I said this to my son, Ben: "I'm trying to come to grips with whether I can genuinely, deeply believe that Marnie is fully present in a conscious, aware, active way in my life. If she is, if she can see me, hear me, and feel my feelings then my world is transformed in a positive way. If that is not true, then the world (for me) is bleak and empty. "Can I believe? Can I live a life fundamentally based on faith?"

I knew that ultimately, I had to answer those questions for myself. I wanted to break free and move forward with my life. I had experienced so many "coincidences" that argued for the reality of Marnie's presence. But they didn't bring me <u>certainty</u>. I needed to make a choice in the face of uncertainty and have the courage to live out that choice.

I made that choice. I made a fundamental declaration of reality which I share with you here.

Declaration of Reality: my Fundamental Conclusions

1) Marnie's presence is real and alive. She is fully aware of me and she loves me.

2) God is real and loving.

3) The love that Marnie and I built was profound. We were one. We are one. We will continue to be one. Our love is a reflection of the divine. In our continuing love, we participate in the divine.

4) I live and love now as us -- as Marnie in me, with God in us.

5) In our oneness we forged a bond of oneness with nature. In that bond with nature, we discovered magic together. Living on with Marnie in me, I will continue to discover magic in nature and it pass on to our grandchildren.

6) My life from this point forward is a gift of love for Marnie that I experience with Marnie. I will live love for her. I will live love with her as us.

7) No more doubting the reality of these things. I will recognize hurt and pain as the real hurt and pain of no longer physically having Marnie with me. I will weep with sadness but not with doubt.

It is time for me to move forward. I will. With my strength and intelligence, with Marnie's strength and clarity, and with God's strength and guidance, I will.

There are those who will doubt or even scoff at all of this. But I make it as a choice, a declaration of reality, and a commitment from today forward. I keep my commitments.

I will keep affirming Marnie's real presence, God's love and reality, and our bond of love and oneness until it becomes absolute, unwavering conviction. I already have the absolute conviction about the unbreakable reality of our love. The rest will follow.

Making those declarations didn't create instant healing. The pain and sadness from missing Marnie so profoundly continued to come over me in waves. Sometimes those waves can be so powerful that I feel like I am drowning. I don't know if I can stand it. I have to acknowledge it and accept it as real. I cry out (literally) to Marnie and God for help. But in not letting the pain alter my fundamental , faith based, definition of reality, it no longer leaves me as profoundly lost as I was when I questioned the reality of Marnie's (and my) essential spiritual being.

The day after I wrote my declaration of reality to Marnie, I wrote the following:

"I am, we are, just one little speck in this universal infinity, Marnie. I am, we are, our love is the center, the core, the heart of this universal infinity. We are a part of God. We are a reflection of

God. We are individualized dimensions of God. We reflect the whole. In our love, we participate in the divine."

Though that felt like a significant insight, the following morning started with grieving. I wrote, "It seems that every morning I have to feel the sadness, Marnie. I have to let the sadness out. I have to talk to you about the sadness. I have to express how much I miss you, darling. I miss you and weep.

I have to go through this to be able to get on with the rest of the day and start dealing with the world again. Grieving does not automatically end with understanding ultimate reality. I love you Marnie! I miss you Marnie!"

As you can see, the process of grieving went on for me. It still does even now after another year has passed. Each day seems to just fly by. But the days seem to stretch on and on endlessly. When your love is real and intense the missing never seems to go away completely. But it can be combined with a new level of joy in being and in believing in the joy and fulfillment that will come with ultimate, spiritual reality.

On a very fundamental level, I don't believe I'm different from any of you who are suffering your loss. In the weeks and months since I made my basic declaration of reality, the waves of pain continued. Their frequency diminished, but not their intensity. Talking with Marnie, talking clearly from my heart to my best friend in my daily walking rituals has made the pain more tolerable. Sharing my pain out loud with Marnie helped release it. Weeping with her helped release it. Asking her to wrap me in her love helped ease it. Affirming the reality of my profound sadness helped limit the pain to the realm of physical loss.

Believing in and feeling the presence of Marnie's soul and feeling her love and awareness makes the physical loss more tolerable. It helps define that physical loss as nothing more than a speck of time in the infinity that awaits us in our spiritual being. When I think about that clearly and feel it in my heart, my pain eases. And I often feel a genuine shiver of Marnie's presence when I clearly think these thoughts.

Still, it's not easy. The waves come. They still wash over me as I'm sure they wash over you as well. But you can, you will survive them. Make your declaration of reality. It is worth it.

I wrote these words to Marnie:

"You are my heart. I, in you, me. I, in me, you. We are one. Our love is a bond of joy and oneness. Our oneness is eternal. Our bond cannot be broken. I carry you in my heart and soul constantly. I carry you forever. I love you. Our love has not, nor will it ever diminish. I will nurture our love every day for the rest of my physical life until we can be rejoined in absolute oneness, with full conscious awareness of one another and our love for one another, for all eternity.

Our bond was not and could not be broken by the death of your body. I carry you in me. You carry me in you. So of course you are here, watching over me, one with me. I think it. I believe it. It is the only thing that makes sense to me in ultimate reality. My task now is to translate my belief in our bond to the heart level where I feel it with certainty as absolute conviction that I carry with me always. That gives my life meaning and purpose. It gives me the joy and peace to love as us for as long as I remain on this physical earth.

A oneness has been created, that can never be destroyed.

I feel intense sadness in missing your physical presence here beside me, Marnie. I miss putting my arms around you. I miss looking into your eyes. I miss running my fingers through your hair. I miss kissing you. I miss holding your hand. I miss making love with you. In missing all of those things, I will need a regular influx of love and energy from you and from God to be able to carry on until the day that I too can leave this physical world behind. Then I will rejoin you in absolute recognition, in absolute awareness, in absolute consciousness, in absolute love, in absolute ecstasy, in total oneness for all eternity.

I affirm that. I pray for that. That is the cornerstone for living my life from this moment forward. I will live love to earn the right to rejoin you on your spiritual level.

All these words come from my heart, Marnie. I don't need to think about them. They just come out. They come from some deep source inside of me that taps into reality. It is you. It is your life. It is your love. It is my need to stay connected to you, to stay connected to your love that has caused me to tap into that source. You have brought me to God.

The death of your body has been the most painful thing I have ever experienced or could ever imagine experiencing. But it may be the springboard for my being able to make the transition into eternity, into the world of spirit, of soul, and supernatural reality.

That's where I need to go to come home. Because you are and always will be my home. And ultimately, I need to come home. I love you...."

I urge you to make your own declaration of reality. I urge you to speak your truth to your beloved from your heart. I believe it will be transformative for both of you.

Chapter 17: A Summary of My Keys to Building Faith

I'm not sure if telling you what I had to learn through experience, will be enough to prevent you from having to repeat my experience, but I hope that what I have to share here will at least help you to be gentle and patient with yourself in building your feeling-level contact with your beloved.

I had to have **heart-felt faith** for my life to continue to feel worthwhile. I needed to feel in my heart that Marnie's presence was real. When I **feel** that, then I feel that a loving God who is alive and active in my life is real. Then I feel that the eternal soul is real. Then I feel that our continued, active relationship is real. I need to feel Marnie's presence. It is the key that counterbalances the intense loneliness, the intense feeling of missing Marnie that can come to dominate my emotions and my awareness.

I built my fundamental beliefs on a foundation of reason. What I needed to do next was to translate that foundation into heart-felt belief. I used every psychological tool I had available to me to achieve it. This is a summary of those tools:

1) **I consciously focus my thinking on my love for Marnie and on my belief in the living, conscious presence of her soul in my life now.**

I focus my conscious thoughts there over and over again. I do so repeatedly, relentlessly, every day without fail. I don't allow my mind to dwell in doubt or negativity.

2) **I affirm my love for Marnie and the reality of our continued living, loving relationship incessantly when I walk, when I exercise, at sunset, and whenever I feel free to roam in my mind.**

I affirm repeatedly, relentlessly. I cannot overemphasize the importance of affirmations.

3) **I affirm as truth everything I want to be true about Marnie, God, and our relationship together**.

Reason tells me that these beliefs are true. I need to feel them as true. So I say these affirmations with intensely felt emotion repeatedly every day. Again, I cannot overemphasize the importance of affirmations.

4) **I visualize what I want to be true about Marnie and me in our next lifetime together**.

I'm a more auditory person than I am visual, so this is harder for me. But there are some visions about rejoining with Marnie after my death that are so strong, so vivid, that I repeat them every day with heart-felt intensity that often generates genuine tears. If you are a strong visual person, visualize what you want over and over again with heart-felt intensity.

5) **I strictly control my external, suggestive environment**.

I surround myself with pictures of Marnie everywhere. My home, my car, and my travel trailer are filled with Marnie's pictures. I carry pictures of Marnie in my pockets and in lockets I wear around my neck. I press her picture to my heart whenever I'm feeling lost or hurting. That is truly important to me.

I listen to music that fills me with love for her. I primarily talk with people who support my beliefs and hopes and who truly honor the love that we had together. I treat other people with love, respect, and kindness, but I try to minimize my contact with people who doubt and question the beliefs I am working at building and strengthening. I look for reading materials that confirm the reality of the living soul without demanding a whole set of religious beliefs and practices to go along with it.

6) **I open myself to and search for external signs in the natural world that confirm my beliefs and confirm Marnie's presence.**

7) **I talk out loud with Marnie every day.**

I treat her as my best friend. I treat her the way I treated her when she was with me physically. Sometimes I have little to share beyond where I've been wandering in my mind. It's nothing earth shattering. Sometimes I just share what I'm thinking about doing that day. But sharing my thoughts, sharing my observations, and sharing what I've been feeling (or not feeling) is vitally important. It keeps us connected on a soul level the same way we were connected when Marnie was physically present. It keeps "us" real.

8) **I exercise every day.**

I walk and run and bike and swim. They keep me sane. Running and swimming are the best for me. They lift me. And I can chant in my mind, "I love you girl, I run for you. I love you girl, I run with you." And I feel Marnie's presence and I feel better.

Sometimes I just want to walk. It doesn't give me the endorphin lift, but in the walking, I can talk with Marnie. Sometimes, as I'm walking, I can get lost in talking with her – just talking and talking. I'm not thinking about it. It's just coming from me spontaneously, and at some point I realize it. I realize that I'm talking with Marnie and I recognize how good I feel when that's happening. It makes "us" feel absolutely real.

9) **I discipline myself.**

I discipline myself to consistently live the rituals and use the tools that I have outlined each and every day. I discipline my eating. I discipline my exercise. I do everything I can to keep my world in balance. None of this is to say that I am perfect at doing all of this all of the time. But when I find myself having been off track, I do everything in my power to bring myself back on track immediately.

10) **Rituals are vital.**

I urge you to develop your own unique set of rituals that you can and will follow every day without fail. They are crucial in building your heart-felt belief in God and your ongoing, heart-felt connection with your beloved. As with affirmations, I cannot overemphasize the importance of rituals. Combining ritual with affirmation has been a profoundly powerful tool for me.

11) **Prayer.**

I pray every day without fail. I ask God to strengthen my faith on every morning walk. I ask for wisdom and guidance in my writing and in my interactions with people. I ask for His love and strength and an increase in my feeling of Marnie's presence when I'm lost in the pain of grieving. And, most importantly for me, I have a whole ritual of prayer that I speak to God every night on my prayer walk.

I talk to God from my heart as I would to a real friend. But I always share the same combination of things. I ask Him for a continued strengthening of my faith. I thank Him profoundly for Marnie – for bringing her into my life, for keeping her in my life, and for taking care of us as we built our bond of love and oneness. I thank him for our eternal souls. I ask that we be absolutely rejoined upon my death. I ask that we be able to share in resurrected, spiritual bodies in the afterlife. I commit myself to living His will for me throughout the rest of my physical life on this earth and throughout eternity together with Marnie.

And I ask God to totally wrap Marnie in his love. I ask Him to fill every fiber of her being with love, joy, peace, understanding, and perhaps excitement about our rejoining. I ask God to let Marnie see me, and feel me, and hear me, and feel the profound depth and intensity of the love that I feel for her. I ask that my love glow within His love and fill Marnie to overflowing.

Then, as part of my prayer, I talk with Marnie. I share with her in intricate detail every dimension of my love for her, and my absolute commitment to her for the rest of eternity. And I often weep. (I will share parts of my prayer for faith with you directly in chapter 21.)

Doing all of this every day is not easy. I wrote these words to Marnie when I was reflecting on my desire to be with her again:

"I'm not ready to rejoin you yet. I need and want to fulfill the promises I made to you before I can rejoin you. I will try to love our grandchildren to the very best of my ability until they each have a profound, unshakeable, deep down feeling of worth, and the skills to build the kind of love in their lives that we shared in ours. And I want to finish my writings as a gift for them, a gift to you, and as a gift for everyone and anyone I can touch through my words. Then I will be ready to rejoin you.

I want to rejoin you as soon as I possibly can. I wish I could do it this very minute. But I want to rejoin you when I'm sure you that can receive me back in your arms with absolute joy, with absolute pride, and with absolute delight in all that I did and gave on your behalf. I. want you to receive me back in your arms without hesitation, without reservation, in absolute ecstasy for all eternity. Then I will truly be back home."

"When you were physically alive Marnie, I was happy just being. I felt at peace simply being in your presence, and I carried inside me a basic feeling of happiness. All I needed was to have you in my life.

Now that you're not here physically, I have to discipline my life to feel that sense of peace and happiness. My morning, nighttime, and sunset walks are essential to fully maintaining my connection with you, to really feeling it. Being outdoors in nature with you at those times keeps your presence alive for me."

Sometimes it's still hard for me to go out on my walks, Marnie. It's hard for me to get up and go outside. But I really need this time with you. I need this time to grieve. I need this time to connect with you. I grieve and connect with you simultaneously. Then I can go forward and deal with the rest of the world. But I have to feel my sadness and my love first. Then I can carry you with me as I go forward.

And I need the daily exercise to keep my mood up. And I need to do my work, my writing as well as my time with the children. It makes my life feel purposeful. I need to eat well, but not over-eat. Comfort food is not necessarily a comfort to me. Even if I get too tired, I can sink into sadness.

I need to manage and balance it all to keep feeling that sense of peace that came so naturally when you were here with me physically. I really do miss you, Marnie. But I love you. So it's all worth it."

Despite the fact that it is not easy, I urge you to design and follow a program similar to the one I outlined above. Create and balance every dimension of your own healing program. The love and connection that you will feel with your beloved will make all the effort and discipline worth it. Ultimately rejoining with your beloved will be the result. Trust in God. Trust in your beloved.

Chapter 18: Grieving

Grief

*I had my own notion of grief.
I thought it was the sad time
That followed the death of
Someone you love.
And you had to push through it
To get to the other side.
But I'm learning there is no other side.
There is no pushing through.
But rather
There is absorption.
Adjustment.
Acceptance.
And grief is not something you complete,
But rather, you endure.
Grief is not a task to finish
And move on,
But an element of yourself –
An alteration of your being.
A new way of seeing.
A new definition of self.*

Gwen Flowers

Strength

You never know how strong you are, until being strong is your only choice.

Bob Marley

Grieving has been the most painful, difficult, confused, jumbled chapter of my life. So it makes sense that this is the most difficult, confused, jumbled chapter for me to write.

Grieving is woven into the fabric of every chapter of this book. It must be so. When you have lost someone profoundly important to you, as Marnie was to me, grieving lives at the very center of who and how you are. So I thought it essential to devote an entire chapter to grieving before moving any deeper into the process of building faith in God and coming to fully feel the continued, living presence of your beloved – the process of healing.

There are many who won't and perhaps can't understand my continued grieving and my writing about it. Healing is what they want for me. Ultimately, healing is what this book is all about. But healing can't happen unless grieving is recognized, acknowledged, expressed, and accepted. It is only in acknowledging, owning, recognizing, and declaring the real pain of your loss, the continuing pain of your loss, that healing can begin to happen. You can only heal from grieving by going through it.

Grieving is essential to healing. And grieving is not a short term process. It's not something to be completed, something that will be over and done with at some point. Grieving is an ongoing process that co-exists with healing. For me, grieving may very well continue throughout my lifetime on this earth, even though for me, healing is happening.

In this chapter on grieving, I will try to show you what grieving looked like, sounded like and felt like for me without censorship. It's not pretty. When it is most intense, there are times when I sob and drool and my nose runs simultaneously. I cry and I cry out for help. My knees buckle, and I just want to fall down. I question if I can or if I want to survive. I beg for help. I beg Marnie to pull me through. She does. I beg God for help. He sends it.

At other times the grieving is less intense. It changes constantly for me. Some days are much better than others. Some days are much worse. Sometimes it changes profoundly during the course of the day. But it is all real. I hope that by sharing this, you will come to know me better and be able to see from my perspective what the most difficult part of my world looked like and looks like.

And I hope it will make you feel ok about your grieving and how you do it. There is nothing wrong with you. There are no grieving standards. We are indeed each different. How you grieve is ok. It's real. It has to be done. It has to be gone through. It is only in going through it that you will heal.

In parts of the chapter, I will write about Marnie and my grieving for her. In parts of the chapter I will talk directly to Marnie, because it is in talking to her that I release my grief by sharing it with her. Throughout the chapter I will move back and forth between these two perspectives. As I did in Chapter 10, I will quote passages from my journal. They are direct statements of my grief. They may not flow together in smooth, coherent paragraphs. But neither does my grief. I hope that what I share with you will feel real. I hope it will feel genuine in a personal way and in an understandable way despite its lack of smooth flow.

(As an aside I think it important to mention that I always feel better in talking to Marnie rather than talking about her. So I prefer to write from that perspective. On some level, talking about Marnie objectifies her. I wonder if she doesn't think, "Hello! I'm here." And talking *about* her feels like it puts her in the past. I end up feeling disconnected from her living presence in the present moment. Then I feel really sad. Then I have to grieve even more and work at rebuilding our connection.

And there's a problem with language. I find myself having to add the word "physically" over and over again. As in, "I so wish you were here with me now 'physically'". It's just plain difficult talking with or about someone who is present, but not physically present simultaneously.

It's difficult enough talking with people who don't understand why I can't let Marnie go and move on. It's even more difficult when just the process of talking to her or about her can be so inherently difficult. Perhaps you understand.)

In this chapter, thoughts about healing will be interspersed with the focus on grief. The two are inextricably connected. Healing will be the primary focus of the remaining chapters of this book, but in this chapter, the primary focus will be on the grief that has to be gone through to achieve healing.

Again, I know the description of my grieving will seem like a jumble of confusion at times, but that's how grieving has been and still is for me. I can't tie it all together in smooth, coherent paragraphs and still portray the ongoing ups and downs of emotion, the ongoing confusion that I feel. My writing in this chapter will be disjointed. My thoughts and feelings are disjointed. What I share with you here are my actual thoughts and feelings.

My Grieving

Some days I don't feel like going on. I will. I will because I promised Marnie I would. And I feel that the sadness, the loneliness, and the emptiness that I feel are my cross to bear. I hope they will atone for my selfishness and self-centeredness, and for the hurt that I caused during my lifetime, so that when I die I can rejoin Marnie immediately.

I said to Marnie, "When I'm at my lowest, I don't want to keep living any more. I want to lay down and give up. You're the only one I can talk to about this, Marnie. I'm afraid that if I were to kill myself I wouldn't get to be with you. So that's not an option. And I promised you I would keep going, so I will. But without you in my life, I don't have confidence in myself. I don't know what I have to offer to the world. I question if my writings have any value. I question if I'm even worth loving still. I find it really hard to think of doing anything really meaningful without your support. And I don't know if I can do it on my own. Somehow your love for me made me whole. It made me willing to go forward and do. I didn't get lost in fear.

I know I have to face the death of my body at some point. That doesn't trouble me. I'd like to face it soon. But going forward, without you, that's hard to face. I need you with me. I need you to wrap me in your love when I hit these places where I just want to curl up and fade away. Please wrap me in your love. Send me your strength. Let me earn the right to be with you again.

The world was more beautiful when you were in it physically with me. The world is still beautiful. I'm discovering that again. I'm just not as happy or at peace in my soul the way I was when I could physically hold you."

You, my sweet, were far more kind, far more loving, and far more special than me. You had faults. You caused some hurts. But your cancer more than atoned for all of that. So I have no doubt that you are wrapped in God's love and filled with joy. My dream, my hope is to rejoin you immediately upon my death, and to go forward in love with you and loving with you for all eternity.

But for now, the stronger I feel my love for you, Marnie, the more fully I feel absolutely in love with you and tune in to your presence, the more profoundly I miss you. It's one of those contradictions that seem so inextricably bound up with the loss of your body. Your presence brings me joy, and your absence brings me sadness. And they happen simultaneously."

Healing from the profound grief that comes from losing Marnie so often feels like one step forward and two steps back. I vividly remember coming back to St. Joseph Peninsula State Park. I wrote to my son, Ben about it.

"This is a hard place for me to come back to emotionally, Ben. It's a beautiful park. It's on the ocean. But it was the first park we stayed in in Florida when Marnie was suffering the effects of her cancer before we even knew that she had cancer. She sat on the beach here and cried because her back hurt so badly and she couldn't run with me.

Now I'm here alone. I miss Marnie so badly. I weep. I sob. I so want to believe Marnie's here, beside me. It's so hard thinking and feeling that we'll never share this beach (or any beach) again in this lifetime and believing she's right here with me simultaneously. It makes me feel crazy, sad, confused, lost, and desperate. I just had to beg Marnie for help to keep going. As soon as I did, the intensity of the distress eased. She must have heard me. She must have intervened.

But it's still so hard to believe when I can't see her. I can't hear her. I can't feel her touch. It's so hard, Ben. So hard.

I just realized that I've been sitting here paralyzed for the last hour. Thinking of nothing really. Just lost. I guess I'll go walk. I write to you because I need someone to understand what my world can be like. Please, just keep hearing me. I need that badly. I need someone who will hear me and not try to fix me or push me to do something else to feel better. When people do that, the implicit message is that there's something wrong with me, that my hurting and my struggle are somehow not ok. And it's hard enough trying to get through this and build genuine faith.

This is the hardest challenge I have ever faced. I can't pray to make the hurt go away. It doesn't. It won't. I can only pray for the strength to handle it. And, by the way, I won't do some inane job to distract myself (as some suggest). I have to genuinely get through this and find a meaningful path for the rest of my life.

I won't give up, though sometimes I want to. I can't/won't fail at this one."

I wrote these words to Marnie at Hillsborough River, one of our special places.

"I don't understand Marnie. I don't understand the complexity of the feelings I have. How can I feel your presence and still miss you so very much? I go from feeling full to feeling totally empty. I go back and forth, over and over again. I feel so sad remembering little things we did together and feeling like they are gone, that they live only in the past. And then I'll think, but I'm here with you and it's beautiful and I'll be able to pass it on to our grandchildren and I feel good again.

And then I weep and I weep and I miss you. So I ask you to wrap me in your love, and soon I feel an infusion of strength that almost overwhelms me. I go from weeping intensely to all of a sudden feeling alright. You must have something to do with that. It's just so hard to know."

I was biking down a road called (ironically) "The Dead River Road" near Hillsborough River. I wept and said to Marnie, "It seems like such a long, empty road ahead of me, Marnie. It feels like a reflection of my life -- like there's a long, empty road ahead of me. I need to have you travel beside me, darling. Please stay with me. Please let me feel you. Please lend me your strength so I can make it to the end and back to you."

In leaving Hillsborough River I wrote, "It seems like I've gotten confirmations of your presence, over and over and over again. And yet I have felt profoundly sad and empty and lost today. Perhaps it's in leaving a place that was so special to us. I don't know. I wish the hurting, the profound loneliness, the emptiness, the missing you so deeply could quit. I miss you so much, Marnie. I miss you. I wish the feeling of your presence could grow strong enough to overpower the sadness, at least most of the time."

"When I'm outside talking with you in the mornings, when I'm outside, talking with you and God and praying at night, when I'm talking to you at sunset, when I run or bike and talk with you, I'm OK. The world feels good. But in between those times, I can get so lost, so sad, that I don't know if I can go on. I don't know how much longer I can stand it. Sometimes I just don't want to keep going.

Please help me. Please help me. Please..... I feel like I'm trapped in quicksand and there's no way out. I'm just going to sink and sink and sink until I die. It's hard to feel that way."

"All the beauty in the world is cloaked in sadness and tears for me. I miss you darling. I wish I was physically holding your hand, tight in mine. Hopefully, the cloak of sadness will fade over time, and the sadness will be transformed into deep joy and peace. I love you no matter what.

The moon and the sun are up together. You and I are one. Oh my darling, I love you."

"I don't know how to live without you. I'm doing it, but my world lacks richness. That's why I have to be outside so much of the time. I have to have nature to fill in the richness that I had, just being in your presence, no matter where we were."

"It's hard for me to understand the feelings that I carry with me in my body when I walk with you in the mornings. Tears are definitely right there below the surface. And there's a hollowness, an emptiness, a tension – I don't know quite how to describe it – but it's a feeling that is unique. It's not pain exactly. It's a sadness or melancholy on some deep level. But it's uniquely tied to you not being here with me physically, not holding my hand while we walk.

I hurt baby. I hurt. There's nobody I can turn to. There's no one who can really understand how badly I hurt except you. There's nobody who can make it better. So I turn to you and I turn to God. I have to trust. I have to believe. I need you, just to survive."

"Maybe I have to be willing to fully go through the pain, the deep pain and sadness of separation from you while continuing to try to feel your presence with me, my beloved. Maybe I have to go through that pain to be able to fully appreciate the joy of your presence and, ultimately, the joy of rejoining you for eternity."

"Peace is tinged with melancholy for me, darling. I know what home is. Home is in your arms. I just don't know exactly where that is right now. We were meant to be together, you and I. I believe God ordained it. I believe our souls chose one another. I live, from this day forward, as us. I live with you. I live for you. I live as us. I love with you. I love for you. I love as us. We are one, and I am better for it. I love you. I thank you."

Still, even after thinking these uplifting thoughts, the next morning I was plunged back into sadness. As I walked I thought and said, "You're never going to be here physically again in this lifetime are you sweetheart? I miss you so much. I miss your beautiful body. I miss sitting in bed and drinking coffee with you in the morning. How do I sit and drink coffee alone? How do I do anything alone? I loved living with you. I never wanted to die. I wanted to push our death back further and further and further. I thought it was hard turning 50, thinking half my life was over. But then I thought, well, I can live to 100. Then I wanted to live to 113. I loved living with you. I didn't ever want to die.

All I have now are pictures of your beautiful body. I'll never be able to touch your body again in this physical lifetime. I miss your physical presence. And I have to be able to distinguish your physical presence from your spiritual presence. And that's hard. Talking now, talking to a spiritual presence, not being able to look into your eyes, not being able to touch you or hold your hand, not being able to see and feel your response, that's so hard. It's so hard not to feel like I'm just talking into empty air.

I love you, darling. I need your help. I need God's help. I need help to go on, to feel like it's all worthwhile. I know physical death had to come at some point. I say I know that, but I never felt it. Your physical death is still unreal. It was real. I saw you suffer. I saw you shrink. I saw your skin turn paper thin. And if I believe that there is real life, real consciousness, a real soul that lives on after physical death and is connected to God, then I know you're better off. It's just so hard staying here alone.

I wish I could have made the transition to the next life with you. I wish I could still be absolutely with you, without any questions, without any struggle, without any separation.

I don't want to believe that there is any ultimate separation between us. But we are living in different realms of existence right now, even if that's only artificial because I can only see what I see with my physical eyes. But I miss you so much…I need help to stay connected on that spiritual level. Please send me any help that you can. Please God, help me believe and make it through.

But for some reason, believing that you're still present, doesn't make me miss you any less. It doesn't make the pain any less. It feels like it should, but it doesn't. I miss you so badly, darling. I miss you so badly. I don't know when it will ever end."

"It's a particularly lonely morning. I feel like I shouldn't be here without you, Marnie. I miss you, sweetheart. I miss you so very badly. I didn't know living could be such hard work."

"Every morning I grieve. I wish I didn't have to do that. I guess it's real. I've been caught up in "me" this morning, feeling sorry for myself, instead of seeing things for you. It's when I'm seeing things for you that I feel good. It's when I'm looking at "me", feeling sorry for myself, feeling lonely, that I feel bad. It's such a struggle."

"There is a huge void inside of me. It's the place that you used to fill, Marnie. And no other person will be able to fill that void. Ever. I'm going to have to love lots of people who can fill up little chunks of the void. I don't know if there will ever be enough to fill the whole thing. But I need to do lots of loving, and I need to do that as us in order to keep going. And maybe just feeling your spirit, your presence, and your awareness of me more strongly will help fill part of that void.

Every morning, I miss you, Marnie. I miss you deeply. I miss you profoundly. And that's when I feel that void, that melancholy. I miss you, Marnie. I love you. I really hope that you see what I see, and hear what I hear, and feel my love for you."

"Physical death does not diminish our love whatsoever. It does cause hurt. I love you. I think it takes self-discipline to love you now, to not give in to the hurt and the sadness, to work at staying positive, to work at loving without you being here physically by my side; to work at knowing that you're here, by my side, to not let myself just collapse in hopelessness and sadness. I love you Marnie.

I seem to feel that strange mix of feelings every day, Marnie. I don't know how to describe it exactly. If you can mix melancholy, sadness, love, desire, awe, beauty, emptiness, fear, confusion, richness, wonder, and hope -- if you can somehow mix that all together, that's what I'm feeling. That's what I feel when I walk, with and without you. A deep feeling of connection and love and sadness and missing, simultaneously -- that pervades my world these days."

"Some days are so much harder than others. Some days I just want to curl up and go to sleep and not have to deal with the world. What's strange is that can be after having a beautiful afternoon talking with you, sharing everything, feeling totally connected. And then, an hour later, I'm so low. I don't understand. Maybe it has to do with wishing I had loved you so much better during your lifetime. I don't know.

I do carry regret. You were so exquisite. And I don't know if I told you often enough. I don't know if I expressed frequently enough how gorgeous I thought you were, how special you were and are to me, how you made and make my life feel worth living. I know I said those things, but not as often as I wish I had, not as often as you deserved. I'm so sorry for getting so lost and caught up in the demands of material world. I'm so sorry for being caught up in my self-centered needs.

I feel like I'm loving you now every day, every minute, better than I ever did when you were physically alive. I so wish I had been this way with you when you were here physically. I hope you knew how very much I loved you. I believe you did. I believe that we built something really beautiful. But still, I wish I had given you so very much more, darling, so very much more."

"I have to tell myself to get up. I have to tell myself to walk. I have to discipline myself. Sometimes I just sit and feel paralyzed, sweetheart, just lost and paralyzed. It's so easy to get lost in regret when I can't look into your eyes and touch you. When I can't be certain of what you are feeling."

"I'm tired. Sometimes it feels like I'm always tired. I'm emotionally tired. Sometimes I feel like giving up. But I don't really know what that means. Because I know I won't give up on life. I promised you I wouldn't. But with every new place I go, the realization hits me that you will never be there or anywhere with me again physically in this lifetime. Then I feel so profoundly lonely and empty.

So I go out and walk and talk to you, and cry, and feel your presence with me again, and I'm OK. Then I can go on, move forward. It is such a repeated process. I wonder when or if it will end. It seems like no time at all, and it seems like forever since your body died, Marnie. It seems like a never-ending struggle living with and without you. Maybe that's why I'm so tired. I just feel tired. Maybe that's part of the essence of grief, just feeling tired."

As I walked along a trail that had been very special to us I saw devastation from a hurricane that had passed over this area. I said to Marnie: "I'm sorry for the broken trees, Marnie. I'm sorry for your broken body. But the new life of your soul has sprung forth from it, just as new life is springing forth from the broken trees.

It's difficult for me, Marnie, seeing all the damage from the wind back here. I sure miss the big trees. I sure miss your body. It's hard carrying the sadness, Marnie. I just have to keep walking through it.

I'm tired. It seems like by the end of the day, I'm always really tired. I think grieving and missing you, Marnie, are really draining. I feel tired, but it's not really late. I don't want to go to sleep. I could curl up and just sleep away too much of the day. But I have to keep things in balance."

"Sometimes I feel disturbed—strong and then weak, happy then sad, confident and then lost, lonely and choosing to stay alone, virtually unending contradictions and virtually unending tears.

I feel like I've become bipolar. I flip flop from intense joy to crushing sadness. One moment I feel so profoundly in love with you and so deeply connected to you that I weep with joy. I feel like my life is profoundly blessed. And the next moment I miss you so much that I can't stand it. I'd like to end my life. But I know I won't. I can't risk doing anything that might block our reconnection. And the tears fall."

"I believe that you are happy, Marnie. I believe that you are reconnected with those who died before you. I believe that you are aware of me and my profound and ever-growing love for you. I believe that you are no longer limited by time or space. I believe that you are aware of what the future holds for us and are joyful in your awareness of eternity. I believe that you are aware of our children and grandchildren and are aware of my absolute commitment to loving and healing them, to finding a way to help them each feel fundamentally loved and worthwhile. I know that you are no longer physically suffering or being profoundly limited by the cancer in your body. And I believe that you are connected with God – all of that and more. You are fulfilled. So why should I be sad?

Why should I feel sad? I feel weak and disturbed, and tired."

"I am perpetually torn between my sadness in missing you and my desire to feel joy in your joy and fulfillment. I have to believe. I have to bring that belief deep down into my heart. I have to bring that belief all the way down into my soul and feel it with absolute conviction. If you are in a state of joy and fulfillment, if I can see that in my mind's eye, if I can feel that, if I can believe that deep down inside, then I'm more than OK. But I still miss you. I love you.

"It's morning now. I'm sitting here by a pond, in the sunshine, listening to the birds, looking at the pine forest. I don't quite understand the sense of peaceful melancholy that I feel. Maybe it's being out here with you in this beautiful, natural world, but not having you right here beside me to touch, to feel your head rest on my shoulder. So the world is a mixture for me. It might always be so for me. It might be the new normal for me. I don't know. Oh darling, I do love you so….

I just sit here in silence, darling. I don't know if I'm lost in meditation. I don't know if I'm lost in thought. I don't know if I'm lost in you. I just sit and the time passes. Then suddenly I come back to awareness. And I wonder, 'Is this alright?' I'm not quite sure what the feeling is. There's a certain quiet, peaceful melancholy to it. I feel a bit lost."

This is the hardest challenge I have ever faced. I can't pray to make the hurt go away. It won't. I can only pray for the strength to handle it.

After I got home from my "healing trip", I would still sink into deep sadness. I wrote, "I get to feeling so desperate, Marnie, so churned up inside. It's like everything is urgent. I need to feel you so badly. I just feel so lost, so empty. I need to feel you. I need to feel our connection. I need to feel that you're here, that you're still watching over me, that you still see me, that you still hear me, that you still love me."

When I can feel that, I'm OK. When I question that, I just start to get crazy. I get really frantic and I have to beg. I weep. I beg Marnie for help. I beg God for help. I beg God for faith. And in a while, not too long, I calm down, and I feel a greater sense of peace inside. Either Marnie or God or both are watching over me, and they help me get through. And then I can walk again and I can breathe. And I can talk to Marnie and I can pray to God, and I can feel hope.

"I love you, Marnie. I need you."

    Sometimes it feels like a real accomplishment just to have made it through another day. I don't think I've ever felt more alone. I have to work and struggle to keep going through the day, finding tasks to do. I have to feel Marnie's presence; I have to feel God's presence. I have to keep working.

    Sometimes I just break down and cry and cry. And sometimes I pray. I ask God for help. I beg God to be real, not a figment of my hopeful imagination. Because if God is real, then Marnie is real. And then I have a reason to keep living.

    If I believed that Marnie was no longer, that she was just gone, then I would have no desire to keep living at all. I am living now as an act of love, for and with Marnie. I promised her I would keep living. I told her I would go on. I promised her I would love the children. And I have to find other ways to love too. I need to find some way to bring love to peoples' lives.

    It is the promises I made to Marnie that have kept me alive. And it is walking the bridge of faith, believing that God is real, and that His daughter Marnie is real that keeps me alive. When I can feel that those beliefs are real deep down inside, then I feel peace. When I struggle with that, I struggle with living. So I have to keep praying. I have to keep working. And as I'm doing now, I have to keep walking. I have to keep working on building faith. And sometimes I have to just keep surviving another day.

    A few days later when I was again plunged into sadness. I wrote, "I have never experienced so much paralysis. I sit on the couch and it's as if I can't move. It's as if I'm frozen in place. I think of getting up. I think of doing something, but I just sit.

I start to get dressed and I stop midway through. I just sit. So much paralysis. I cry as I write these things.

And I'll walk out to the end of our driveway to go for our walk and when I get there I just look up at the sky. And I don't know which way to go. And I just stand there and cry."

I needed to use a scissors today, and I picked up Marnie's scissors. And I realized it was her scissors, and it just threw me for a loop. I wept. I spent the next half hour just lost.

People used to call me all the time, or text, or email. They don't call very often any more. And I get very few emails. I think people have tired of my sadness, of my grieving, of my focus on Marnie. My sadness, my focus on Marnie doesn't end as theirs does. Or at least it is not the center of their world as it is mine. It's hard going on, still having Marnie being the center of my life, and having almost no one understand that and having no one feel it with me. It's lonely.

Here are excerpts from a letter that I wrote to members of Marnie's family in trying to explain to them my grieving and my journey of faith:

Marnie was my heart. I didn't care what kind of work I did. I didn't care where we went. I didn't care where we lived. As long as I was with Marnie and loving her and doing whatever I could to support her, I was really happy. Marnie asked me if I still had dreams, if there was anything that I'd really like to do, if there was any place that I'd really like to go. And my answer was, "My life is just about perfect. In you I have everything that I want. I don't need anything else. I don't need to go anywhere else. The only thing I would change is that we would work less and have more time to focus on and be in love with one another.

That was absolutely real for me. When Marnie's body died, it felt like my heart was ripped out of me. There was a huge hole in me that I wasn't sure could ever be filled. There are still days when I feel that overwhelmingly. I feel a massive emptiness. I feel a crushing feeling in my chest. I feel a crushing feeling in my heart. I feel a crushing sadness -- in missing Marnie, in missing her physical presence. I just want to lay down and give up. I have no desire to keep living.

I know that I won't give up, because I promised Marnie that I would live on. I promised her that I would be OK. I promised her that I would love the children, that I would love the grandchildren for her, as she would love them. I promised all that. I told her that only her body was dying, that we would be together again.

But that hole in my heart is still there. I don't know if it will ever fully be healed until I am rejoined with Marnie after my death. I see it as my responsibility now to love as many as I can, as deeply as I can, as fully as I can – to fill that hole in my heart with as much love and joy and goodness as I possibly can. So that's how I will live the rest of my life. I do that as a gift of love for Marnie.

Marnie was the most pure, loving spirit I have ever known in my lifetime. We truly became bonded as one, in and through love. And so if Marnie is with God now and is filled up with love and *peace and understanding, then that's what I want for her. That is what she deserves. And if she is receiving love from you, from all of the family that has gone before her, from all of the family that still lives, and from our friends both living and dead, if she is being filled up with love every day, then I'm OK. I just have to keep living love myself to move up to the level that I believe Marnie is on, so I deserve to be with her in our next chapter of eternity together.*

But at the same time I grieve the loss of her physical presence every day. How can I not? I think of her every day, constantly, throughout the day. Every special place, every beautiful sight, anything can trigger a special memory, and it brings her back to me vividly, and I miss her. I have to shift my thinking to feel the presence of her soul, to feel the presence of her essential spiritual being, so that I'm sharing the beauty with her here and now. But I still miss touching her. I still miss looking into her eyes. It's in keeping her vividly alive that I ensure both sadness and ultimate hope.

I can still get consumed with doubt and fear. I question if all my beliefs about God and the life of Marnie's soul, of her continued being, are simply wishful thinking. But then I think that if what happens when we die is that we just die and that's it, it's over. Well even then I really have nothing to lose. I won't care when I'm dead, and while I'm alive I will have spent every day loving Marnie. And that gives my life purpose and direction.

And it's in loving Marnie every day for the rest of my life, it's in giving her all the love I have to give, that I have so much more love to give everybody else. It's one of those fundamental contradictions seem so pervasive in my life now.

And if Marnie is alive, if God is real, if the soul really does live on after physical death and Marnie really is present and seeing me and hearing me and feeling me, and knowing the profound depth of love that I have for her, then I am making her happy now.

And nothing means more to me. And I am earning the right to rejoin her when my body dies.

So that's how I'm living my life. I hope it makes sense to you.

Love, Bill

It seemed strange to me that no one really responded to that letter. I guess they just didn't know what to do with it.

Living Now

The process of grieving that I've tried to share with you continues in my life now, more than a year later. I don't think it will ever end completely. I'll always wish that Marnie was here, physically sitting beside me.

I wrote to Marnie, "I look forward to my days at home alone. They are my days with you, Marnie. My days alone in the wilderness with you are my happiest days. It's strange to be looking forward to being alone. But it's in being alone that I feel my connection with you most strongly, Marnie.

And yet, with the connection comes the sadness. It's such a jumbled mix. It's when I'm alone that I can really focus on you, that I can focus on our relationship, and that I can talk. I can focus on feeling your presence. That gives the greatest meaning to my life. But in focusing on your presence and in feeling our connection, I also feel the absence of your body. And I grieve.

But I choose to be home alone to be with you. It's like ultimately wanting to die so I can be with you permanently and live our connection above and beyond faith. But I still have work to do here on this earth. I know that. So I'm not ready to die. There is so much contradiction. It seems like there is contradiction inherent in everything that is still going on in my life.

There was no contradiction when you were here physically. I just plain loved you, and there you were. Now, I love you more, and I have to believe, deep in my heart, that 'here you are'. You are with me. I feel that the strongest outside.

When I first get up in the morning and am drinking my first cup of coffee, I wonder if you're with me. I have to work my way through the morning thoughts and the morning sadness.

But even then I know there is nothing I can say with greater feeling or greater truth than, 'I love you, Marnie. You are my heart.' That is ultimate truth for me. And it is in that truth, that I have the deepest hope that we are indeed reality, that spiritual being is reality. Someday I will move beyond this body, and then I can rejoin you all the way. That for me, will be heaven."

After writing that last entry, I again got lost. I wrote, "Sometimes not being able to go home and just hold you is devastating to me, Marnie. I can have such clear insights, but they just fade and I miss you so very much.

I sat alone in a field last night, a mile away from home and wept. I just cried and cried and cried. I felt so very inadequate. I recognized how profoundly I miss you, Marnie. You have been, were, and are the very center of my life, the very core of my being.

I've heard much from many about God loving you, about Jesus loving you, about the beauty of the universe you're in now. And I just begin to feel inadequate. I begin to feel like I have nothing to offer by comparison. Why would she still love me? And I love you so much."

The feelings of emptiness, of sadness, of inadequacy almost overpowered me. All I could do was just weep, and weep, and weep…and pray that Marnie knows how very much I love her. And that somehow, that still touches her deep in her soul.

Sometimes I feel like I'm in a pit so deep that I can no longer see the top, and I don't know if I'll be able to get out.

We have a poster in our home that says, "Do not pray for an easy life. Pray to be a strong person."

I think my personal poster now would say, "Do not pray for an end to your grief. Pray for a strengthening of your faith. Faith is where joy lives."

In addition to all of the intense feelings of sadness that I've tried to share honestly in this chapter, there's been one more feeling that I thought perhaps I should share simply because it's been real for me.

I've experienced a recurring, remote, far off feeling of muted sexual tension, some sort of sexual loss that has come with the loss of Marnie's body. It's strange, it's not any kind of intense feeling. I no longer have any kind of intense sexual desire. But there's a strange emptiness, a remote, far away tension. It's hooked into loss. There's so much loss. I would love to make love with Marnie. But when I think of rejoining her, that's not what I think of first. I want to hold her. I want to hug her. I want to kiss her. Those are the things that I miss so profoundly. I want to be able to look into her eyes. I want to be able to kiss her deeply and just hold her tight. I want to hold her hand. That's what I look forward to in our rejoining.

It's been a strange feeling that's real for me, and I thought I should share it. If you've lost your spouse, perhaps you can relate to it. Maybe it's related to knowing that I will never make love again in my physical lifetime, and I don't know what will be possible in the next lifetime. There's a sadness in that. I don't know. I don't understand it. I find myself saying that a lot since Marnie's body died – "I don't know."

Overall Conclusions

That's a brief snapshot of some of my grief and the process of grieving that I went through and continue to go through. I'm sorry if it seemed like a jumbled mess. That's how grief has been and is for me – a jumbled mess. Yours may be very similar to mine. Yours may be totally different. But no matter its form, grief is real. And we have to be patient and gentle with ourselves in going through it. The process can't be hurried. The pain can't be denied or avoided or pushed aside.

It is in owning the pain, in expressing the pain, in fully feeling the pain that we release it. For me, it is in sharing the pain honestly with Marnie that I release it best. I believe that it is in directly expressing your pain to your beloved that you too will ultimately be freed from it.

Your beloved will understand even if no one else does. Your beloved sees you from a perspective and with a level of understanding that transcends our earthly limits. I believe strongly, that expressing your pain is a gift of love to your beloved, not a source of hurt for them.

You are saying, "I love you. I love you enough to bare my soul to you. I trust you enough to believe that not only will you love me in spite of my pain, but that you will embrace me even more fully because of it. I love you enough to trust you with the depths of my heart and soul."

That is a beautiful message to send to your beloved. That will be a treasured part of your eternal bond of love together. The depth of your hurt, the depth of your confusion, the depth of your fear are all a reflection of the depth of the love. Your beloved will receive it all in love.

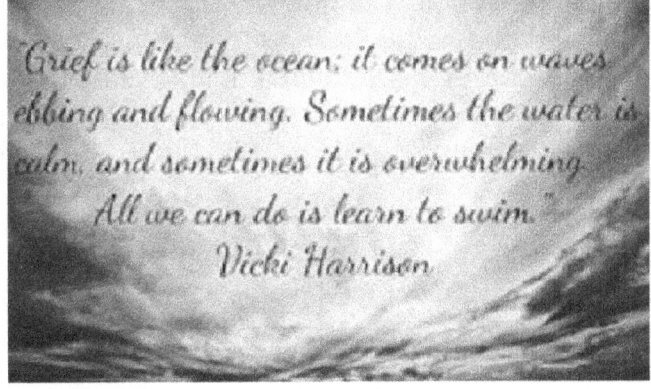

"Grief is like the ocean; it comes on waves ebbing and flowing. Sometimes the water is calm, and sometimes it is overwhelming. All we can do is learn to swim."
Vicki Harrison

Chapter 19: The Struggle to Heal

She's Amazing

*If she's amazing, she won't be easy.
If she's easy, she won't be amazing.
If she's worth it, you won't give up.
If you give up, you're not worthy. ...
Truth is, everybody is going to hurt you;
You just gotta find the ones worth suffering for.*

Bob Marley

As I'm sure you could see in the sharing of my grief and the process of my grieving, the road to healing has not been a smooth one for me. It has been one of ongoing struggle. It has been a struggle in my mind and heart. I've had to face hurdles that were never there for me before. I had to face doubts within myself that I never felt before. I knew the road to healing would not be smooth or easy. But I never dreamed it would be so difficult. I've never faced so much struggle.

Partly I think the difficulty has come from the fact that the process of healing is not a smooth, linear continuum. For a while you feel like you're moving forward, like you're really healing. Then your progress comes to a screeching halt. It feels like no matter what you do, you go nowhere. If you think about it in the context of growth, you've hit a plateau. You can know in advance that growth comes in plateaus. But in the context of healing from the loss of your beloved, the plateau can be unbearable. It feels like the hurting will never end, no matter what you do.

Eventually you begin to move forward again and you feel like there is hope. You feel like healing can be real. Until you fall back. Then you feel like you hurt worse than you've ever hurt. It feels like the hurting will never end. There is no hope. Healing is just an illusion.

Again, that is part of the process of growth that occurs whenever you try to learn any new skill, any new behavior. Know in advance that there will be periods of time when you don't just hit a plateau, you actually regress. It's normal. It happens to everybody. That is so easy to say in an intellectual analysis of the learning process. It's virtually impossible to remember or accept in the process of healing from the physical loss of someone in your life that you loved profoundly. The feelings are simply too intense.

But you have to keep going. Suicide is not an option. I considered suicide virtually every day for the first year after Marnie died. I still think of it occasionally. But every day I choose to keep living. I make that choice because of the promises I made to Marnie. I won't let her down. I wouldn't want her to be disappointed in me if I get to rejoin her after my death.

But I also made that choice because I absolutely couldn't risk the possibility that suicide somehow might block my ability to fully rejoin Marnie in total consciousness, in total awareness upon my physical death. Feeling my continued connection with Marnie after the death of her body has been hard enough in this life. I simply couldn't risk the possibility of losing our connection (perhaps forever) in the next life.

And suicide would negate the profound positive impact that Marnie's physical death has had on me. The death of Marnie's body has affected the way I think about everything. It led me to God. It led me to belief in the immortal soul. It led me to belief in Marnie's continued real, living presence in my life. It caused me to look closely at every regret I had about how I lived with and loved Marnie when she was physically alive. Every one of those regrets has become a lesson for me. They've become a guide as to how I want to live my life differently now, and how I want to live differently the next chapter of my life with Marnie in eternity.

And I believe that I have more lessons to learn from Marnie's physical death. I've begun to look closely at all of my faults and shortcomings. I want to see them clearly and address them. I don't want to carry them with me into eternity. I don't want them to impact or diminish my rejoining with Marnie. Marnie's physical death has demanded that I learn and grow. I've had to ask myself, "What are the lessons I need to learn to be able to fully rejoin Marnie on her level in the afterlife?"

I think we can each look closely at the lessons to be learned from the physical death of our beloved. We will each be rejoined with our beloved in the afterlife. And we each want to be the very best that we can be in that rejoining. It's a gift of love for our beloved.

With all that being said, again, even with having intellectual clarity, the hurt, the loneliness, the pain of missing Marnie is still so intense. Plateaus and periods of falling back are profoundly difficult to deal with. Just as with coming to believe in the reality of a loving God, I have to tell myself the sound intellectual reasoning over and over and over again in order to believe on a feeling level that healing is happening. Heart-felt belief is the key to healing. Getting to heart-felt belief is a difficult, ongoing, and sometimes (it feels like) a never-ending struggle.

Through what I share with you in this chapter, I hope to give you a clear picture of how that process of getting to heart-felt belief has looked for me in my struggle to heal. I will share both my thoughts and direct conversations with Marnie in my attempt to do so.

I've realized that my sadness comes when I focus on me, on what I have lost, and my memories of the past. I get profoundly sad. I miss Marnie intensely. I feel deeply lonely. My life feels empty.

When I focus on Marnie now, when I focus on loving her, then my feelings shift. When I think about what I want to give to and share with Marnie now, I feel a renewed sense of determination and purpose. When I focus on moving beyond this lifetime and rejoining Marnie then I feel a sense of excitement and joy. When I feel her love and presence, I feel at peace.

Marnie's happiness is the most important thing in the universe to me. So when I focus on Marnie first, not me, I feel so much better. I turn to God. I ask Him to absolutely fill every fiber of her being with love, with joy, with peace, and understanding. I ask that He fill her with love from every source possible. I ask that she be fully connected with and feel the love from all those who love and have loved her, both living and dead. I pray that she glow with love and joy. I remember that it is Marnie's joy and fulfillment that matters more than anything to me.

I wrote these words to Marnie in thinking about it.

"I'm still terribly self-centered aren't I? I get lost in my own feelings instead of rejoicing in yours. I want you here with me now. I think about all we had together. I think about not having that anymore. I want it again so badly. I miss you. I want you. We had such beautiful times together. Everything. We shared everything. I never did, I never had to do, alone. We drank coffee together in the mornings. We exercised together. We sat across from one another and looked into each other's eyes in restaurants. Everything felt beautiful together. And now, I'm by myself…. That's all me focused, focused on what 'I' don't have.

When I shift my focus to you, on loving you, on moving forward in living as a gift of love for you, then I'm not sad. I want you to make you laugh. I want you to turn you on with my fantasies.

I want to fill you to overflowing with my love. I begin to feel peace in my heart when I think of giving to you again. I want to be a central part of your heaven. But most of all I want you to feel my love for you every day."

I think this shifting back and forth between the "me" focus and the focus on my beloved is probably normal and natural. I think it will be true for each of us who have suffered a deep loss. It's in recognizing it and taking conscious control of where we focus our thoughts that we move more deeply into healing.

There's another issue that I've had to deal with in my struggle to heal that I also believe affects each of us. When I'm with people I care about, especially our grandchildren, I'm really with them. I'm totally in the present. And in that present, I am positive and often happy. But to stay happy I have to come back to Marnie. I have to reconnect with her to have the energy to continue to be with them. The depth of my happiness ultimately depends on my feeling Marnie's presence. I need to feel the deep-seated confidence that Marnie is real. Ultimately I need to feel that God is real. That God loves me. That Marnie and I will fully rejoin after the death of my body.

So in my alone time I work at focusing my thinking and training my heart to feel that deep-seated confidence in our continued oneness. That is what allows me to be truly present and love others when I am with them. That deep-seated confidence is at the core of everything for me. But it's a mental challenge. It requires that I constantly discipline my thinking.

I wrote these words to Marnie. "I look forward to my days at home alone. I have to have them. They are my days with you, Marnie. They are my days at home alone with you in the wilderness. It's strange to be looking forward to being alone. But it's in being alone that I feel my connection with you most strongly.

And yet, with the connection comes the sadness of being alone with and without you simultaneously. It's such a jumbled mix. It's when I'm alone that I can really focus on you. I can focus on our relationship and I can talk to you. I can focus on feeling your presence. That brings the greatest joy and meaning to my life. But I also feel the absence of your body. And I grieve.

So for me, living each day is a push-pull between needing to be with others and needing to have time alone to connect with my beloved on a spiritual level. I believe that may be an issue that we each face. It requires an ongoing balancing that more than likely will be a life-long process.

For me, every day involves tears. Some more than others. Some days I feel a real sense of peace and hope. But no days feel quite as rich and full as they did when Marnie was here with me physically. I said to Marnie,

"I had such confidence when you were alive, when you were here with me physically. I would go anywhere. I would do anything. Somehow, just sharing it with you let me know that everything would be ok. I don't feel that confidence any more. I'm surprised at how fearful I am. I doubt myself. I find myself being afraid of going to new places, afraid of trying new things. I have a level of fear that

I never had when you were with me, Marnie. I don't understand all the fear. Perhaps it comes from being alone so much, from feeling alone. I have to feel you being with me, even while I'm feeling alone, to be able to go forward and face the fear."

I don't know if fear and doubt play a significant role in your life now after the physical death of your beloved. But if they do, know that you are not alone in these feelings. It is in refocusing on the living presence of my beloved that I find the courage to trust in myself and move forward. I believe the same will be true for you. Courage comes in faith.

For a very long time I struggled to join with Marnie. I tried to do so in every way that I could. I felt desperate to feel certain of the absolute reality of my connection with her presence every day. I believe that you too may struggle. I believe that each of us who have experienced profound loss struggle in our own unique ways. Struggle is real for each of us. Since Marnie's physical death, much of my life has felt like a struggle. Too much struggle.

I would like to share with you one very special, very specific experience that I had in my struggle to connect with Marnie on a feeling level, here and now. I hope it illustrates to you the reality and the intensity of the struggle to heal inherent in the process of grieving and healing. But on a significant level, it gave me more reason to hope.

But please remember, you will have your own experiences. Yours will be totally different from this one I'm sure, but yours will be no less real. Yours will be no less meaningful. This is mine:

There's a mountain lake near our house that I bike to regularly. The lake is fed by mountain streams, so the water is cold. Marnie was a really good swimmer. She loved to swim across that lake and back. I'm not a really good swimmer, but I would swim with her. I always felt that she was there to protect me, to save me, if I needed help. And I loved swimming with her. I loved looking at her as she swam. It was a beautiful, sexy experience for me.

August is the warmest time to swim the lake in Montana. So on an August day just a little more than a year after Marnie's body died, I decided to swim the lake to honor her. I would do so in honor of who and how she was -- in honor of her special connection with the water.

We were always happy being in the water together, no matter where we were. I can't ever remember being unhappy being in or by the water together. Swimming across the lake has been a special, positive (though frightening) experience for me. But that experience proved stronger today than it ever has. It was significantly unusual.

I swam in a different place than I normally swim because of boating activity on the lake. I went up near the mouth of the lake where the mountain streams feed into it. The water is shallower there so the boats tend to not come up that far. But the water is also significantly colder and the lake is wider. It was a much longer swim than my usual.

I debated whether or not I really wanted to do it. I thought I could wait till another day. I thought the weather might be warmer and there might be less boat traffic. I thought maybe I could go back to where the lake isn't so wide and the water wouldn't be so cold. This just looked like a huge, daunting swim. But I got in the water and swam.

I swim with a mask and snorkel, so that my breathing is comfortable. And with every breath, I chant, "I love you, Marnie. You are my heart." I repeat this chant (or similar ones) all the way across the lake and back, with every breath I take. It profoundly intensifies my feeling-level connection with Marnie.

This time, however, I got really, really cold especially on the way back. I became increasingly frightened. I wasn't sure if I would actually make it. But I discovered that the water was shallow enough that I could actually stand on the lake bottom on my tip toes and walk. So I walked and swam the second half of the return trip. When I finally got back to the shore where I had started, I was shivering almost uncontrollably.

I said aloud, "Marnie, I was trying to reach you. I had to do it. I was trying to reach you." And when I said that, I suddenly felt like I had almost reached her. I felt her presence in a different way. I felt like she was right there, just beyond my touch. I could almost reach out and touch her, but not quite. She seemed to have just slipped away from me. When I no longer felt in my mind's eye that I could reach her or touch her I began to sob. I sobbed and sobbed and sobbed uncontrollably. I couldn't move. I could only cry. I was so glad I was all by myself. I just wept and wept and wept.

It was an overwhelming feeling. Perhaps it was from having been so close and yet not quite being able to reach her. Perhaps everything was intensified because I was so cold. But the thought hit me that maybe there was something real in this. The swimming made Marnie's presence feel more real to me. She felt closer than she feels when I'm walking on the roads. She felt closer than she normally feels to me living in faith.

I felt like I had almost gotten to her. I felt like I had almost gotten to the level of reality where she lives now – that higher level of frequency and vibration. I wondered if it was possible that I had shifted to a different level of reality, to a different level of frequency, and vibration. I realized that I had been living in a different medium. I had been living in the water, where Marnie was so at home. I had been in the water, seeing virtually nothing. (The lake isn't very clear. You don't really see anything in front of you or on the bottom.) There's only the water, directly in front of you, with beams of sunlight streaming through.

It's being in a whole different physical realm – almost like being in a different dimension. And I had been calling out to Marnie the whole time that I was in that different dimension. I repeated over and over again, "I love you, Marnie. I love you, Marnie. You are my heart." I was in a different realm, and my focus was absolutely on Marnie. So when I got back, perhaps it made perfect sense that my perception of reality had shifted.

I hadn't joined Marnie on her soul-level of reality, but I did live for a brief time in a different level of reality. And I was joined with Marnie in my heart the whole time. It made the possibility of different spiritual levels of reality seem much more real and believable to me. I had just experienced it.

I carried a sense of disorientation with me on the 11 mile bike ride back home. It was a real feeling of disorientation. I bike that road all the time. But this time, it seemed so long. It seemed unfamiliar to me. At times I didn't know where I was. And my strength was incredible. I had already biked 11 miles to get to where I did my longest lake swim ever. But I simply didn't tire. My legs didn't tire. I pedaled hard. I kept peddling and peddling and it never felt difficult. I didn't breathe hard. Even going up the steepest hills my breathing never became as labored as it normally does. It was virtually an effortless bike back. I was in a different world.

When I got back home, I felt warmer. I took a hot shower. I put on warm, dry clothes. I no longer felt the disorientation. Things felt pretty normal again. But something had changed. Something had shifted. Something felt different. And it felt precious. I felt like I had received confirmation that Marnie living in another dimension of reality was not fantasy. It was real.

I decided to swim the lake again the next day wearing a wet suit so the cold wouldn't be a factor. (My oldest son wondered if I had begun moving into hypothermia and that this could have affected my thoughts and perceptions.) But I wanted to be in that other world again. I wanted to be calling out to Marnie the whole time I was in it. I wanted to see if there would be a shift in the level of reality that I experienced. I wanted to know if I could consciously make the shift from "normal" reality to a different plane of reality -- to a different level of frequency and vibration that would bring me closer to Marnie.

I swam the next day. Magic didn't happen. I didn't feel a reality level shift as I had the previous day. But I did feel a deeper connection with Marnie.

It's nice, feeling that Marnie is here, just on that different plane of reality. She's living on a level of frequency and vibration that we don't experience. But she is here. She is real. I can reach out to her here and now. I want to touch her. I want to feel her touch – if not physically, at least deeply in my heart. And I want to feel that intensely. So I will continue to swim.

That was my experience. Though it was unique to me, you (I believe) will have your own unique experiences in your struggle to heal. You can feel blessed by those experiences. You can know that the lessons contained in those experiences are valid, just as your connection with your beloved is and will continue to be real.

A year and a half after Marnie's death I chose to go on essentially the same healing trip I had gone on 4 months after she died. I thought it would be easier being on this trip this time. I thought the positive feelings would be more intense. I thought that Marnie's presence would feel strikingly real to me.

I was wrong. It was not easier. That was very hard to take. The struggle continued for me. The pain of missing Marnie felt unrelenting. I often felt bathed in sadness, doubt, and fear.

There was a morning early in the trip when I didn't want to go out on my walk with Marnie. Those walks have always been so vital to me – uplifting – a time when our connection feels deeply real and alive. But I was afraid to go. What if I didn't feel the connection? What if it wasn't uplifting? It is in our connection that I feel hope. If I didn't feel the connection, then there would no longer be hope – no longer be a reason to keep going, to keep living. I was deeply sad, frightened, and troubled.

I don't know why that happens. I don't always understand the reasons for my thoughts or my moods. My prayer walk the night before had been profoundly uplifting. Maybe that's part of it -- I'm afraid it won't stay that way. I'm afraid that I'll fall back into sadness. So I create it. I don't know.

I went out for the walk. How could I not? It is some of my most precious sharing time with Marnie. And she's still my best friend. I still share everything with her. I'm afraid that everyone else tires of hearing my sadness and my struggles. Everyone else wishes I could move on. So I don't often talk to anyone else. Not really. Not totally openly. I don't want to burden them with my hurt. I talk with them, but I don't share everything that's in my heart.

Marnie never tired of hearing me share my heart in our lifetime together. I believe that she never tires of hearing me share my heart with her now. So I talked to her. Honestly. From my heart. I wept. I asked for her help. Almost immediately, I felt a sense of peace. (Thank you my darling.)

On the one hand it feels so strange talking when there is no one else physically present. Just talking, when there is no one to see, no one to touch. There is a sense of unreality to it. But on the other hand, I'm doing exactly what I always did. Marnie and I would walk and talk. We would walk and share the beauty and majesty and magic of the natural environment. We would sit at home and talk. We would move in and out of our daily tasks and then come back together and talk some more. We would go on long drives together, sometimes sitting in silence, lost in our own thoughts, sometimes lost in a meditative state. And then we would talk. We would share dreams, hopes, plans, insights, fears, desires.

As I walked and talked with Marnie my sense of peace was restored. Then I began to weep intensely at how profoundly I missed her – how profoundly I missed being able to look into her eyes and to touch her. (That's one of the reasons I'm glad that I live in the middle of nowhere and spend so much time alone in the wilderness). I cried and cried and told her how much I love her. I asked (as I often do) that she experience this pain and sadness as an intense statement of the depth of my love for her – that it be for her a source of deep joy in feeling my love and knowing what is to come for us when we are rejoined and again share the same plane of reality.

Then it suddenly struck me that I was talking with Marnie exactly as I always did. I was sharing my deepest feelings. I was doing so on this walk. I do so at home. I do so when I run or bike, (in my mind and heart, and out loud when I can, in between breaths). The only difference for me is that only Marnie's soul is present, not her body. So I have to talk in faith until we can be rejoined again on the same plane of reality.

I thanked Marnie. I thanked God for the insight. I felt a profound sense of relief. I felt a shiver run down my spine. I wept – this time with joy. The rest of my walk was wrapped in the beauty of the nature surrounding me – seeing things that I shared with Marnie or that perhaps she sent to me. I never really know which of those is true, or if they both are. But I always offer what I see and experience as a gift to her, hoping that she can see it and experience it along with me (perhaps on a far deeper, more intense level).

After walking for a while longer, I realized that my mind had been silent, that I had been in a meditative state, just being in nature together with my beloved. Again, I thanked God and I thanked Marnie. I am walking a bridge of faith back to my home – Marnie's arms. My life is profoundly changed and not changed at all, simultaneously. I'm still scared at times. I'm going through a fundamental shift in how I view the world, in how I view reality. I still so miss being able to hold Marnie in my arms. But I hold her in my heart, in my soul, and in my mind. She is forever my soul's mate. And our time on earth is infinitesimal in the context of the eternity we will share.

But even after experiencing these insights, after feeling so positive, I found myself sinking back into sadness and doubt the very next day. I was virtually drowning in sadness.

I had to ask God for the strength to deal with the loss of Marnie's physical presence to go along with the faith in her spiritual presence. Otherwise the sadness can be so overwhelming that it makes me question the faith. How can I be so sad if Marnie is really still alive, consciously aware, and watching over me?

I have to build the strength to deal with missing having Marnie physically present in my life. Virtually every minute, for 32 years, she was the physical and emotional center of my being. Not having her to look at, not being able to see her smile, not being able to hear her voice – it all leaves me profoundly sad and empty.

All of those things are gone for now. So I grieve deeply. And when I do, I start to question, "How can I have faith and still be so sad?"

I have to have the strength to carry the sadness (which may never fully leave) and still build and maintain the faith in the reality that our essential being is spiritual. One can be healing and grieve simultaneously. That's so hard to remember when you're grieving.

After writing this I fell back into sadness again. I feared that my writing was nothing more than lofty, grandiose rhetoric. But as I considered it more deeply I thought, "This is all real. I think it is all true. I think what I have to say is accurate."

And then I realized that when I'm writing, I'm OK. When I'm with Ben and Nellie and the children, I'm OK. When I'm exercising, I'm OK. When I'm walking and talking with Marnie, I'm OK. When I'm walking and praying, I'm OK. Sometimes I weep profoundly when I talk to Marnie or to God, but even in that, I'm OK. When I'm actively reading or studying, I'm OK. Even in being caught up in menial tasks like cleaning the car or cleaning the house, as long as I'm "doing", I'm OK.

It's when I'm not <u>doing</u>, it's when I'm just <u>being</u>, that sadness can wash over me. Then I can get lost. Then I can feel purposeless. I can even begin to fear that my doing is nothing more than an escape. I can feel like seeing the children is escaping. Exercising is escaping. And there is something that's not right about escaping. I don't fully understand where that thinking comes from, but I know it is off track.

So first I started writing. I wrote, "When you were here with me physically, Marnie, just being was peaceful. I was happy. Everything felt right. Just being, no longer always feels that way.

Maybe my faith isn't deep enough yet. Maybe it's just a natural part of missing you that will heal with more time. I don't know. But it takes real discipline to pull myself out of the abyss."

I stopped writing and biked. It took over 3 miles of biking hard uphill before my mood started coming back up. I recognized it happening. Then I knew I could keep biking and that I would be OK. But finding the discipline required to force myself to go out and do the bike ride was hard.

I came back home and wrote, "When I'm walking and talking with you, when I get lost in real in-depth conversation with you, when it feels like I really am talking with you, then I'm more than OK – then I'm joyful, and life feels good all over again. But even then I can question, "Is this real?" I have to pray to God, "Please! Please God make this real!" It's so difficult, sweetie. It's the biggest challenge I've ever faced. It's a challenge I have to meet day after day, hour after hour, sometimes minute after minute.

But I will not let you down, Marnie Winn. I will never give up. I'll keep struggling. I will do whatever it takes to stay connected to you. It's all grounded in faith. Faith, my belief in God and in you, has to be the bedrock of my being. You are the heart and soul and purpose of my life. I have to live in faith to stay connected to you. I love you."

The next morning I wrote, "It's funny, I never know what I'm going to say to you when I go out on our walks. I never really know what ideas are going to come to me. But it's vital that I do these walks. It takes discipline to get myself up and go out. But the intensity of the emotion that I can feel sometimes is just stunning to me. And the insights, the feelings that I have about our lives together, the love that I feel for you, Marnie, the profound depth of appreciation and admiration that I have for you can all come clear in memories and thoughts.

It's vital to keep nurturing our connection, to keep our love alive and in the forefront of my mind and heart – to not let it fade into memory, into the distance. I need to keep you present every day in my life, so that when I finally do make the transition back to you after the death of my body we'll be right there together. You'll be ready and waiting for me. I love you Marnie.

Still, I sometimes want to cut our walks short. I don't know where those feelings come from. I don't know what that's about. I just know it's important that I not give in to those feelings, that I not do that. It's vital that I keep on going. That's the way it is trying to walk the bridge of faith back into your arms, sweetheart. I have to keep on going no matter how hard it feels.

I discover the worth as I travel the path. And I need to travel that path with you, now, because it is the path to you.

It's so ironic that the more I feel like I'm with you as we walk together, the more sad I can feel. I miss you so very much. I profoundly want to rejoin you and be with you absolutely again. The sadness makes it all the more important that I be out walking with you or biking with you to feel your presence now in our spiritual connection. But it can make me miss your physical presence all over again. It's such a jumble of emotion.

But we are one, Marnie. Our relationship continues. I will not allow a break in our connection. (And I have a pileated confirmation of the wisdom of that decision.) When I feel a shiver (and it really feels like it's a shiver of your presence) or when the pileated woodpecker suddenly appears at just the right moment, it means so much to me. It requires faith to believe in the shiver. It requires faith to believe in the pileated woodpecker. And at the same time, the shiver and the woodpecker confirm the faith. It's another one of those ironies."

As I was traveling a bit later in the trip I said to Marnie. "We discovered pelicans together, Marnie Winn. We discovered so many things together. I saw my first pelican, my first cormorant, and my first great egret of the trip today, Marnie. I'm traveling alone sweetie. I have to carry you in my heart. I have to know that I am not traveling alone. I have to know that you are traveling with me, to make traveling alone be OK.

I'm happy when I'm with you. And I'm with you now. I'm happy when I can feel your presence, when it seems real to me, when I can talk to you genuinely.

And I'm happy when I'm loving others, when I'm doing for others, when I'm doing. I don't have to be aware of you constantly, just as I wasn't aware of you constantly when you were here physically. We would come back together eventually. In its profound change, our relationship hasn't changed.

I have to maintain my connection with you, Marnie. It's the key to everything for me emotionally. And the key to my being able to believe in the reality of our connection is my faith in God and God's love for us. It's the essential foundation for my healing.

You bring me to God, Marnie. God brings me to you. You and God are inseparably bound together. It is in that bond and in our bond with one another that I will ultimately find lasting healing."

As I hope I have shown you clearly, healing has been a profound struggle for me. It may be for you as well. But I have come to believe that you will ultimately find healing in faith. It is in God that you will find peace. I never dreamed that I would say anything like that. But that has become truth for me. It is a truth born directly from my experience. Look closely and carefully and see if it is truth for you as well. The transition from struggle to healing will come through faith. It is indeed a gift from God.

Chapter 20: Transitions

Death is a pathway, a passageway to ever deepening love. But death is also a transition, the most profound transition any of us will ever face.

For me, transitions have always been really hard. The transition into living a life without Marnie's physical presence in it, is the most difficult transition I have ever had to face. For each of us who have lost our beloved there will be multiple transitions that we will have to deal with.

I thought a lot about this. I'd like to share that thinking with you. I will share my personal experience – perhaps you will be able to relate to it. And I will offer some thoughts about it that hopefully will be relevant to your life.

Travel days have always been hard for me. Whether it be going to a new place or a special place that Marnie and I had shared in the past, I feel real sadness, a real emptiness in traveling without having Marnie sitting beside me, holding my hand. It's the transition. Once I get to the new place or the old, special place and can be there for a while, then I can make peace with it.

I've always had trouble with transitions. Marnie and I would be looking forward to going on the road and doing a series of art shows. I'd be excited about going and doing them. I'd plan for the trip in detail. But then, as it came time to actually leave, I wouldn't want to go. I wouldn't want to leave home. Once we got out on the road, once we were on the trip, then I'd be really happy to be there.

When it was time to go home, I wouldn't want to go home. I'd want to stay out on the road, in love, feeling the romance of it all. The transitions have always been hard.

Now, with Marnie's physical death, the transition to dealing with her solely in a spiritual world is the most profound transition I've ever had to face. It's really, really hard for me. I so want to hold her hand and have her support me through this transition. I actually want to make the transition to the next world myself – though I'll probably be afraid of that too and resist when that time actually comes. But I want to be back in Marnie's arms.

I know I've got to stay and love for both of us though. I know that. I've got to stay and do what I promised -- that which Marnie would want me to do. I've got to stay and do what I believe is God's will for me, before I can go back home to Marnie.

Sometimes I look forward to it -- to doing the loving and living on whatever path I think Marnie and God would want me to follow. But it is so hard adjusting to this world without Marnie's physical presence in it.

I've come to realize that even going back and forth to be with family is a difficult transition for me. For one thing, when I'm with family, I talk about Marnie instead of talking to her. Talking <u>about</u> someone implies that they are not there. Talking about Marnie creates a level of disconnection from her. I end up feeling really lost and alone when I go back home. I feel like I have violated Marnie in not continuing to feel our connection.

On another level, when I'm with family I'm living in a world that doesn't require faith to know it's real. Leaving that world of physical certainty and going back to one that requires spiritual reconnection and re-immersing yourself back into faith can be both difficult and painful.

The key for me has been recognizing that reconnecting with Marnie requires reconnecting with my faith. I can't see Marnie. I can't touch her. I can't hear her. I can hope that she sees me (and sees with me). I can hope that she hears me and feels me. But I can only <u>know</u> these things in faith. It's such a blatant transition from just having spent time with family when seeing, touching, and feeling are all physical realities in which you can know the reality of love without needing faith.

Recognizing that it's time to move back into faith is the key to helping me come home, to helping me <u>feel</u> that I'm back home with Marnie again. It is only then that I fully feel good about living again.

From a third perspective, living in the physical world is not as easy as it used to be for me. Loving my grandchildren is not a simple task. It is not a smooth, easy road where I have all the answers and immediately have the exact impact I've been hoping to have on their lives. And it's loving the grandchildren well that is my primary responsibility in fulfilling my promises to Marnie.

Some days I feel like I wasn't good enough with them. I didn't know exactly what to do. I didn't do things decisively or effectively the way I wish that I had. Then I feel like I failed both Marnie and the children. When I feel disconnected from Marnie on top of that, I get really lost and sad.

It's never really clear cut or simple being with children, touching their lives in precisely the way that you wish you could. That was true for Marnie and me when she was here physically, sharing that experience with me. But on the way back home, we could talk. We would process everything that went on. We would share it all together. We would reconnect with one another in the process of focusing on what we wanted to do the next time we were with the children. We would reconnect with one another, reconnect with our love for one another, and make the transition back into the world of being in love with one another.

Processing with someone who is not physically present to your senses, processing with someone who can't respond verbally and share her perspective out loud, is so much more difficult. You have to be able to listen beyond words. You have to be able to listen in your mind and heart. And you have to be able to listen for thoughts and insights.

Marnie is still my best friend. Marnie is still the mother whose insights and way of being with children I value more than any other person's. Marnie is still the person with whom I can speak my own thoughts and feelings absolutely openly and honestly. So I need to process with her. I need to talk out loud with her both to get clear about future directions and to reconnect. Talking is essential.

A side point that I have learned is that I can't stay too late. I can't be driving home when I'm too tired. When I do, I can't listen effectively in my mind or listen effectively for insights. I get lost inside myself. I get lost in sadness. I get lost in feeling like I failed – both the children and Marnie. Then I really have to work the following day to reconnect, to make the transition back into the world of faith – to come back home to Marnie again. It is only then, in our reconnection, that life feels worthwhile again

We each, in our own individual ways need to move back and forth between the realities and the necessities of living in this physical, material world and the reality of the spiritual level connection we have with our beloved. I have found that it is in maintaining my spiritual level connection with Marnie that I am a far more loving, far more effective human being on this physical plane of being.

I suggest that this may be true for each of us. It is in maintaining an active connection with our beloved that we are connected on a higher level of vibration that enriches who and how we are as human beings. And in keeping the connection with our beloved alive, we find an increasing measure of healing and joy in living. Even if transitions in general haven't been a problem for you as they have been for me, making the transitions back and forth from the world of physical reality to the world of faith can be difficult. Yet it is vital to make those transitions consciously.

It is in facing and going through the transitions (both the profound and the daily transitions) that our relationships with our loved ones flourish. And it is through those relationships that our lives maintain their full meaning and purpose.

And though I fear and resist transition, I look forward to that one final transition when I will finally be back home in Marnie's arms again. It seems so far, far away. But in my mind's eye I will hold her again, and kiss her and kiss her.

Chapter 21: A Prayer for Faith

We each need to have our own prayers. I'd like to share with you just a part of mine. Perhaps there may be parts of it that you would like to borrow and adapt to your life and your relationship. Perhaps it will make you feel even more at peace with your own prayer.

A Part of my Prayer

Please God, help me to believe deep down in my soul, in the very core of my being, that you are real. That you are loving. That you are our creator. That you are the source and substance of our being. That you love us.

Help me believe that Marnie is fully alive. That her soul is real and eternal. That her conscious awareness is fully alive in her soul. That she is aware of me. That she is with me. That she loves me. Help me believe.

Help me to fully believe that our love is absolutely real and alive now. That our bond, our oneness, our commitment are all absolutely alive.

Help me believe that Marnie sees me. That she hears me. That she feels me. And that she feels the profound depth and intensity of my love for her. Help me believe that she absolutely glows with the intensity of my love. That my love fills her to overflowing. That being loved so deeply makes her glow with pride.

Help me feel Marnie's living presence with me now. Help me feel it so strongly that it creates a deep sense of peace in my heart. Help me feel that peace so strongly that I can tolerate the pain of missing her (body) so deeply.

Help me to believe that our love transcends the boundary created by physical death. That our love transcends the boundary between the physical and the spiritual planes of being. Help me believe that our oneness cannot be severed by physical death. That our oneness cannot be severed by living on different planes of reality.

Help me believe that Marnie still loves me and wants me. I need her so much. I love her so much. My love has not diminished. It keeps growing stronger every day. And I miss her so much. I need to believe. Help me believe.

Please, strengthen my belief that Marnie is joyful, that she is fulfilled, that you have wrapped her in your love and are filling every fiber of her being with love and joy, with peace and understanding, and perhaps excitement about our coming rejoining.

Help me believe that she is reconnected with all those who have gone before her, who love her and who she loves. That she is bathed in the love of family and friends. That her world is full and rich. That she is filled with every possible source of love.

Help me believe that Marnie is vibrating on a far higher level. That she is able to experience your love, and the love of all those others, but that she is still aware of me, and deeply feels my love. Help me believe that I am a special part of her heaven. Please God, help me strengthen my belief in all of that.

And help me to believe that when my body dies, Marnie and I will be rejoined in total awareness, in total consciousness, in complete recognition of one another, in absolute love for one another, in total oneness, in total ecstasy for all eternity. That is my deepest prayer.

And if we can have resurrected, spiritual bodies that we can share with one another, I want her to run and leap into my arms. I want to wrap my arms around her and twirl her and kiss her and kiss her. And I want to look into her eyes and I want to say from the depths of my soul, "Oh my darling, I love you, I love you, I love you, I love you, I love you."

And I want to be able to say from the bottom of my heart, "Thank you God, thank you, thank you for fulfilling the gift of love that you opened to us, which you gave to us so many years ago. Thank you for fulfilling my heaven.

Please God send me strength, directly and through Marnie, to keep my faith, to strengthen my faith, and to hold on to belief in everything that I've said in the face of all my sadness and my missing Marnie.

My heart is filled with love sweet darling – you are my heart. Our souls are one in love sweet darling – our souls are forever one.

Chapter 22: On Healing

My hope is that in this chapter I can share with you more, perhaps slightly different perspectives about my path to healing. It is a path that I believe you can follow. I know I'm repeating myself, but it is essential to remember that healing is a process. It's an ongoing process. It's a long term process. I'm still in the midst of it. And it is vital to remember that healing is like learning. There will be plateaus. There will be times when you fall back. You will see that clearly as I describe my healing journey in this chapter.

But I am healing. I am not yet fully healed. I don't believe I will be fully healed until my physical death. But I know I am healing. Hopefully, as you have traveled along with me on my path of grieving and healing, you've experienced healing happening too. The key is faith. If you maintain your faith, if you persist in faith, healing will happen.

At some point every day I say aloud to Marnie, "In my mind and heart, I put my arms around you. I kiss you. I feel your body pressed against me. And boy do I look forward to experiencing that again physically in our resurrected bodies in the next chapter of our never-ending love story."

I'm able to say those words to Marnie because I'm healing. It's been an infuriatingly slow process. I still cry every day. I still have days that are dominated by melancholy, but I am healing. My belief in the living reality of Marnie's soul, is increasingly becoming genuine conviction. With that, my world is filling with a greater sense of peace and hope. I think there are several keys that have fueled this transition. I share them, not in order of importance, simply in the order they come to my mind.

First, I have surrounded myself with photos of Marnie. They are in every room of our house. They are in our van. They are on every wall of our travel trailer. I carry them in my pockets every day, everywhere I go. I carry them in lockets that I wear on a chain around my neck.

I see Marnie everywhere I look. This keeps her totally alive, totally front and center in my consciousness. The photos allow me to look into her eyes. (And I have come to believe that the eyes are indeed the window to the soul.) They give me a stronger sense of her presence when I talk to her. I address the specific photo that best matches the mood of the particular moment.

I have a much stronger sense of being "at home" when I am surrounded by Marnie. And the photos remind me of the myriad of special, loving, joyful experiences that we shared together – an accumulation of love that far outweighed the mistakes, the hurts, and the regrets that stood out so powerfully in my mind after her physical death. They remind me that our relationship was primarily a journey of love and joy together.

When I'm out walking and feelings of sadness and missing Marnie start to envelop me, I reach into my pocket and take out her picture. I press it to my heart. I tell her how profoundly I love her. I ask her to wrap me in her love. I hold her picture on my heart until the pain eases and I can go on walking, talking, and sharing my love with her again.

Second, I can't overstate how crucial walking and talking with Marnie have been to my healing. The ritual of my two mile walks and talks with Marnie every morning and night, and our walk and talk together at sunset are vital. They make our connection <u>feel</u> real. Not simply a product of my desire and imagination.

For one thing, the more I talk with Marnie, the better I feel. She is my best friend. I can share anything with her. I did throughout our physical lives together. Doing so now only feels right. And she is the only one with whom I can share my sadness over and over again without feeling utterly self-centered. The intensity of my sadness (which others want to alleviate) is a testament to the intensity of the love I feel for her. And I trust that Marnie can see it that way. I trust that Marnie, from her perspective in the afterlife, can experience my sadness as an expression of love, knowing that I am keeping our love intensely real. And because of her special perspective in the spiritual realm she has a clearer vision of what is to come for us as a result of our love.

So when I walk and talk with Marnie, and feel like I am engaged in a genuine conversation with my best friend, I feel joyful. I look forward to those walks. I look forward to our talks. I look forward to planning together the tasks that I need to accomplish to complete my time on this earth so that I can come home. As I have said, coming home, for me, is coming back into Marnie's arms. That for me is the definition of my heaven. I like thinking about heaven with her.

When I express my love for Marnie and believe in my heart that she hears me, that she sees me, that she feels me, and that she feels the intensity and the depth of the love that I have for her, when I believe that I am making her heart swell with joy and pride, then I am happy. I feel genuinely happy. Then life is good. Then I feel like I can wait to rejoin Marnie while I complete my work on this earth. I am still loving her now, and she feels it. I am bringing Marnie joy now. I am a central part of her heaven. That makes my continued living worthwhile.

When I expressed all those things out loud to Marnie I got a shiver. It ran down through my body. It was a shiver of Marne's presence. The shivers tell me that she is here. They tell me that she is with me. They tell me that what I am saying or what I am doing is on track, and that Marnie is with me in it.

The shivers are a confirmation – a confirmation of us, a confirmation of Marnie's reality and a confirmation of our shared connection. They affirm that we are indeed still joined. They affirm that our love is indeed still real. They affirm that our love is still a two way love. They affirm that we are indeed still one, here and now. In that, I feel joy. With that, my resolve to stay here and continue my work on this earth is strengthened. I am healing because Marnie sends me shivers. I experience the shivers because of our walks and talks together.

Third, I pray to God every day in both my morning and nighttime walks. I ask him directly to deepen and strengthen my faith in Him as real and loving and as the source and substance of our being. I affirm that our souls, our consciousness, our awareness, and our ability to love are created directly from His being, from His essence. In that, they are eternal. In that, Marnie's soul, her consciousness, her awareness, and her love are fully alive. They are eternal.

I affirm that Marnie is truly God's daughter. Each time I go deep into prayer I feel noticeably uplifted, stronger, and more at peace when the prayer is completed. I feel the movement from belief to conviction happening (ever so slowly) inside me. And with that, the feeling that Marnie is not gone grows inside me, so much so that at times I weep with joy.

Fourth, I read. I start each day by reading a short one or two paragraph spiritual meditation. I have read a variety of books that affirm my growing belief in God, in the soul, and in an eternal afterlife. These books were written by authors ranging from medical doctors, to mediums who communicate messages from souls in the afterlife, to a Mormon elder.

"Life after Life" by Raymond Moody Jr. M.D., and "Proof of Heaven" by Eben Alexander, M.D. were written by medical doctors who had no preconceived, deeply held religious beliefs or agendas about God and the afterlife. Dr. Alexander's book in particular touched me. He (Dr. Alexander) spent 7 days in a coma with no measurable brain activity in his cerebral cortex. Yet with no medically measurable activity in what is considered the thinking center of the brain, his consciousness remained fully alive and carried him directly into an extended experience with God and the spiritual reality of the afterlife.

I read the book "Lessons from the Light" by George Anderson after I had completed several drafts of this book. He is a practicing medium who shares what he calls "discernments" -- direct communications from souls in the afterlife. These communications directly and profoundly confirmed for me the validity of my thinking, my conclusions about Marnie and her living soul, and my continued relationship with her. That, for me, was a true blessing.

I continue to read other books that reinforce the belief that not only is spiritual life real, but that it is ultimate reality that far transcends our brief stay on this earth. Surrounding myself with intelligent thinkers and believers (as opposed to doubters or religious "true believers") reinforces the growth and development of my own thought-out, spiritual beliefs. It helps give me confidence in moving forward on the path of transforming hope and belief into confidence and conviction.

Fifth, I maintain strict self-discipline. I have to. All too often I've wanted to give up. All too often I am virtually overwhelmed by my feelings of deep loneliness in missing Marnie. She was the center of my world. She was my heart and soul. There are times when I just don't want to get up off the couch – when I feel like I can't. I'm paralyzed. There are times when I'm out walking that I just want to lay down on the road and let whatever comes come.

I don't allow myself to lay down. Sometimes I have to beg Marnie and God for help. I beg them to wrap me in their love. When I do, strength returns and I can move forward again. And after that, I talk extensively with Marnie and pray sincerely to God, and my mood is transformed. But I have to go through the process. I have to maintain the discipline. I don't believe that anyone else can or does help me the way Marnie and God do. And each time I experience their help, my faith grows a little stronger. Belief moves a little deeper towards conviction. It is through the discipline that I experience that.

Sixth, I'm looking for ways I can share in a positive, loving, joyful way with more people in my life. I text and talk on the phone with family members and friends who don't live nearby. But that's not enough. When I was thinking about this I spoke to Marnie. I said: "I really used to love going out to dinner with you, Marnie Winn. Just you and me, sitting in a quiet little restaurant across from one another, looking into each other's eyes and talking to one another. (Usually eating chips and salsa and drinking a really good beer in a little Mexican restaurant, and looking forward to a special dinner together, just you and me.)

I miss going out to dinner with you. I have to find a way to do that again. No way am I going out to dinner alone. I would miss you and feel profoundly sad. I've taken Ben and the family out to dinner multiple times. But it's not the same. It's too difficult shifting my focus between four children each wanting attention simultaneously. And it's too expensive. So I have to find real friends to go out to dinner with. (And I'll share it with you.)

I know you want joy for me in this lifetime as well as when we rejoin. So I'm trying to open myself to others who I can love without pushing you aside or replacing you. You can't be replaced, you know. You are my soul's mate. You are my forever wife."

Seventh, I cry. I cry a lot. I cry every day. I still miss Marnie so much. The pain is real. I have to express it. I have to feel it. I have to hurt with it. I have to weep with it. I have to let it out. Only then can I move on into appreciating the day. I have to go through the pain to heal. I have to cry.

Going forward has been a struggle for me. But each day, as my belief increases that I will be fully rejoined with Marnie upon my physical death, my feelings of peace and optimism grow deeper and stronger. Carrying Marnie and my belief in her continued, conscious presence in my heart allows me to move forward in a loving way with everyone I touch in this world. And that, I believe, will earn my right to rejoin Marnie fully in our heaven.

There's nothing magic about my walks with Marnie being 2 miles. From our house going one direction it's a half mile to a place we called "barky dog's house." Marnie and I used to walk up to see barky dog and then come back. And going the other direction from our house it's a half mile walk to a bridge over the West Fork River. I love standing on that bridge, seeing the birds that Marnie loved so very much, and experiencing the world from that perspective. So if I combine those two walks, it's a two mile walk. It was just a logical distance. It became my ritual.

What I discovered in doing it though is that two miles is just about the perfect distance for me. It translates into about 40 minutes. For me, that's enough time to break through to a real heart-felt connection with my emotions. It takes me a while to get there. And once I'm there, it takes me a while to fully release that emotion and again feel peace in my heart.

On virtually every morning walk I grieve. It's hard realizing I'm beginning another day without being able to hold Marnie or look into her eyes. I have to let go of the sadness that comes with that realization to be able to get on with the day. But, for me, it's essential that I get in touch with that sadness and go through it to be able to release it. Then I can feel a renewed sense of peace in my heart and be fully present for what I need to do that day.

You may not need to walk at all. You may be able to sit and meditate or just sit quietly and talk sincerely with your beloved. And you may not need 40 minutes to get in touch with your heart and feel your heart level connection with your beloved. But as with exercise, I do believe that it does take at least 20 to 30 minutes to get to that point – to get to the point where you experience the full value of connecting with your beloved on a heart level. It is that daily heart level connection that is vital. There can be no substitute for that.

So I believe it's essential to create and maintain what you choose as your own special rituals. They affirm the value of your beloved. They become a living testament of your love. There can be no substitute for that.

As I've described, it seems like I've gone through a seemingly never-ending struggle to believe deeply enough in my heart and soul to find healing. Struggle. It's been a struggle to believe, a struggle to heal.

Initially, I accepted my sadness, my loneliness, and my struggle as atonement for my past failings, for the hurt that I caused

Marnie and others in my life. I decided that I simply needed to develop the maturity and the patience to be willing to wait for my rejoining with Marnie. I thought, "I can do that." In spite of my sadness and missing her, in spite of sometimes feeling like I simply didn't want to go on with this life, I knew that I wasn't ready for this life to end. I knew that I would go on with this life. I chose it. I took full responsibility for it. It was a struggle. But I chose the struggle.

I knew I was not yet ready to rejoin Marnie because I needed and wanted to fulfill the promises I made to her before she died. I want to love our grandchildren to the very best of my ability until they each have a profound, unshakeable, deep down feeling of worth, and the skills to find and build the kind of love in their lives that we shared in ours. And I want to finish my writings as a gift for them and as a gift to each person to whom I can perhaps bring healing through what I share.

I want to touch as many people as I can, as deeply as I can with love and kindness. Then I will be ready to rejoin Marnie.

But going on has been a struggle.

I do want to rejoin Marnie as soon as I possibly can. I wish I could do it this very minute. But I want to rejoin her when I'm sure that she can receive me back in her arms with absolute joy, with absolute pride, and with absolute delight in all that I did and gave on her behalf. I want her to receive me back in her arms without hesitation, without reservation, in absolute ecstasy for all eternity. Then I will truly be back home. So I chose the struggle.

Struggle. Surviving Marnie's death was a profound struggle. Everything felt like a struggle for me.

Perhaps that struggle has finally begun to ease. I was able to say to Marnie, "I like being outside in the wilderness, Marnie. I enjoy it. I started coming out again because I needed to talk to you. I needed to be with you. I was coming out here for you, for us, for our reconnection. It was a way of seeing beauty and experiencing magic as a gift that I could give to you.

But it's grown into me loving being out here for me. I still want to share it with you, but now it's a gift for me again. Through my love for you, I have rediscovered beauty and magic in the world for me. (Thank you, darling.)"

The key to finally beginning to move beyond the struggle (I know I will be repeating myself here, but I think it is worth it) has been to keep going back to faith. I affirm over and over again that God is real. That God is the living, intelligent, aware, conscious, loving source of our being, the eternal, spiritual source of our being. With God as the source and substance of our being, we too are intelligent, aware, conscious, loving, eternal, spiritual beings. We are a part of Him, a reflection of Him. We are the literal children of God. In carrying His essence in us as the essential substance of our being, our souls are eternal. In her eternal soul, Marnie is real and alive, now and always.

Our love is that which makes us a reflection of God. Our love defines us as a part of God. Our love is the fundamental core of our spiritual essence. Our love, therefore, is eternal.

The bonds of love that we forge in our physical lifetimes define who we are. They give us our unique identities as individualized parts of God. And the bonds of love that we make in our physical lifetimes are spiritual bonds. They will last forever. Only the body dies. The soul doesn't. Death is the separation of the body from the soul. It is a separation, a transformation, a passageway, not an ending for the soul. The soul rises above the body. It transcends the body. Every element of our spiritual being is eternal. It is undying.

I believe, therefore, that Marnie, my beloved wife, is fully alive, fully aware, fully conscious, fully loving. The bond of love that we built with one another is real and alive. It transcends physical death. It transcends the boundaries between the physical and the spiritual planes of existence. Marnie was a gift from God that I was profoundly blessed to receive. And a gift that God has given cannot be taken away.

I know now that the more I love, the more I participate in the divine. The more I love, the more like God I become. Marnie was the most loving human being I (personally) have ever known. Marnie was the most Godly. Marnie was the most divine. Marnie was ready to rejoin God. Loving was the core of her being, the center of her identity. She was a loving part of divinity.

I now move forward in this life, loving with Marnie and God in me. As I do so I become more divine. With Marnie in me, I am less selfish. I am more Godly. The more I can love with her, loving as us, the more I will be ready to rejoin her on her level of being in her heaven.

In this reality, in this understanding, I have found healing.

As I walked outside one morning, thinking these things, magic was everywhere. There was a great horned owl in a tree, not 15 feet away, right above me. He didn't move. He just watched me. And I saw robins. It was almost mid-October and the robins were still there in the Montana Mountains with me. As I went on, a huge flock of small birds flew towards me. They kept coming and coming. They flew over me, around me, and landed in a tree directly beside me. And then I came upon wild turkeys – 19 of them. I remembered the first time Marnie and I saw a flock of wild turkeys together in the Swan Valley. And now they came here – to where we are.

And there were Clark's nutcrackers everywhere. They were flocking in the trees. They were covering the ground. I watched them eat and could hear the beat of their wings as they flew over me and around me.

Seeing all the birds, hearing their sounds seemed so magical. I said, "Are you seeing this Marnie? Are you hearing it? Am I sharing this with you? Am I giving this to you? And then I realized that it's for me too. It's for you. It's for me. This whole thing that I'm experiencing is a gift from you for me and from me to you. It happens because I'm out here wanting to give to you, wanting to share with you. And it enriches my life.

I need to be with you, Marnie. I need to give to you. And that need is bringing me out into the wilderness which is your way of giving back to me. It's that irony. It's that mystery. It's the continued mutual nature of our love for one another. In giving to you, you're giving to me. In giving to each other, I'm one with you, though we are separate individuals.

There is a level of mystery, of magic, of depth in this world. You and I are one in love. You and I are one in God. You and I are one. And yet you and I are separate individuals. Individual and one. In giving to you, you are giving to me. It's magic. It's divine reality. Everything has truly moved to a higher level, Marnie. I love you more than I've ever loved you. I love you more than I have ever loved. I'm seeing more beauty than I've ever seen. Everything is richer even though your body is gone from me.

What I look forward to in death is the rejoining of our resurrected bodies with this higher level of love and awareness. I don't think our love could get any deeper. I don't think human love could get any deeper. It's pretty magical. It's pretty special. It's the gift, the perspective that has come with your physical death. I love you Marnie. You are my heart. The shivers are coming with greater and greater frequency. Thank you darling. Thank you God."

There was one more experience that played a central role in my moving beyond struggling to a finding a greater sense of peace in healing. It was time for my afternoon exercise. I was tired. I didn't really want to do it. But I put on my running shoes and got ready to go for a run. I walked for more than a half a mile. I just felt like walking. I wanted to talk with Marnie. I didn't feel like running. But I thought to myself, "No. I need to run. I need to stay disciplined. I need to force myself through this. I need to keep running to keep my emotions up. I need to stay in a positive place emotionally. I need to do the run."

So I started running. I was tired. My legs felt heavy. And within the first 25 seconds, I tripped over a root, fell hard, and rolled. And I realized that I was forcing myself to run – that this was a <u>struggle</u>. This was not a joy. I would feel a whole lot better walking and talking with Marnie, instead of forcing myself to run.

So I got up and started walking. I realized that it's been the same way with building faith. It's been the same way with healing – I've been <u>struggling</u>. I've been trying to force it. I've been striving to achieve faith. And that's when the thought came to me that if I were in Marnie's place, if I were the one whose body had died and she was still here, there is absolutely no question that I would be there for her every moment. I would be watching over her. I would be doing everything that I possibly could to make her feel OK. And suddenly it felt just like the run.

There is no need to force anything. Marnie is here. Marnie loves me. Instead of struggling to have faith in Marnie's presence, I need to relax and accept it. I can know and trust that it is there. I receive faith, I feel Marnie's presence in peace, not in struggle. When I thought this, I felt good. I felt connected to Marnie. I felt a deep sense of peace in my heart, knowing that I no longer had to struggle to be with my beloved.

I am with her in my heart. And because the soul (her soul) is real, she **is** with me. There is no need to struggle. She is here and she loves me deeply. And God loves me. I don't have to fight for faith. I simply have to open myself to it and receive it. God gives it to me.

It felt like I crossed a threshold. I felt a new sense of peace inside. That was some time ago now, and the peace hasn't left. Marnie is here. Marnie is real. Marnie loves me. God is here. God is real. God loves me. I simply need to let it be, let it glow, and let it flow out through me. Thank you Marnie for the insight. Thank you God for the peace.

Because of this, I made the decision that I'm going to experience joy in every way that I can every day. I'm going to experience beauty in every way that I can. And I will give it all as a gift of love to Marnie. I don't need to work so hard at fitness. I'm fit. I need to exercise joyfully. I'm going to eat an ice cream cone now and then in special places and enjoy them and think of Marnie sharing them with me. She would like that.

I no longer need to push really hard when I bike. I did that too much with Marnie when she was alive (physically). Now, I just want to feel strong and enjoy the ride, together. I love you Marnie.

Today as I walked and talked with Marnie, I didn't struggle. I accepted our relationship peacefully. I accepted God peacefully. I realized again that if our positions were switched, I would absolutely be there for Marnie. I would love her. I would watch over her. I would do anything and everything I could to love her. And she loved (and loves) better than me. So she is here. She's doing the same. I don't need to struggle to reach her. I just need to relax and feel the peace that comes from her. I need to let her love flow over and into me.

I thought about Marnie's cancer. I thought about sleeping in a chair next to her bed in different hospital rooms for 21 days. I thought about not being able to hike together or run together or go for long bike rides together. I thought about scheduling and monitoring as many as 12 different medications simultaneously. I can remember washing her, cleaning her, turning her over, and lotioning her dying body. I remember sleeping on the floor beside the adjustable bed that hospice provided to her in the days before her body died.

None of it felt like a burden to me. It absolutely never felt like a burden to me. It was purely an act of love for the woman who was my heart and soul. Never in our 45 year (physical) relationship did Marnie ever feel like a burden to me in any way.

We became absolutely one in love in our years together. We are one in love and one in God now. So I can pretty much absolutely trust that for Marnie loving me, watching over me, and sending me love and strength from the afterlife every day is not a burden to her. For her it is an act of love and joy, freely chosen, just as it was for me. I could have done it no other way. I don't believe that Marnie would do it in any other way. In that, I can feel at peace.

I'm no longer struggling to achieve connection. I accept it. I find wisdom in the words "Let it be." Let it be and trust. I've done the thinking. I've done the searching. I've done the soul-searching. I've done it over and over again. I've done the struggle. God makes sense. The soul makes sense. I don't need to keep struggling and trying to have faith. I need to relax and let the faith flow over me. I need to let Marnie's love flow into me. I can trust her absolutely. I need to let God's love flow into me. I can trust God's love and wisdom absolutely. I've turned a corner in my healing.

I need to recognize in writing this book that I can influence, but I can't control outcomes. I'm not responsible for how anyone reacts to what I write. And I don't have to defend myself or defend my writings, I simply present them. In being simple, in being gentle, in being loving, and in being accepting, I find peace. In doing those things I live as Marnie in me.

I have crossed over a threshold moving into faith. I feel a sense of peace. I feel a sense of trust. I asked God to have His permission to have the hand of His daughter, Marnie in <u>eternal</u> marriage, and in my mind I heard the answer: "Yes, my son. You may. You have my permission."

I really believe I have crossed a threshold, and I am deeply grateful. Thank you God. I love you, Marnie.

Struggle, I believe, was a necessary part of my grieving, of my growth, and of my healing. It was a struggle to maintain the discipline in both my thinking and my actions as I moved forward along the path of healing. Sometimes it felt like a never-ending struggle. It felt like the rest of my life on this earth would be a struggle. But it was a struggle that I was willing to face because I believed it was required of me to find my way back home to Marnie.

Moving beyond that struggle has been the step that has made me feel that healing is real, that healing is possible, and that I am indeed on the road back into Marnie's arms.

I don't know if you will need to go through that same process of struggle. I hope that my writing about it may help to short-circuit that struggle. I hope that your path to faith in God and in the eternal soul of your beloved may be more direct than mine. I hope that you will feel the presence of God and confidence in the presence of your beloved much more quickly than I did.

But if your path proves difficult, if your struggles seems to stretch on and on, know that if you persist in your quest to maintain your love for and your ongoing relationship with your beloved, you will succeed. Persist in your rituals. Persist in using all the tools for building faith that fit for you. Persist in reaching out to God. And above all, persist in actively loving on a level even higher than you did when your beloved was here with you physically on this earth. Persist, and you will not fail.

Persist and you will (eventually) reach a point where your need to struggle will come to an end. Peace will return to your heart. You can count on it. Trust God. Count on Him. Trust your bond of love with your beloved. Trust….

"Discipline is remembering what you want."

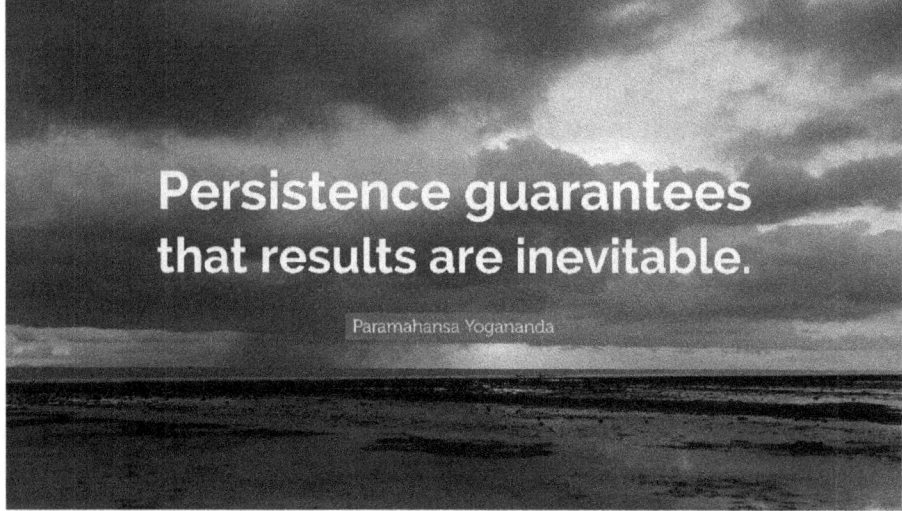

Persistence guarantees that results are inevitable.

Paramahansa Yogananda

Chapter 23: Living with the Soul of My Beloved

In this chapter I hope to share with you my experience in keeping Marnie's soul as the center of my universe as compared to what life was like for me when Marnie was the physical center of my universe.

Keeping Marnie alive on a feeling level has required a fundamental adjustment to and a disciplined focusing of my thinking. It's so easy to get lost in sadness. It has been a profound challenge to stay centered in relating to a purely spiritual being. It has required not only disciplined thinking, but a disciplined use of the tools I outlined for building faith as well. There has been so much pain inherent in losing Marnie's body that grounding and re-grounding myself in faith has been essential to being able to live joyfully, and at times, vital to my very survival.

However, in relating to Marnie's spiritual being I've recognized that on some very fundamental levels, our relationship has not changed. What I shared with Marnie when she was physically alive is what I still share with her soul. One of the things that has changed though is the impact that relationships with other (physically) living people have on me and on my relationship with Marnie. I've learned that I need to consciously connect with Marnie both before and after my interactions with other people.

I think it is vital that you become aware of these kinds of things in your life. In keeping your relationship with your beloved alive, I believe you will face many of the same challenges to your thinking, to your behavioral discipline, and to your relationships that I have faced. But it is in keeping the relationship with your beloved alive that (if you are like me) you will be able to find healing and a rebirth of joy in your life.

It is with this in mind that I offer you my thoughts about the similarities and differences involved with living with a spiritual being as opposed to a physical being, and my experiences in trying to cope effectively with those differences.

When Marnie was physically alive, I was bathed in her presence. I could see her and touch her. She filled my life every day. I felt deep peace and contentment in her presence. I never doubted or questioned my sense of purpose. My purpose was to love and support her.

Now, when I don't have her physical presence, when I can't look up from where I'm working and see her or reach over and touch her, I have to fill in that void with thoughts. I say these thoughts out loud. It gives them a greater feeling of reality for me. I don't know if Marnie can see or hear or feel inside my head (though I invite her in). Speaking out loud ensures communication for me. And I have to do that a lot.

Marnie's physical presence in our world was omni-present for me. So now I have to say my thoughts to her out loud, every day to fill the gap that the loss of her physical body has left. I have to. I have to speak with Marnie. For me personally, I often have to go outside to connect with her most effectively. That may very well be simply a personal limitation of mine. I don't know. You have to see what works best for you.

Our daily walks, my daily exercise, and our sunset times are vital to keeping the same felt level of loving presence alive for me. It's a real commitment of time, but, for me, that time commitment is worth it. It keeps the feeling level of my belief in the reality of our relationship alive. It's then that I speak to Marnie most spontaneously from my heart. And that sharing with her and the feeling level belief that it engenders, keeps me alive.

As I've said, it's essential for me that my faith, my belief in Marnie's continued living presence be "heart-felt." When I feel her presence in my heart, then I know that only her body is gone from me. That in and of itself is profoundly hard to deal with. I have to feel Marnie's presence to counter-balance it. When I do there is still true richness in my life. I can, in a more limited way, continue to experience the joy and peace that permeated my life when Marnie was physically here with me. I love her enough to be willing to wait for physical fulfillment again in our next lifetime (eternal lifetime) together.

Another realization I've come to is that in our physical lifetime together, we each worked independently on our own tasks. We weren't always focused on one another. We worked beside one another. We each did our own jobs. When we would stop, then we would focus on one another again and share our world.

We talked with one another when we needed to or wanted to. That was even true in our travels. We worked a lot. But when we would stop we would talk. Then we would go off and explore together. We discovered a world of magic together. We played together. Marnie climbed in the trees and hid in the trees. We found hawks eating snakes. We found alligators. We found magic together.

What struck me is that this is still true now. Our fundamental relationship has not changed. There are times when my sole focus is Marnie. I actively express and feel my deep love for her. There are times when I am working in my own world, and I occasionally speak to her. There are other times when I am busy loving others for and with her.

I don't know what Marnie's focus is now while I'm working. But I can still call out to her and talk with her as I did when she was physically present. She will hear me and respond. And we will go off together and share, seeing this beautiful world through my eyes. We will discover new magic together, and I will pass it on for us

Something that has changed for me in the course of maintaining my spiritual relationship with Marnie is the effect that my conversations with other people have on my overall emotional state. As human beings it is natural to talk and share with the people who are physically present in your life. But I often want to talk about Marnie because she is so important to me. She is such a central part of my life.

However, I fear that most of the people with whom I have regular contact have tired of hearing me talk about Marnie. They simply do not and perhaps cannot understand her continued, overwhelming importance to me. (Some have called her "my obsession.")

Even with those who do listen and don't come across as wishing I'd move on to some other subject, I can still come away from our conversations feeling distressed. I'm talking *about* Marnie instead of talking *to* her. Doing that can feel like I'm objectifying her. Even in writing this book, in writing about my relationship with Marnie, it's as if I'm objectifying us. I'm creating this entity that's out there, that somehow feels separate from us, separate from the living reality of who we are.

That can make me profoundly sad because it implies a level of separation. For me, **separation brings sadness**. I've had to recognize that and talk to Marnie about it. I have to talk with her. Whenever I'm distressed I have to talk with her. I have to bring her here, into my life, now. That often involves going through profound sadness and pain because in bringing her here, I realize how much I miss having her here always. But it is in bringing her here, in talking with her here, and sharing with her now, that I find my way back into joy and meaning in my life.

I have to remind myself that Marnie is here. She's here now. She's always been here. I need to bring that back into my consciousness. It is my consciousness that defines my world. It is my definition of the world that creates my feelings. And that is a constant, ongoing process.

When I was out on one of my "Marnie" walks, I said this to her, "When I'm feeling strong it's like we're in separate rooms near one another. I can call out, and you'll reply. You're there. You're always near, and we can be absolutely together at a moment's notice.

That's how it really is now, even though at my level of awareness, it's only real in my mind and heart. Sometimes I feel like we're together walking hand in hand seeing things virtually through the same eyes, feeling things together. Sometimes you're nearby and I need to call out to bring you to me. And you'll be there. You'll wrap your arms around me with your love and we'll go forward together."

Though I cannot yet know the emotions, the experiences, the levels of awareness, the journeys, or any of the other realities of Marnie's life on her current plane of existence, I believe that she remains fully aware of me and fully connected with me. And I believe that without the limits of her physical body, without being limited by time and place, that she can have an infinite world of possibility, potential, and experience, and still be present with me and fully involved with and in love with me as she was in her physical lifetime.

It felt like these thoughts came to me as an insight that Marnie had sent to me. I felt a shiver run through my body. It feels like a shiver of being physically touched by Marnie's presence. Shortly thereafter a beautiful hawk flew over me and landed in a tree behind me, looking over me. As I expressed in chapter 11, these "coincidences" in nature come repeatedly and are what I believe to be a sign of Marnie's real presence.

The conclusion I've come to, is that nothing beyond the absence of her physical body has changed in the relationship between Marnie and me as long as I keep talking to her. When I talk to her enough to feel our connection in my heart, I experience peace and joy. I can go on with my work with a sense of genuine purpose. In that, I feel peace and satisfaction.

It is when I'm weak that I have problems. If I let myself get too tired or sick, or even if I overeat my emotions can crumble. That didn't happen when Marnie was physically alive. I could get off track. I could get lost in an emotional funk. But it would be limited. Now, without Marnie's physical presence, I can get totally lost.

I start missing Marnie intensely. I cry and cry and cry. I have to struggle to resurface. Discipline is vital. There is a degree of difficulty in maintaining your emotional center when dealing with your beloved on a soul level that is far greater than it was when you shared one another's physical presence.

I have to force myself to go outside then to walk and talk or ride my bike and talk. I have to talk. I have to reconnect with Marnie to not get lost in the depths of depression. So I go out. I talk to God. I ask him to strengthen my faith. I ask that He bring me heart-felt belief in Marnie's continued, real, living presence. I ask that He bring me heart-felt belief in the reality of her living soul.

Then I talk with Marnie. I share what I've been feeling. I sob the intensity of my love for her. I affirm it in all the details that have become my mantra. I keep affirming until my heart is healed again. I affirm, "I love you, Marnie. You are my heart. You are my soul's mate. You are my forever wife. You are my forever love. You are my forever ideal lover. You are my forever perfect partner. You are my forever ideal playmate. You are my forever best friend. Our souls are one in love sweet darling. Our souls are forever one."

There have been times when my life has felt like it's shrouded in a veil. I love people actively, especially our grandchildren. I do everything in my power to make them feel loved, valued, special, and worthwhile. I try to do that as Marnie would – as Marnie in me. I feel deep, genuine warmth and affection for them. It makes me smile when they are happy. I can feel good inside when I'm on my way home and I feel like I succeeded in making them happy.

But all of that is what I promised Marnie I would do. I feel it to be my responsibility. I feel like loving itself is my responsibility. It can feel more of a responsibility to love than a desire to love. I don't necessarily feel a sense of real joy in it. I don't always feel the sense of joy in living as I did when Marnie was physically alive and sharing life with me.

That's the veil – that lack of joy. My happiness can feel muted. I fulfill my promises to Marnie. I do so lovingly. But I don't necessarily do so joyfully. Finding joy can be a far greater challenge when you no longer live in the physical presence of your beloved.

As I walked and prayed last night I realized that when Marnie was physically alive my joy in living had come from loving her. Loving Marnie and loving with her was the source of my greatest joy in life. And I realized that my deepest joy since Marnie's death has come in my walks and talks and prayer time with her. It clicked in my mind. I realized that I do have times of real joy then. It is when I feel Marnie's presence as absolutely real – when I feel that I am actively connecting with her and loving and living for and with her that I am still joyful.

So it comes back to faith. <u>Faith is the essential key to my healing</u>. Faith is the key to my living joyfully. When I believe on a feeling level that Marnie is fully alive in her soul, when I believe that she is aware of me and loves me deeply, when I believe that she feels my love for her, when I feel that we are truly still connected, then I feel real joy.

To genuinely feel those things I need to believe, on a feeling level, that God is real and cares for me personally. That a loving God gave me Marnie and gave us our eternal souls. Because of that Marnie and I can be in love now and forever.

Marnie and God are inextricably tied together for me. I remind myself repeatedly that Marnie was created from and of God's essence. As such she is an eternal, spiritual being. The bond of loving oneness that we built together is fully alive now and always will be. Therefore, loving Marnie, and loving for and with Marnie now makes my world make sense. And now I know that God's love is fundamentally interwoven into our love as well. My joy can go even deeper – as long as I have faith and live with that faith as the bedrock of my being.

So every day and every night I pray for a deepening and strengthening of my faith. I pray that I be able to walk the bridge of faith until I can die into Marnie's arms and finally be home, wrapped in her love and God's together.

It's only when I lose sight of that faith that the veil returns. That's when my life becomes shrouded in sadness again. When I tap in to my faith, joy returns to my life. The strength of my belief is the key to the level of joy that I feel. It goes back to disciplining and focusing my thinking. I can lose myself in self-pity or rekindle myself in faith. It all depends on where I focus my thoughts.

As long as I have faith, when I focus my thinking on faith, when I feel faith, joy is and will be real in my life. It is in faith that I believe that Marnie is wrapped in God's love. It is in faith that I believe that Marnie wraps me in her love. In faith there can be a feeling of oneness that transcends even what we shared in our physical lifetime together.

With these insights I shivered.

Talking with Marnie is the most natural thing in the world to me. Talking to Marnie without being able to see her is still strange. It's part of living in faith. And it's so hard to feel confirmation of the reality of the faith without seeing her and without touching physically. But I talk with Marnie in faith. Even though there is no direct verbal response, the results indicate the reality. I'll ask for help. I'll ask for insight. I'll ask for direction. I'll ask Marnie to guide my words, to guide me in wisdom, and it happens.

When I talk with Marnie (as the conscious center of my awareness) I believe that she comes to me in her awareness instantaneously. Because of the bond of loving oneness that we built together in our physical lives (with, I now realize, God's help) Marnie's conscious awareness as a living, spiritual being is fully linked to mine. I implicitly call her to me when I directly express my love for her. And I now realize that if I call her into my awareness before I write, or before I engage in loving others, or when I am outside rejoicing in the beauty and magic and majesty of nature, that she will be there with me and for me. Then I am living exactly as I did when Marnie was physically alive. And now I am loving much more consciously, so the depth of my love is deeper and the depth of my appreciation of nature is more profound.

I'd like to give you an example that illustrates how Marnie comes to me when I need her and ask for her help. I'm trying to enrich the lives of my grandchildren. I'm working at strengthening them. I'm working at strengthening them sometimes in the face of their parents doing things that don't accomplish what they (the parents) would really like to accomplish. I don't always know what to say or what to do. I don't know how to intervene most effectively.

The intent of the parents is totally positive. But their words can achieve just the opposite of what they are trying to achieve. In being critical, in telling the children what they aren't doing and how they aren't being what they should be in a judgmental way, they generate feelings of guilt and inadequacy. This in turn blocks the children from moving forward in the positive direction that the parents were looking for in the first place.

So I'm working on strengthening the children so that they are able to hear the positive intent and can define the critical negativity as nothing more than that -- critical negativity. They don't have to take it in. They don't have to take it on.

I find that I often need direction not only in strengthening the children, but in interacting their parents in a positive way without being critical of them and pointing out to them what they are doing wrong, in the same way that they do it with the children.

I'll ask Marnie for guidance. When I do, I find that I say what I need to say and I do what I need to do. The result is there. I do things the way Marnie would do them – with gentleness, with kindness, with patience, and with wisdom – wisdom that is beyond my natural style.

You can reach out to your beloved as they live in the spiritual realm, and they will reach back to you offering any and all the help that they possibly can. Just as you still love them, they still love you and wish you only joy, success, and fulfillment.

Sometimes I will ask for help with a situation where I'm troubled or struggling. I'm trying to figure out what direction to take. Then circumstances will arise that are totally out of my control. They push me in a specific direction. They (the circumstances) come up out of my request for help.

So, although her physical presence is no longer here, and I don't see or hear her response to my requests in my conversations with Marnie, the outcomes that I get from those conversations indicate that I was heard. I am given direction. My faith in our real relationship results in a real response in terms of insight and direction. It works. It confirms the two way reality of the conversation.

I find that when I have my conversations with Marnie, things haven't fundamentally changed. I still talk to her in the same way I talked to her when she was here in her physical body. I still have the same issues in my life that I had when she was physically here. I still struggle with the same things. The world is really very similar.

    What has changed is that my love for Marnie has intensified. It has deepened. It is significantly stronger. Both of us are vibrating on a higher plane of being. And, my focus now is not nearly as much on this physical world as it used to be. My focus is now on the spiritual world where Marnie lives. And in the spiritual world, love is the only thing that really matters. And since that is my focus, my love is deepened. And we remain a perfect reflection of one another.

    My love for Marnie was always there, but I could get so lost in the day to day needs and requirements of the physical, material world that I'd lose track of us. Now, the physical world just isn't significant to me, not the way that it was. Now my connection with Marnie is my most profound, overarching need and focus. That's a need that is real on a spiritual level. And that's where love lives.

    The specific tasks that you face in your world will be different from mine. What you need and hope to accomplish in this world will be different from my needs and hopes. But your ability to stay connected with your beloved, your ability to receive direction and input from your beloved will be every bit as real for you as it is for me -- if you allow yourself to be open to it.

If you take the time, if you make a regular ritual of continuing to talk with your beloved, you too will find that on a profound level, the world really hasn't changed. You can share your thoughts. You can share your questions. You can share your needs as you always did. The reply will come in a different form than it did when your beloved was present in physical reality. But the reply will come if you open yourself to it.

If you actively express your love over and over, day after day, with heart-felt emotion, your relationship will stay strong in your mind and heart. And it is in and through this bond of love that a greater, living level of two-way communication can and will be achieved.

The depth of your love will increase, and the wisdom of your actions will increase proportionally. The caveat is that it must all be done in and through faith. You have to work on faith constantly in this spiritual dimension of reality in a way that you never had to when your beloved was with you in the physical world. But as I have discovered, when you do the work (on building faith), it works – you get the results you need.

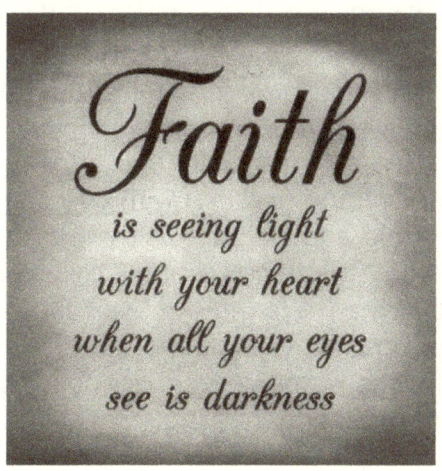

Faith is seeing light with your heart when all your eyes see is darkness

Chapter 24: How Relationship, Nature, Children, and Purpose Can Keep You Connected with Your Beloved

As I described in the chapter on Marnie and me, Marnie and I were "different" in many respects. I think you have to be willing to be different to be able to follow the path of healing that I'm outlining in this book. To choose to believe in God, outside the confines of religion, that in and of itself defines you as different.

Being willing to think and consider possibilities that seem out of the realm of "normal" is, I believe, essential to keeping your relationship with your beloved alive. Choosing to keep your relationship with your beloved alive is already living outside the realm of "normal". But remember, it is only in living outside the realm of normal that you can become exceptional.

Marnie and I always took the path less traveled on, both physically and emotionally throughout our relationship. It's how we discovered so much and how we grew into one another so deeply. It's the path we're still traveling now after the death of Marnie's body. We will continue to travel that path together into eternity.

In this chapter I hope to share with you some of the special ways that I think Marnie and I lived outside the bounds of "normal". I want to share some of the things that we believed that were different and some of the ways that we lived that were different. I believe those differences played an important role in our love. And most importantly, for the purposes of this book, I believe they have played an important role in my healing.

I will share some of the choices we made that shaped our world both before and after Marnie's physical death. I will offer ideas about our relationship and the role nature and children played in our relationship, and about the role they continue to play now in shaping my life. And I will share my thoughts about finding my life's purpose after the death of Marnie's body.

I hope you will look at these ideas and our differences from the norm and see what you think of them. See if they seem like important differences to you. See if adopting any of these differences might be beneficial to your healing. It is purely your choice.

I have conversations with Marnie virtually every day. Much of what I will share with you in this chapter comes directly from those conversations. Though the conversations skip forward through time, I hope the overall impact of the conversations will be coherent.

Our Relationship

In our wedding ceremony Marnie and I read excerpts from the book "The Little Prince". In the spirit of "The Little Prince," Marnie and I chose to bond with one another. We chose to establish absolute ties. We chose to tame and be tamed. We chose to observe the proper rites. We created rituals that we would follow throughout our relationship. We chose not to possess one another, but we chose absolute commitment.

We grew more deeply into that commitment every year. As we did, our bond became absolute, unbreakable. Bonding, fully achieved results in the exponential growth of love. Once achieved, it can never be undone. It is built upon a base of honesty and results in the desire for absolute openness with one another.

Whenever there was an issue between us that we feared sharing, no matter how uncomfortable we were about sharing it, we shared it with one another. It was a fundamental rule in our relationship – whatever you fear sharing the most is the most important thing to share.

Sometimes that sharing caused real hurt. Sometimes it caused real conflict. But we always kept going through the hurt and conflict until we could find a way to end both (the hurt and the conflict) and be back in love with one another again. We would never stop. That was the second fundamental rule in our relationship – every conflict must be resolved. And conflict is resolved only when both people are satisfied with the outcome. Sharing fears and resolving conflict helped create our magic.

I believe we are doing it still, together, now, after Marnie's physical death. No matter how deep the hurt I feel, I share it with Marnie. No matter how deep the shame and regret I feel about past events in our relationship, I share them with Marnie. I talk with her. I weep with her. I keep going until I feel lovingly and joyfully reconnected with her again.

In our physical life together we shared our hearts and souls freely and absolutely no matter how difficult it was. Sharing my heart and soul with my beloved now, after her physical death, brings me healing. I believe the same will be true for you.

And I believe we are (still) discovering ultimate meaning through our relationship. I believe that ultimate meaning is found in relationship. To love Marnie now, after the death of her body, my love has to spread out to the world. Prior to loving Marnie, my love was too self-centered. I loved, but I only really saw things from my own perspective. In meeting Marnie, in learning to love her, in growing into really loving together, in raising our children together, I learned to truly love. I learned to see the world through the eyes of the other.

My task now is to go forward and love as us, with Marnie in me. Marnie taught me to love without expecting anything back.

Loving is a gift. It's a gift we gave to our children. It's a gift we gave to our grandchildren. It's a gift I give now, because Marnie gave so freely. She taught me to truly love, and now loving is my sole reason for continuing to live in the world. Our love has brought me to the world.

I believe you will find that to be increasingly true for you as you affirm and nurture your ongoing relationship with your beloved. No matter what your specific path through life, your love and your loving will be increased through your ongoing real, spiritual relationship with your beloved.

The Role of Nature

One of the ways that Marnie and I could be seen as different, was that in loving one another, we chose as part of our lifestyle to bond with nature. (I described some of our nature experiences in the chapter on Marnie and me.) Our bond with nature was incorporated into our bond of love. Marnie and I found beauty together in nature. Every day we would spend time outside in the wilderness. I even remember cross country skiing together on Christmas Day in Montana when it was 18 degrees below zero. So now, every day and every night I walk in the wilderness and talk with Marnie. It feels real. It feels special. It feels right.

You have to be willing to put yourself out there, to make the physical effort to be out in the wilderness, to let that magic happen, to have it come to you. Marnie was always willing to do that. She was always willing to make the supreme effort. And magic surrounded her. So now I follow her lead.

Depending on where you live, nature may not be as accessible to you as it is for me. Nature may not have played as central a role in your relationship as it did with Marnie and me. But I believe that being out in nature whenever you can will help you heal.

For me, just being outside helps me. Being in the wilderness definitely helps me. Being out in the dark at night when no one else is out, or being out alone in the early morning, that all helps me. When I'm outside looking at the stars and I look towards the city, I can't see anything clearly. When I look away from the city, that's when everything becomes more clear and bright. I wonder if there isn't some profound truth in that.

I had a truly magical experience that helped confirm for me the importance of being outside and maintaining your connection with your beloved no matter where you are.

Earlier in the year I had been walking in Fort De Soto Park when I came to a magnificent field of clover. It was a luxuriant blanket of clover. I had just been singing the song to Marnie, "I Want to Lay You Down in a Bed of Roses." And I immediately realized I wanted to change the words. I sang to Marnie, "I want to lay you down in a field of clover." I felt that. I desired that. I hoped it would be possible for us in some future dimension of our lives.

Later in my trip, I was camped in what (for me) was a very unspectacular state park. There were no real, walkable trails in the wilderness that weren't muddy bogs. It was a fine place if you wanted to go fishing. But I felt no real magic or magnificence there.

Late one night, even though I was tired, I went out and walked along the road that overlooked the lake where people fished. I'd been feeling really sad. I missed Marnie so much. I needed to walk and talk with her. In my sadness and tiredness I began feeling like laying down on the road as I walked. I just felt like laying down. So I began singing, "I want to lay you down in a field of clover." Everything was tied to "laying down."

Instead of laying down on the road, I walked over to and a little ways down the sloping bank that overlooked the lake. I thought I would lie down for just a little while. It was totally dark. There was no moon. When I sat down and laid back I found myself in a massive field of clover. It felt like a blanket. It felt so magical. It felt like Marnie was telling me that she's with me, no matter where I am. Even when I don't feel that sense of magic and magnificence, she's still there.

Back home in Montana I wrote, "I like being out in this magnificent wilderness with you Marnie. God is its source. I feel a sense of awe. I feel a sense of humility in being in the presence of magnificence. And that's what I want to give to you every day – a sense of magnificence. It's how I feel about you. So it's what I want to give back to you. And I love being in the presence of all of these birds.

With birds, there are so many times when you can't see them. You can only hear them, but you still know that they're real. That's the message of faith about God and your soul, Marnie. Just because I can't see them, doesn't mean that they're not real. I've been learning that lesson over and over again. It's reinforced repeatedly so that I can believe in your living soul. So I can believe in God."

In spite of all my insights, I'm not always strong. When I'm weak, I struggle. I hope that if you've lost someone profoundly special, you understand. I'm talking without seeing. I'm walking without holding Marnie's hand. I'm talking to her and asking questions of her, without hearing the sound of her voice in response. That's all so different from what it used to be. And sometimes, that's all still so difficult....

In one of my weak times, walking and carrying a feeling of sadness, I asked Marnie, "What's the world like for you now? What's it like living beyond your physical body? What's it like in a spiritual realm? What do you see? What do you experience? What are the possibilities for you? It's all so baffling to me. Eternity is so baffling to me. I don't understand exactly what or how you are as a soul. I don't even know what you look like any more. But all that really matters to me is that 'you are'."

When I said those words, I looked up and a great blue heron landed and perched in the tree directly in front of me. He didn't move in spite of my presence. It's just too coincidental. It's you telling me through nature that you really "are". Thank you, Marnie.

Being out in nature has been and continues to be a magical experience for me. In it and through it I feel connected with Marnie. The magic doesn't happen every day, but I have to keep putting myself out there, as Marnie and I did together, to enable it to happen. I hope I've shared a slice of that magic with you. I hope it encourages you to give serious consideration to being out in nature to talk with your beloved whenever that is possible for you.

Children

I believe that one of my purposes in still being here on this earth is to love and heal our grandchildren children. They carry wounds from their birth mother abandoning them. They carry fundamental feelings that say, "I'm not good enough." And whenever anything happens where they feel criticized or feel like they have failed in some way, it taps directly into those "I'm not good enough" wounds. My job on this earth is to help heal those wounds, so that they feel special, loved, and worthwhile, and hence capable of building loves that will keep them fulfilled throughout their lives.

That's a building process. That will take time. I do it in lots of little ways -- from working on math to help my grandson feel successful, to working directly on communication skills with my granddaughter. But to a large extent, it's in how I communicate with them and how I ask them to and expect them to communicate with me that makes the greatest difference in their lives. It's in building their communication and relationship skills that they will gradually come to feel better about themselves.

And I want to teach them that no matter how things appear on the surface, on the level of the soul, everything is OK. I want to teach them that death cannot end a relationship grounded in love. I want to teach them that love lives on, that their Grammy, Marnie lives on. I want to teach them that Grammy and I will always be there for them. I want to teach them that God will always be there for them. All they need to do is reach out and we will respond.

Modeling my continued active, loving relationship with Marnie and God will make it profoundly easier for them to feel and understand this lesson. If I can teach them this, and if I can teach them how to build the kind of love that Marnie and I built together, then my life will have been a success. And Marnie's death will have achieved an even greater purpose.

But that's a process. That's going to take time. That will happen over months and years. And I have to remember that to feel good in my heart about still being here alive. "I can rejoin you, Marnie, when that job is complete. And I hope you will be really, really proud of me for doing it."

Children demand loving. A bond with nature is fundamentally a loving bond. Children and nature were and are my realities. In some ways, that makes my continued reason for being on this earth much more simple and straightforward. Loving is my continued reason for being.

I don't know what role children have played or play in your life. I don't know how much of this description of my relationship with my grandchildren is directly relevant to your life. But I do know that the need for loving is the fundamental lesson contained in that relationship. And I now understand that love is the fundamental reason for being for each of us. The need to love is the fundamental lesson of death.

Purpose and Direction

Each day I hurt. But each day my faith grows stronger. Each day my belief in Marnie's continued life, her continued conscious awareness, and the continued life of her soul grows a little stronger. And my belief in God and God's love grows along with it. I believe I've make a transition. I believe it has been Marnie's love and God's love that have carried me. They've helped me believe that there is a real world beyond our bodies, and that our love transcends this physical world and will keep us joined as one in the next world.

Having come to believe that, to feel that, and to share that, maybe that's my purpose in still being here on this earth. Maybe sharing that understanding with others is my new task in this world. I don't know for sure, but maybe so.

I know that my love for Marnie extends way beyond the physical. My love for her is intense and real. Even without getting anything back physically, it has not diminished. It has increased. Our love transcends everything.

God brought Marnie into my life. It was totally out of my control. God kept her with me when I didn't deserve it. God allowed us to build the exquisite love that came to fill my whole universe. Because of the living reality of Marnie's soul, that love was not terminated by Marnie's physical death. God is teaching me that love is eternal. It transcends death.

The love and oneness that Marnie and I shared was a reflection of God's love and oneness with us. Our continued love and oneness demonstrates the essence of what ultimately matters. Our love did not die with the death of Marnie's body. It will not die with the death of mine. Our love vibrates at a higher level now because of Marnie's physical death. It will reach its peak when we rejoin as one after mine.

One of my purposes now on this earth may simply be to say "Thank you!" to God in every way that I can for the ongoing (eternal) gift of love that He gave to me (in Marnie).

Still, each day I hurt. The hurt is real and intense. I weep with it. Each day I miss Marnie profoundly. Each day I feel sadness. But each day I talk with Marnie. And the more I talk with her, the better I feel. Each day I grow a little more impatient to move on beyond the hurt and find a way of living and loving that will make her really proud of me and fill her with the joyful knowledge that my love for her is bringing greater love to the rest of the world.

I have a deep-seated need to believe all of this. I have a deep-seated need to believe in God. Maybe it's a fundamental human need to believe, that comes from the very core of our being. Maybe without that belief we'd be lost. Maybe God put it there, so that we could find out who and what we really are.

"What do you think, Marnie? Am I on track? Is this my path back to you? Am I meant to be a spiritual teacher – at least for our grandchildren? Maybe your physical death was in part God's way of helping me find both my true nature and my fundamental purpose for still being here on this earth.

It's okay with me, as long as it leads me back into your arms. You are my home, Marnie. You are my heart. I love you. I can't wait to be rejoined with. I feel sad that I'm not yet fully rejoined with you and that our rejoining seems so far away. What I need to focus on though is not the rejoining, but the work that I need to complete to fulfill my purpose for being here on this earth. Then our rejoining will come.

You know I talk with you every day. You're my best friend. I have to talk with you. I have to have conversations with you. And the way that you can talk back to me is through nature, the shivers, and the insights that come to me when I'm discussing questions with you that really matter and when I really need your input. Something comes. A magical experience or a shiver or an insight comes. That's an answer. That makes it a dialogue, not just a fantasy monologue."

Whether it be a brother or a sister, a parent or a child, or a beloved spouse, when you talk with that person and ask that person questions, something will happen. You will feel it. Then you will have confirmation of the continued reality of your living, ongoing relationship.

I can't speak to the fundamental purpose of your specific, continued relationship with your beloved. But there is a purpose. And I am certain that that purpose will be fulfilled in loving. Your continued connection with your beloved is an act of your faith and love. The continued life of the soul of your beloved is a direct expression of God's love. Your beloved's continued relationship with you is a direct expression of the love they had and have for you.

With the physical death of your beloved, love itself becomes the focus. Love is the center, the essence of the real meaning of being. It is love that keeps your relationship alive. That is transformative. It is in bringing love to the very center, to the core of your being, that death becomes a blessing. The pain of loss, though profoundly intense, is ultimately temporary. The bond of love that you are actively forging, is eternal. And so will be the joy that comes with it.

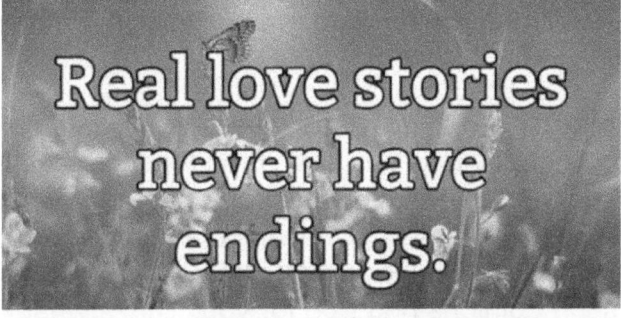

Chapter 25: Dealing with Helpful Suggestions – More Thoughts on God, Faith, and the Afterlife

On my journey of grieving and healing, I have been presented with, and in some cases virtually assaulted by opinions from people wanting to give me directions for healing. I listened to all the feedback I was given. I didn't want to make any mistakes. I didn't want to discount anything that someone told that might contain truth. I didn't want to do anything that might hinder my being able to reconnect with Marnie. Our reunion is the most important thing in the world to me.

Though it's hard to do, I had to remind myself that these were only opinions. Unless you have died, experienced the afterlife, and returned to earth, what you believe about the afterlife is opinion. All of the input I was given was opinion. What I'm writing here is my opinion. You have to look into your own heart to determine which opinions ring true for you. That's what I had to do.

What I write in this chapter about God, faith, and the afterlife are the conclusions that I came to in response to the opinions presented to me by others. I don't know how much you have had to deal with "helpful" suggestions and opinions. I hope that much of what I write about will be opinions that you haven't had to deal with. Maybe there are things that you've had to deal with that I've never had to face. Just remember that the only truth that really matters is the truth that you find in your own heart.

I was told that I had to move on beyond Marnie. I was told that I should sell her things and consider selling our house and moving into a smaller place, closer to our grandchildren. I was told that Marnie is finding her happiness now in Jesus. That she no longer needs me. I was told that I need to find my own happiness in a new relationship. I was told that Marnie is now in a state of universal oneness in which our personal relationship no longer matters to her. I was told that my continued focus on Marnie was limiting the quality of her experience in the afterlife. My continued focus on Marnie was causing her distress, not joy. The only thing I could do in this lifetime to make Marnie happy was to be happy myself and to move her into memory.

I was told much. I was told too much. And I really took in all the feedback I was given. I took it in far too deeply. I let it worry me. I let it distress me. I let it raise doubts about whether I was loving Marnie well.

But ultimately, I looked into my heart and came to conclusions about what felt true and right to me. I share these conclusions with you in this chapter. Though I hope that you will agree with my conclusions, I urge you to look into your own heart to determine what feels true and right to you. (And I really hope you haven't had to live through all the unhelpful "helpful" feedback that I was given. It does make you stronger though, when you can let it go. ☺)

I know that I have talked about this over and over again, but I think it's essential that I deal with it one last time. The most frequently repeated "helpful suggestion" that I knew I had to deal with was the repeated opinion that to heal from my grief I would ultimately have to let go of Marnie and move her into memory. That suggestion was repeated to me multiple times in multiple ways by multiple sources both subtly and blatantly.

It felt wrong. First of all, I knew I wasn't willing to do it. But the more I thought about it, the more I came to believe that it was only trusting in a loving God by living in faith that any of us ultimately find healing. And in that same faith and trust I could believe that I would achieve my ultimate goal of rejoining with Marnie. Here is a description of the process I went through to arrive at that conclusion:

As I was walking and talking with Marnie one night, I was thinking about how death just doesn't seem real to me. I simply couldn't imagine my dying. I couldn't imagine Marnie dying even as her body was clearly failing. Then it struck me – of course I can't imagine dying, death isn't real. Death is an illusion. Only the body dies -- the body which is a temporary vehicle designed to let us build our personal identity as the unique dimensions of God that are our real essences. The "I" does not die. Marnie's real essence did not die.

That's a pretty esoteric thought. And since I'm still living in my body, and I can't "know" the truth of it experientially, I have to believe with faith. But it rang true for me. It felt true. I have had numerous intuitive awarenesses in my life. I always discounted them (or had someone explain to me why I should discount them) even though they felt true. But they each turned out to be correct. To have listened to them, to have acted on them would have required faith. Belief in a truth that cannot be confirmed physically, in the moment, requires faith. Faith is neither blind, nor passive. Faith is an action. Faith is a choice. Faith is an intelligent decision based in trust. Faith is an act of intelligent trust in ourselves or in a friend that we believe in.

I can have faith that my friend will do what she says she will do. The deeper the friendship, the more solid the experiential base of that friendship, the more solid will be the faith. When Marnie was alive (physically) I had absolute faith in her.

When it comes to the issues of life, death, eternity, and the meaning of being, that friend can only be God. My act of faith now, though very difficult, particularly in the context of the pain of the physical loss of my best friend, is probably the most important action I can or will ever choose to take. It is through an active act of faith in God, in the reality of God, in the reality of God's love that my life continues to have its purpose, its center – my love for Marnie, my loving in the world for and with Marnie.

It's always going to be faith – no matter how much the signs in nature tell me that Marnie is watching over me (unless I have a profound transformative vision), it is always going to be faith that will be the key to the rest of my life. Faith is the key to continued meaning in my life.

These insights on death, trust, and faith felt significantly important. If I can trust that God is my loving friend and creator, then I can be sure that he ultimately wants joy and fulfillment for me. He wants the best for me. And He gave me Marnie. He kept me with Marnie. He protected us as we built our love and oneness together. He gave us love. He gave us our souls. Those gifts are eternal. Because of that I can know that both my continuing relationship with Marnie now, and my ultimate rejoining with her in the next life are an extension of His love for me and His will for us.

None of this involves moving Marnie into memory. It all involves keeping her and us alive now and always through an active act of faith, love, and trust.

The second conclusion that I came to had to do with the feedback I was given about Jesus being the only pathway to God, and ultimately, the only source of Marnie's fulfillment.

I sat one night amongst the trees in Highlands Hammock and talked with Marnie about my pathway to God through her. I said: "You and this wilderness, Marnie, are my church. You in this wilderness, Marnie, are my pathway to God. There is magnificence in this ancient forest, Marnie. Magnificence and profound stillness. I feel the presence of God here. It's humbling – the magnificence and magic. It's humbling in the presence of God. I never would or could have been here without you, Marnie.

I don't think God would criticize anyone's path to Him. I think God is much more understanding than those who have written to me and criticized my path to God through you. I think we each have to find our own way to God. It has to be through a genuine heart. You are my pathway to God. You fill my heart. You fill my soul. To feel you still being here, I need to believe in God. You are my pathway, and I don't think God judges or condemns me for that.

I don't believe that Jesus is the only pathway to God. He may be a real pathway, but I don't think he's the only one. And I don't think Jesus would condemn me or anyone for finding a different path to his Father.

God is all-knowing, He knew our commitment to one another. He knew the intensity of our love for one another. He knew that our love would not and could not end with the death of your body. He knew that I couldn't quit loving you. He knew that I couldn't quit feeling you, being aware of you, and carrying you in my heart and consciousness. He would have known that I would not move on from you.

He would know that you love me deeply. He would have known that you would choose to stay and watch over me. He would know that I need you, that I need you profoundly. God would know all of that. He would expect it and plan for it to be a real dimension of your heaven, and a central dimension of my pathway back to Him. It comes back to trusting in a loving God. It comes back to trusting in the wisdom of a loving God.

Faith does not have to come from the bible. Faith does not have to be based on Jesus. And faith need not be blind. Faith can grow from clear seeing and clear thinking. There is a sense of awe and wonder and magnificence in this ancient hammock forest. Faith can grow from awe and wonder. But clear thinking and awe and wonder need not be mutually exclusive paths. You can walk the trail of awe and wonder with reason and clear thinking.

Magnificence, awe, wonder, profound love – they all argue for the existence of God. And if you haven't had faith in God, it makes sense to think, to use your reason. And reason argues for the existence of God. And if both reason and awe and wonder argue for the existence of God, then it makes sense to work at building belief until true faith is achieved. True faith can come from a foundation of reason and magic intertwined with one another.

Reason, awe, wonder, and magnificence intertwined together bring me to God. And God brings me to you, darling. To you. I love you. I immerse myself in you. I am surrounded by you. I carry you."

"Intelligence need not negate belief and psychology need not negate spirituality." When I said these things there was a flash in the sky. I don't know what it was exactly, but it was an unmistakable, bright flash. That was a confirmation.

"I love you. There is nothing that I feel with greater depth, with greater intensity, or with greater certainly. For me, it is absolute truth. Our bond of oneness grows stronger every day. Our bond of oneness transcends the boundary between the physical and the spiritual realms. Our bond of oneness insures our joining in divine oneness for all eternity.

I have faith that God understands our connection and my path to Him through that connection. I trust that He approves. I trust that Jesus does too."

God knows you and your beloved as well as He knows Marnie and me. I believe that you can trust fully in His love and understanding to bring ultimate fulfillment to your continued relationship with your beloved as He has to ours. What it requires of you is an active act of faith.

A Personal God

In one of the books I read described "God consciousness" as being impersonal, meaning it is not tied to "me" or to my personal view of reality. It gave me the impression that God is an impersonal, albeit profound source of the power of creative consciousness. It talked about unity – about the oneness of all beings with and in God. It talked about a universal reality, not a personal reality.

I may be misinterpreting the words or the meaning intended in the book, but I find myself disagreeing with it. I find God to be totally personal. I view God as "universally personal". With God being both the source and the substance of our being, we are one with God. We are ultimately one with one another in and through God. It is a universally shared oneness. But it is a <u>uniquely personal</u> oneness for each of us. I believe that God is uniquely personal for me.

In the context of eternity, infinity, omnipotence, omniscience, creating the entire universe (or multiple universes) God is an overwhelming presence, seemingly far too large and all-encompassing to be personal. But we are each a unique dimension of God because of the life he gave us from His essence.

In God everything is oneness. He encompasses everything. Yet we are each unique persons within that oneness because of the unique lives and the unique set of experiences that He allowed us to have while living on this earth. Our unique lives, our unique experiences have woven the fabric of our unique identities. God knows and sees that uniqueness. God knows us and loves us personally within the context of his unfathomable power and his absolute love for all of us in oneness because **we are each a unique part of Him**. Therefore, I believe there is a unique part of God for each of us to relate to personally.

This stuff is overwhelming to talk about. I feel like I may be talking far above my level of intelligence and understanding. In so many ways, God is absolutely incomprehensible to me. But within the context of that incomprehensibility, a God who knows me personally and to whom I can relate personally, makes sense to me.

We are individual human beings who we are ultimately one with God. We are not separate from Him. We could not exist separately from him. Individual and one, in and through God -- the one, absolute, eternal being. It's pretty overwhelming thinking that God knows each of us personally. It's especially overwhelming considering that there are billions of human beings who each have a unique, individual, eternal soul shaped from a myriad of unique experiences and real loves in what amounts to little more than a speck of time in eternity. And those souls exist in the context of countless galaxies and multiple universes.

Yet we are each one with God. He is the source and substance of the being of each of us. We each have a personal relationship with God because each of us was created by Him as a unique dimension of Him. As unique parts of God Himself, He has to know us uniquely – individually.

It's overwhelming. God is overwhelming. Infinity is overwhelming. But it is only in the context of an infinite God that life makes sense. It is only in relationship with a personal God that the soul makes sense.

So I have come to believe that there is a real, personal, loving part of God that is available to me and responds to me personally as my parent – as the personal (yet infinite) source of my being. And as my parent, as the source and substance of my reality, God loves me intensely and wants the absolute best for me. As my parent (my creator) God would want only love, joy, and fulfillment for me. And God gave me Marnie....

My connection to Marnie is absolutely, uniquely, and intensely personal. Your connection with your beloved is absolutely, uniquely, and intensely personal. We are each one with God. We are each one with one another in and through God. But because of the bonds of love that we built in our physical lifetimes together, the bond that we each share with our beloved differs from the bond that we share with all the rest of creation because of our unique "personalities". The unique "identities" that we developed in the course of living and loving one another in our physical lives together made our souls eternal mates.

I say to Marnie, "You and I are one in love, Marnie. You and I are one in God. You are my soul's mate."

I can absolutely love everyone. I believe I will throughout eternity. But Marnie is my soul's mate. That does not make her more special than others in God's eyes, but it gives her a special kind of connection with me that we will carry forward with us throughout eternity.

I believe that you have a special connection with your beloved. You will carry that bond as an inherent part of your soul based on the love that you lived and shared in your lifetime.

Another concern that I had to face was the suggestion that my needing to maintain a connection with Marnie, that my calling out to her in the afterlife when I hurt deeply, could be truly "perturbing" even hurtful to her. It could keep her from moving forward to the new experiences that await her in the afterlife.

This suggestion troubled me deeply. In my grieving I had looked over and over again at all the ways I had "failed" Marnie in our physical lifetime together. The thought that I might be failing her in her afterlife was devastating. I had to look at that possibility deeply and repeatedly. Finally I was able state unequivocally: "I disagree!" I offer you the thoughts that led me to my conclusion.

My love for Marnie is real and intense. In the bond of loving oneness that Marnie and I built together, we became inseparable on a human level, and we were and are one in and through God. We are individual and one simultaneously.

I believe that with Marnie's death, she moved to a whole new spiritual level of being. I believe that in the spiritual realm where she exists now, she has a new-found connection with, awareness of, and oneness with God that brings her absolute love, joy, peace, understanding, and fulfillment. I believe that in living now in conscious oneness with God, Marnie is in a state of profound, lasting ecstasy.

But I believe that I am a part of that ecstasy. God saw, knew, and understood the bond of love and oneness that Marnie and I built with one another in our shared physical lifetime. Our love for one another became a reflection of His love and oneness with each of us. My love for Marnie is a reflection of and an extension of God's love for Marnie.

In this, because of this, I believe that I am a real, central part of Marnie's heaven. I believe that God, in His personal knowledge of us and love for us, left room for me to be a part of Marnie's fulfillment.

I know that Marnie feels the profound intensity of the love that I have for her. The depth and intensity of that love now, in our spiritual connection, transcends even the love that we had for one another in our physical lives together. Our love now participates even more fully in divine love. And I offer all the loving that I do now as a gift of love to Marnie. I offer all the beauty, majesty, and magic that I see in this magnificent natural world as a gift of love to her. It's all loving.

I don't believe that love can be a limiting factor in the afterlife, in any life. Love can only be fulfilling.

And I believe that Marnie can focus on me and be aware of me when I need her without it limiting her ability to experience new realities, new universes, and new relationships in the afterlife. What I (continue) to share with her in my physical life is infinitesimal in terms of time in the context of eternity. And Marnie is no longer limited by time or place as a spiritual being in her afterlife. I believe that she can travel instantaneously, at the speed of thought. And in the context of eternity she can move back and forward in time, because there is no time.

So if my focus is purely on loving her and wishing her absolute joy and fulfillment (even in sharing my sadness), then there can be nothing limiting or troublesome about my wanting or needing to feel the real presence of her soul here with me as I struggle live out the remainder of my physical life without her physical presence here with me.

These insights came to me in the context of talking with God and asking for his help in my wanting/needing to feel that I was bringing only good to Marnie in her afterlife – even in my neediness. I asked directly for his help. Then these thoughts came. I felt a shiver. I felt a sense of joy, of relief, and being uplifted. I thanked God. And I thanked Marnie for choosing me – for loving me.

I don't believe that needing or wanting to feel connected to your beloved, or needing to feel their loving presence is in any way limiting or perturbing in their experience of the afterlife. I believe it is an act of love. Love brings fulfillment, not limitation.

And I believe that the times I express my deep love for Marnie still bring her joy. I don't think you can hear heart-felt expressions of profound love from your beloved and not be bathed in real joy. There is no one in the world more important to me than Marnie. My heart-felt love for her is still the most intense feeling I have in my life. And I hope and believe that it is so for her as well.

I don't think that you can be offered the gifts of loving or relishing in the beauty and magic of nature without receiving those gifts and having them bring you joy. Our relationship was the very center of my being. I was bonded to Marnie in absolute love and oneness. That hasn't changed on the level of our essential being with the death of her body. Marnie is still the very center of my being. We are still one in love. Our souls are still one in love.

Physical death cannot touch that. So as awareness of Marnie still permeates the very core of my life on this plane of being, in our love and oneness, awareness of me must still permeate the core of her new life on Marnie's plane of being. Neither the death of the body nor existence on different planes of reality can sever our love and oneness. It cannot sever the oneness of our souls.

"I love you Marnie. You may be in a very different realm, but for me, here, now, my love for you, my oneness with you and my commitment to you are the most profound dimensions of my life. Loving you and loving with you continues to be my purpose for being."

As I said earlier in this chapter, one of the reasons that it's been so hard for me to address any of these questions is that God is so utterly beyond my comprehension. I can't conceive of "infinite". On some level (in spite of my explanation) I have no conception of how something so massively powerful, something that's capable of creating the entire universe and all the beings within it – of everything – how something so massive and all-encompassing could have a personal awareness of me or could care for me personally. It's beyond my ability to conceive. But, when I think it through, it makes sense. So I work on believing. I choose to trust.

Though my Christian friends are significantly disappointed in my level of belief in Jesus, I can say to them that perhaps my difficulty with the infinite is one of the reasons God sent Jesus into this world and why Jesus resonates with so many.

Jesus was a person. Jesus had personal relationships. Jesus was a dimension of God (as I am a dimension of God, as Marnie is a dimension of God, as you are a dimension of God). And Jesus modeled a personal relationship with God – an absolutely real, personal relationship. So if Jesus is a model for us, a personal relationship with God, the infinite and almighty God, seems real and plausible.

I've had other thoughts in response to the questions that were raised about how I'm choosing to live my life with Marnie now after the death of her physical body. I'd like to share those with you. I hope they will reinforce your belief in the ongoing life of your beloved and in the living reality of your relationship with your beloved.

The first thought was about how much Marnie and I loved and love our children and grandchildren. God is our creator, our parent. As our loving creator and parent, God would love us the way we love our children and grandchildren. God would never will the eternal death of His beautiful daughter, just as we would never will the death of our children or grandchildren. And as we would never wish sadness for our children or grandchildren, God would never wish (or allow) profound, eternal sadness for his son, by taking away his beloved daughter -- by taking Marnie permanently away from me. Because of that, I can know, I can believe that Marnie is here. She is real. She is alive. She is with me.

I said to Marnie directly, "We are each dimensions of God. God is our essence. We are one in love, and one in God. God is not something separate from us. You are not something separate from me, Marnie. I love you. In our love, you and I are one. You and I and God are one. You and I in our love, are one with God.

We are absolutely one in our bond of love. We are still connected. You are still one with me here, always. I could never, ever not be there for you. For the last forty plus years that has been true, and it certainly is true now. And so it makes sense that you will always be there for me too – especially when you are beyond the limits of this human body. We are one darling. I love you.

And beyond that, as you are living in some other dimension now, that I simply don't know, I think that many of your limits are gone. So I feel like I can call out to you and talk to you at any moment. And since you are beyond time, even if you are somewhere else, with someone else, or even in some other universe, it's like you are receiving a text. That message is there, and you will respond to it. We will have this sharing talk in your time – beyond time. And since you are part of eternity, you are no longer on my clock. You will be there for me, in what is for me, the present moment."

The final thought that I'd like to share with you in thinking about God, faith, and the afterlife is partly a question. I wondered, "Is another reason why hurt is implicit in human life because, in order to live our human lives, we had to experience a level of separation from God. It is through that separation in coming into this physical world that we get to develop our individual identities and the self-concepts that we carry forward with us throughout eternity. But developing that individuality required a separation that was implicitly painful.

And perhaps the higher level of vibration that the soul experiences with physical death comes from reconnection with God. It is in and through that reconnection that deepened love, joy, and fulfillment come to the soul. But that deepened connection with God involves separation again – physical separation from those left behind. This implicitly results in a level of pain for each of us who lose that physical connection with our beloved.

Pain and fulfillment are, on some level, inextricably bound together. It is in going through the pain of separation that we ultimately achieve the fulfillment of eternal oneness. It is in going through the pain of separation that we gain the perspective on how profoundly we were (and I believe will be) blessed by the physical presence of our beloved.

I've written much about Marnie and me in this chapter. I tried to answer the questions that were raised about the way I was choosing to live my life and maintain my relationship with Marnie. In doing so I hope I've brought increased confidence to you in the wisdom of choosing to maintain your relationship with your beloved. I believe that all the conclusions that I've come to about, God, faith, and the afterlife apply directly to your relationship with your beloved.

In presenting these ideas, I wrote almost exclusively about my relationship with Marnie. But I believe sincerely, that the fundamental truths about eternal connection reflected in our love, are absolutely true for your love with your beloved as well.

I'd like to share with you on last experience that for me brought home the reality of God and the reality of Marnie's eternal soul. The confirmation of that reality came to me through the most magnificent morning I have ever experienced.

I went out on my morning "Marnie walk". I began wondering if I'd be able to talk about God and about the reality of Marnie's soul when I went to see my nephew that afternoon. I hadn't seen him in over two years and he really knew nothing about the process of grieving I'd been going through.

I was wondering if I could talk to him comfortably about God and Marnie's soul and feel genuine in doing it. I'd never talked with him about those things and I didn't know what his beliefs were. Immediately upon thinking these things, I saw a red shouldered hawk on my left, standing in a tree. He stood motionless, looking at me. We stared at each other. He never moved. As I finally moved on, when I looked back, he was gone.

I went on to a lagoon where I'd always see birds. This time, however, was unlike anything I have ever experienced. There were at least a hundred great egrets and more than a dozen great blue herons in the trees overlooking the edge of the lagoon. Black vultures and the turkey vultures flew over me. Storks began flying in. Caspian terns were fishing. An osprey flew over me with a fish in his talons while another dove in front of me. Glossy ibises, white ibises, and more storks began flying in. Soon dozens more ibises flew directly over me. A king fisher flew across the pond in front of me calling. A group of cormorants flew over the pond. The birds just kept coming and coming and coming. The vultures flew directly in front of me, so close that I could almost touch them.

And from behind me, I heard the red shouldered hawk calling. When I turned toward the sound I saw, there, at the top of broken palm tree, a pair of red shouldered hawks feeding together.

It was a scene of such magnificence that it was virtually impossible to doubt the reality of God. I felt humbled. It felt like a precious gift to be sharing with Marnie, my beloved. I wondered if she had a part in bringing this to me, or if I was giving it to her. I stood for a long time just watching, feeling awed by the presence, by the magnificence. There was a sliver of a moon over the pond and the sun began rising to my left. It was brilliant. It was beautiful.

And as I finally turned and began to walk back, I saw the red shouldered hawk land in its nest in a nearby palm tree. And a pileated wood pecker landed beside me calling and calling and calling.

I couldn't imagine a scene of greater magnificence. I couldn't imagine a scene that more dramatically demonstrated the presence of God. I hoped with all my heart that I was giving this as a gift to Marnie.

It was a dramatic demonstration for me that I could talk to my nephew about God and the presence of Marnie's living soul with genuine sincerity.

Chapter 26: On Giving to Your Beloved in the Afterlife

As I sat down to write one morning, I said to Marnie, "You are alive Marnie Winn. You are happy. You are healthy. You are absolutely gorgeous. You love me, and I sure as hell love you. We are one." The moment I said that, a red shouldered hawk called outside the window. I hadn't heard a red shouldered hawk for days. I hadn't heard one at all before in the park where I was staying.

"I don't think God would put us on this earth and allow us to learn lessons for no purpose. And I have learned so much since your body died, Marnie. Your physical death has given me a whole new perspective on love, commitment, and involvement. I see so many things that I wish I had done differently. They are lessons I have learned. And I don't think God would let me learn those lessons and then say, 'Tough. Too bad. You learned your lessons too late.' We have something more coming. And in that future together, I will be traveling with real lessons learned.

And I've been thinking about the future, sweetie. If you're in eternity, is it all an eternal now? Can you move from place to place instantaneously, simultaneously? Can we share this world again when I join you? Can we? Eternity is so baffling to me."

Can you continue to give to your loved one in the afterlife, after the death of their body? I believe the answer to that question is yes. I want to look closely at that together in this chapter. I believe that a continued, two-way loving relationship between you and your beloved absolutely makes sense.

They have a living soul. I believe they can hear you. I believe they can see you. I believe they can feel your love for them. And they love you. So it's not too late to share now. It's not too late to give to them now.

And I believe it's not even too late to say what you wished you had said or to share with them what you wish you had done differently when they were physically alive. Your beloved will hear. It is too late to do things differently in this lifetime, but sharing what you wish you had said or done and what you would like to do will bring joy to your beloved, now. And I believe it will increase the likelihood of your being able to do those things together in reality in the next lifetime.

To not share is to carry regret. Regret is poisonous. It lives only in hindsight. But to regret is natural. So it is in transforming regret into a vision of what and how you will share in the life to come (together), that regret is transformed into a loving gift. Share your vision now as a loving gift. Live the vision together in your next chapter of eternity.

That's what I sincerely believe. However, my getting to this place of belief was a process that was not without its struggles. In this chapter, I hope to fully share this process with you. I hope that by sharing it and sharing my struggles, you might be able to avoid having to go through those struggles for yourself.

To get to my place of belief, I began with questions:

Can I actively and directly love Marnie **now** in a way that she can feel? Can I see things for her (when I go out and search for beauty and magic in nature)? Can I say things to her that will touch her heart or make her smile or laugh? Can I feel things for her and express my feelings for her actively now in a way that directly touches her heart and brings her joy. Can I love in this world in a way that will bring her joy-- by loving the children for instance? Can I love her actively and directly in a way that she can feel now?

I don't have to get anything back from Marnie (though I would certainly like it). But if I can believe that I am still actively giving to her, then my world is enriched greatly. Then I can believe that I am a real, active part of her heaven.

But how can I speak with certainty about things I have never experienced, about a world I've never lived in? How can I know what she sees, what she hears, what she feels? How do I write about this as I'm trying to make my way through this world? Everything for me has been a jumbled mixture of sadness, fear, doubt, hope, blossoming faith, and desire to please Marnie -- a jumble of emotion. Sometimes I'm strong and clear, and sometimes I'm just lost and searching.

So how can I know what's real on the "other side"? How can I know what Marnie "sees" on the other side? I'm still on this side. But I know I want to still be able to give to Marnie -- now. I said to Marnie, "I don't think anybody really knows what the world is like for you, now, Marnie. So I'm going to keep treating you like my best friend. You are my best friend. You talk to your best friend. You share with your best friend. You give everything you can to your best friend. The death of your body shouldn't stop that. In either direction."

A Talk with Marnie

I sat on a bench at Highlands Hammock State Park late one night and talked to Marnie about my feelings and my desire to be able to still give to her.

"I want to be part of your heaven, Marnie. I want to be a gift of joy that brings you fulfillment. I wish I could be more eloquent, but I love you with all my heart and soul. I thank you profoundly for all the love that you gave me and all the beauty you brought to my life. I want to live every day, from this day on, as a gift of love for you, Marnie. They may not always be great gifts, but every day that I live, I will live for you, as a gift of love for you. I will live for you, with you, in you, and through you. We are one. I will live on as us together.

I want to believe that you can truly feel the depth and intensity of my love. I want to believe that you are with me, that you're seeing with my eyes, that you're hearing with my ears, that you're feeling with my feelings (even my terror in the dark). If those things are true, then I am still bringing joy to your life. Then our living connection truly is a part of your heaven.

See through my eyes, darling. See through my eyes. Hear with my ears, darling. Hear with my ears. Feel my heart with your heart, sweetheart. Feel me with your heart. I love you. I hope I make your heart swell to overflowing.

It feels so much better to believe that I am giving you love, beauty, and magic in exchange for what you are giving me in strength and peace now, and what you gave me in love and fulfillment throughout our life together. It feels so much better to believe that my love truly is a central part of your joy and fulfillment in the afterlife – that you feel my love now.

My ability to believe these things comes back to my faith in God. God would know how profoundly I would need and love you after the death of your body. God would know that in our love and oneness, you too would feel that need. God would know that you would want to stay with me to take care of me. God would know that you'd want to watch over me. God would design your continued, active involvement in my life to be a part of your ultimate fulfillment in your afterlife.

Believing in an all-knowing, all-understanding, all-loving God is the key to believing that your soul is here with me and that our love continues to be real and alive -- that our active, two-way love is indeed a central dimension of your heaven.

So I affirm that you are here, hearing my words now. You're seeing what I see. You're feeling the profound depth of love that I have for you. I am bringing you joy now, in sharing my love, just as you're bringing me the strength to survive your body's dying. We're still loving one another. God knows it. God knew it would be true. Perhaps this is another unique way that we were meant to bring more love to the world and to one another. It's another lesson we can teach our children and grandchildren and everyone we can touch about loving, about not giving up, about not letting go of your commitment to one another, and about God.

I love you Marnie. Right now. Right here. And I hope you are feeling it intensely, (and hearing the armadillo that's scaring me in the dark from my left side. I hope that makes you laugh, here, now too.) I hope you are bubbling over with joy, in your heaven, from our love, right now."

The next morning I wrote, "I'm outside sitting by a pond, a mile back in the wilderness. There is absolute silence around me -- well except for the crickets. It seems like absolute silence when the loudest thing is crickets. They say there are supposed to be alligators here. Maybe I should be frightened. But I'd happily be eaten by an alligator and come back to you darling. I hope that gives you a sarcastic smile. I really do hope I bring you joy, now."

And the next day I wrote, "I love you girl, I walk with you. I love you girl, I look with you. I love you girl, I see with you. I love you girl, I hear with you. Every morning I walk with you. I walk hand in hand with you (in my heart), and I feel our love. That's how it is in my mind's eye. I pray that's how it is for you.

I hear the squirrels and the little birds. I see the turtles and the armadillos. I hear the silence. I hear the far off sounds of a train in the distance. Every morning is beautiful, no matter where we are. Every morning is magic. I love you Marnie. I wrap myself around you in my mind and heart as I see the branches of the trees in front of me wrapped around one another. I carry you forward with me into our new life together, until I can rejoin you one more time – for all eternity, in absolute oneness. I love you girl."

I continued wondering about my impact on Marnie in the afterlife as I walked to the beach a few days later. I felt the return of some doubt and fears about continuing to reach out to Marnie and talk to her. I recorded this conversation (with Marnie) on my phone as I walked: "I'm walking to the beach. I've been talking with you the whole way, Marnie. I know I've had nothing spectacular to say. Nothing magical or magnificent. Just talking my thoughts. Talking my observations. Just sharing with you and wondering about things. Seeing things out here. (Wishing I had noticed them sooner. Wishing I had pointed things out to you on our previous trips here when you were physically alive.)

And I wonder, Is it OK? Is it OK that I'm pointing things out now? That I'm seeing things now? That I'm sharing them with you now? Is this still real? Does this make your afterlife richer?

I have a hard time when some 'experts' say I should be letting go of you, moving you into memory. Or when some suggest that I am limiting you from more important things in your afterlife by calling you to be with me, to watch over me, and listen to me. So I question, 'am I somehow failing by sharing these observations with you now? Am I failing by not sharing these things with some other living' person, some physically alive person instead of you?

You're on another plane. You're in an afterlife. I don't know what fills your world. But I certainly don't want to be a limiting factor for you in any way. I want to add to your world. I want to bring joy to it. I want you to feel like your best friend is here talking with you. And I want you to experience a peaceful feeling in that, so that I'm adding peace to your world. But if you're already with God and you're already feeling fulfilled and joyous, and peaceful, and loved, then I don't know if I really have much to offer. I just don't know. So I question what I'm doing. I feel bad about it.

I already feel bad about all the ways I wish I had done a better job of loving you in your physical life. I certainly don't want to somehow be diminishing the quality of your afterlife. It's all very difficult. But you were and are my best friend, and I love you. I hope I'm bringing you good things by continuing to love you, by continuing our relationship. That is certainly what I want to do.

Is it somehow a failing to be talking with you? I like talking with you. You're my best friend. I not only deeply loved you, I liked you. I liked being around you. I liked everything about you. And so talking like this is the same kind of talking we would do if we were walking hand in hand before your body died. Are we still walking together?

Is it OK? I want it to be OK. I don't want to feel like I'm limiting you in any way. There is so little that I know with certainty anymore in this life. But I do know that I love you, darling. I want it to be OK"

I realized after my talk with Marnie that I had to turn back to God for it to feel OK. It is in God that I find peace and certainty. I remind myself that an all-knowing, all-loving God would indeed know the reality of the bond between Marnie and me. He would include it in His plans for our fulfillment. And our fulfillment would absolutely be His will for us as His children.

    I shared these thoughts and my concerns in a letter to my son, Ben. His response reinforced the wisdom of my trusting in God. Here is a part of his reply:

    Hey Pops,

    I think Marnie is now more aware of all the beauty and wonder in the world than we can ever comprehend, but the fact that you are noticing those things and sharing them with her absolutely brings her joy. Her happiness is directly tied to your happiness, so the more that you can experience and appreciate the more she is with you in that process....

    Yes, Marnie is with God. She is definitely joyous and peaceful, but that absolutely doesn't mean your love and friendship mean any less to her (they actually mean more). The comparison I like to make is that I feel whole inside because I had the love and support of you and Marnie growing up.

    Being whole inside doesn't mean I can't grow or have my life improved by sharing love with Nellie. It is simply a foundation upon which I can now build more love and more happiness. It is similar with Marnie and her continued love and partnership with you; even though she is with God and feeling joyous and peaceful with Him, the more you can experience and love in your life, the more happiness and fulfillment she gets to share with you....

When you hear people say "let go and move on", try to take it as meaning: "Let go of any regrets, any feelings of doubt. Let go of sadness. Let go of wishing you had done more or been better when Marnie was physically with you. Know that she understands you weren't perfect but loves you for who you really are." Focus on finding as much wonder and beauty and joy in this life as possible, so that she can share in that until you are one, together again....

When I got back home I experienced a concrete example of giving to Marnie (in the afterlife) and its effect on her. I had stopped to pull some knapweed on my morning walk. Marnie would always pull knapweed. It meant a lot to her to try and keep it under control, to keep it from spreading. So I was pulling the knapweed for Marnie.

And the thought came to me that I wasn't just honoring her memory, my memory of her doing that. I was doing it as a gift for her because I think she's watching over me and would appreciate that. And when I said that out loud, I felt a shiver go down and through me. "Thank you for the shiver sweetheart."

Conclusions

So for myself, I've come to the conclusion that I can actively love Marnie in this physical lifetime even while her soul lives in a different dimension. Actively loving Marnie is a profound need for me. I feel that need deep in my heart and soul. I want to give her everything I can give right now. Loving Marnie now gives my life a feeling of purpose and direction. It brings beauty, magic, and majesty into my life. It makes me a more loving human being.

It is in trusting that God would recognize my need and desire to love and give to Marnie still, and believing that God is loving and wants us to be happy that makes being able to give to Marnie in the afterlife make real sense. Trust in an all-loving God is the key to my belief that my active, loving connection with Marnie is still real now, even as we live on different planes of reality. It keeps coming back to an all-knowing, all-loving God. It keeps coming back to faith.

I believe that everything I had to say about the living connection between Marnie and me is true for you and your beloved. Your relationship is unique, but your relationship is every bit as real as ours. And it is every bit as important to God. So I believe that not only can you give to your beloved now, but that doing it is essential to keeping your love fully alive.

I believe that you can trust that God knows and understands you and your relationship with your beloved, and that God would plan for the continued expression of your love to be a part of the fulfillment for your beloved in the afterlife. So in my view, get on with actively loving now.

As to the thinking of those who suggest that you must ultimately move your relationship with your beloved from presence to memory, I suggest that you consider this. Things that you allow to move into memory gradually weaken and fade. Our pets, who were really important to Marnie and me are now just memories. Now, years after they have died, I only think about them once in a while.

When I realized this, I said to Marnie, "I'm not allowing you to move into memory. Our relationship is real. Our relationship is alive. Our relationship is active. I have a responsibility on my end to keep it active. That keeps you alive for me, in my heart and soul and mind, now. It makes my life feel more worth living. You are my center. Loving you and loving with you is my purpose. Letting you fade into memory doesn't make sense."

I urge you to consider those sentiments and see if they fit for you as well.

One other thing that I've had to deal with in working at actively giving to Marnie now, in the afterlife, is that I spend a lot of time alone thinking about her and our relationship now. I share all my questions and doubts and fears with her. I do that out loud. And I feel much more comfortable talking out loud to a spiritual presence alone. So people question what appears to them as my silence and isolation. And it's hard having "living" people question me about the time I'm spending alone with someone who is not physically present.

But Marnie is the most important person in the world to me, and she is no longer physically present. I believe in my heart that she is spiritually present. I believe that her soul is real. I believe that her soul is alive, conscious, aware, self-aware, loving, and real. And because of those beliefs, talking to that soul is truly talking to my best friend. I have to do that. And that happens when I'm alone with Marnie, sharing my thoughts.

If Marnie were here physically, very few would question the amount of time that we spend together. No one would question the talking that we do together, or the thinking that we do together, or the questioning, the wondering, the searching, the dreaming, and the hoping that we do together.

Yet all of that is still real for me now. I am sharing that with Marnie's living, loving soul. It continues to give my life meaning, purpose, and direction. But because her physical body is gone, my way of communicating with her soul is through my mind. And I share those thoughts best out loud, alone with Marnie.

So I do in fact spend a lot of time in my mind, thinking. I do in fact spend a lot of time alone. That is an accurate observation, but it is inaccurate to judge that as any kind of deficiency or disturbance. You have to have lost your beloved to understand.

If you choose to follow my path you will be questioned. The questioning is valid. Any kind of negative judgement, however, is off track. It is a reflection of someone who doesn't understand. Trust your heart.

The path that I have chosen to follow can get lonely though. I wrote these words to Marnie.

"I'm lonely, Marnie. The person I really want to be with is you. But to feel fully connected with you I need to be able to focus solely on you. So I chose to be alone to stay connected. It's one of those contradictions that are so omni-present in my life since your physical death.

When we were married, we each took the middle name, Cantkiya – 'to make one one's heart'. I grew into that name. I took you more and more deeply into my heart. You became my heart. You are my heart. When your body died, my heart died with it. In finding my way to your soul, I have found my way back to my heart. In loving you, in giving you all the love I have to give, in giving you all the love there is in my heart, my heart is filled. I have more love to give to everyone one else in this world because I give all my love to you. It's another one of those contradictions. It's a beautiful contradiction."

When I have my conversations with Marnie, I find that things haven't really changed much. I still talk to her in the same way I talked to her when she was here in her physical body. I still have the same issues in my life that I had when she was physically here. I still struggle with the same things. The world is really very similar.

What has changed is that my love for Marnie has intensified. It has deepened. It is significantly stronger. An insight that I had was, that my love is stronger because Marnie's body is not here in this physical world. So my focus is not nearly as much on this physical world as it used to be. My focus is now on the spiritual world where Marnie lives. And in the spiritual world, love is the only thing that matters. And since that is my focus, my love is deepened. And we remain a perfect reflection of one another.

My love for Marnie was always there, but I could get so lost in the demands of physical, material world. Now, the physical world just isn't significant to me, not the way that it was. Now I deeply need to stay connected with Marnie's soul. And that's a spiritual focus. And that's where love lives.

Each of you has a special bond with your beloved, just as Marnie and I have. It is no less real. Your bond is eternal. So is your love. You can know that. You can be confident in it. Trust it. And you can act on it. Now. In this lifetime. In and through your bond of love, you can give and share now. And in doing that in this lifetime, the level of your joy upon rejoining in the next lifetime will be magnified immeasurably.

In your relationship, nothing essential has changed. You still can communicate with your beloved the way you always communicated. The things that were important are still important. They will always be important. You've lost the body of your beloved, but they've gained immeasurable blessings that we can't fully comprehend. There is for them a far greater depth, a far greater ability to be here in this world with you while living in their new world. They can be with you now. You can share now. Share what you're feeling with them, now. Share in the way that you've always shared together.

For Marnie and me, we were husband and wife. Our sharing was intense. If the relationship between you and your beloved was one between parent and child or brother and sister, you had your own unique ways of communicating. They are still real. Don't cut them off.

I said to Marnie, "I'm going to offer you the world on my journey of healing every day – sharing what I see, sharing what I feel, sharing what's happening in my heart, sharing what's happening in my mind; sharing my transformation from fear, and sadness, and doubt, into a joyful new reality, into a future that I don't yet quite see, but that I hope is waiting out there for me, with you, in us and through us.

I have so much hope, Marnie. I want to travel every inch of this magnificent, natural world and experience it all here, now, in love. It certainly would be beautiful if we could do that together in the next life. But most of all, I just want to be in your arms. I just want to kiss you. I would like that to be real in our eternity. I pray to God every night that it be real. I miss you. I so look forward to rejoining you."

Chapter 27: Soul Mate -- My Soul's Mate

Only Once in your Life

Only once in your life, I truly believe, you find someone who can completely turn your world around. You tell them things that you've never shared with another soul and they absorb everything you say and actually want to hear more. You share hopes for the future, dreams that will never come true, goals that were never achieved and the many disappointments life has thrown at you.

When something wonderful happens, you can't wait to tell them about it, knowing they will share in your excitement. They are not embarrassed to cry with you when you are hurting or laugh with you when you make a fool of yourself. Never do they hurt your feelings or make you feel like you are not good enough, but rather they build you up and show you the things about yourself that make you special and even beautiful.

There is never any pressure, jealousy or competition but only a quiet calmness when they are around. You can be yourself and not worry about what they will think of you because they love you for who you are.

The things that seem insignificant to most people such as a note, song or walk become invaluable treasures kept safe in your heart to cherish forever. Memories of your childhood come back and are so clear and vivid it's like being young again. Colours seem brighter and more brilliant. Laughter seems part of daily life where before it was infrequent or didn't exist at all. A phone call or two during the day helps to get you through a long day's work and always brings a smile to your face.

In their presence, there's no need for continuous conversation, but you find you're quite content in just having them nearby. Things that never interested you before become fascinating because you know they are important to this person who is so special to you. You think of this person on every occasion and in everything you do.

Simple things bring them to mind like a pale blue sky, gentle wind or even a storm cloud on the horizon. You open your heart knowing that there's a chance it may be broken one day and in opening your heart, you experience a love and joy that you never dreamed possible. You find that being vulnerable is the only way to allow your heart to feel true pleasure that's so real it scares you.

You find strength in knowing you have a true friend and possibly a soul mate who will remain loyal to the end. Life seems completely different, exciting and worthwhile. Your only hope and security is in knowing that they are a part of your life

Bob Marley

    This chapter applies most directly to those of you who have lost your spouse.

    When I was younger, "soul mate" was a romantic term. It was a way of saying, "I absolutely love you. You are the one for me." It means so much more to me now. Soul mate still means "you are the perfect match for me. We are a perfect reflection of one another. We are truly one together, one in and with one another." But I now say to Marnie (every day), "You are my <u>soul's</u> mate." We are one together for all eternity. All eternity. Not just this lifetime. It's an absolute commitment. It's a vow to both Marnie and God. For me, it is inviolable.

If you have lost your spouse and you too are choosing to keep your relationship with your beloved fully alive rather than moving on to a new relationship, then I believe that everything I write here is true for you. As I speak to and of Marnie, please hear the name of your beloved in your mind and heart....

There are so many times, mornings especially, when I feel so profoundly sad. In one of my times of sadness, I wrote these words to Marnie:

"My life doesn't feel as rich and full without you here physically, Marnie. I need to be connected with you, to stay connected with you to feel like life is still worth living. Our connection, our bond is profound. It joins us with the divine. We had to nurture our bond. We had to struggle through such a myriad of difficulties to deepen our bond and make it unbreakable.

Our connection grew so deep that I couldn't possibly let the death of your body take you away from me. I couldn't let it separate us. And in spite of the times when I miss you so much that I don't know if I can keep on living, I believe it has not. I believe that the death of your body cannot separate us.

We are one in love. We are one in love in our souls. We created that soul-level oneness through our loving relationship in our physical lifetime together. But we are also one in God through our fundamental spiritual being. In both of those dimensions our souls are one. We truly are soul mates.

Every day I thank God for bringing you into my life, Marnie. Every day I thank Him for keeping you in my life. Every day I thank Him for protecting us, for watching over us, and taking care of us while we built our bond of love and oneness. There has been so much that is so far beyond the possibility of simple coincidence in our lives that I now believe that our souls chose one another in the very beginning. Somehow, our souls knew one another. Somehow, our souls knew, 'This is the one.' Since our essential being transcends our physical bodies, then perhaps our essential being existed prior to the birth of our physical bodies. And in our essential being we had the capability, the intelligence to know, 'This is the one'.

This has been a whole new way of thinking for me. It has evolved from coming to believe that there is a divine level of being that is ultimate reality. Within the context of divine, spiritual reality, our soul level connection, from the very beginning seems entirely possible. And now, our soul level connection beyond physical death seems absolutely real.

On some very fundamental level, we lived a life that was meant to be. We made the choices that our souls demanded. Whenever either of us tried to move out of harmony with our soul-level connection, our souls said, 'No!' and blocked that action from happening so that we could continue to grow into who and how we were meant to be, together.

Our souls were mates waiting for us to come to realize that; waiting for us to declare (beyond doubt), 'You are my soul's mate'.

I now make that declaration to you without hesitation, without reservation, in the presence of God. It is a vow. 'You are my forever wife. I am your forever husband. You are my soul's mate.' In living that, I will find my heaven."

We are spiritual beings, temporarily inhabiting physical bodies. Our physical bodies allow us to make the choices that shape our self-concepts. They allow us to build the bonds of love that ultimately define the fundamental core of our self-concepts and link it inseparably to our spiritual reality. These bonds of love define the uniqueness of each of us in our oneness with God as unique dimensions of Him.

In the bond of loving oneness that Marnie and I built together, we became linked in love as one. We became fundamentally inseparable in our loving oneness. In becoming one with one another we became a reflection of what we are with God – individual and one simultaneously. Living our state of oneness now is participating in the divine. It joins us with the divine.

The special love and oneness that Marnie and I built while she was here with me in her physical body will live on forever in our spiritual lives. That love and oneness is fundamentally spiritual. It will allow us to continue to have our special connection with each other within the overall context of the eternal oneness and perfection that we will share with God and all of creation. We are truly soul mates.

I so want to be with Marnie again in the next chapter of our ongoing love story. I want to see her and know her and have her see me and know me in complete recognition, in total awareness, beyond faith. I want to feel our love for one another. I want to not only see one another, but to see into one another's souls.

Marnie and I were special. We were unique. But our truth is not exclusive. If you hang on to your love, if you believe in your love, if you believe in your beloved, as I surely do, then your bond, your love, will transcend the separations of physical death and living on different planes of being.

Trust in your truth, and rejoice in it. It's nice to be able to rejoice now and then, beyond the tears.

> And then my soul saw you and it kind of went "Oh there you are. I've been looking for you."

Chapter 28: Our Never-ending Love Stories

The Winds

The winds that sometimes take something we love, are the same that bring us something we learn to love. Therefore we should not cry about something that was taken from us, but, yes, love what we have been given. Because what is really ours is never gone forever.

Bob Marley

Those of you who are living through the profound feeling of loss that comes with the physical death of your beloved, now share with me an appreciation of life that could only come from that death. We each share a never-ending love story with our beloved. It is so significant, I can't overstate it. Ultimately, physical death becomes a blessing. It transforms our lives. It can transform our remaining relationships. It can give us a joyful vision of reunion with the soul of our beloved. It is a vision of an exquisite life that could have only been born from the ashes of their physical death.

For me personally, I now have a profound appreciation of how deeply I was blessed in having my relationship with Marnie and in living our love together. Though I wish that I could have lived with the perspective that physical death has provided throughout our relationship, and fully treasured every moment of our exquisite life together, I now realize that in the life to come (in our journey through eternity together) I <u>will</u> have that perspective. I will carry it with me.

It has been in finding my way to God and in coming to see the living reality of Marnie's eternal soul that I have come to this realization. And this realization makes the next chapter and all the future chapters of our never-ending love story truly exciting. And that brings me peace now.

Ultimately, I believe that what is true for me is true for you. Your love story is not over. Its final chapter has not been written. Any regret that you may have been carrying can be transformed into joyful fulfillment in the next episode of your soul's journey through eternity with your beloved. <u>Your</u> unique love story is never-ending. Endings are not in your destiny.

My message to Marnie

I want to share with you the message I wrote to Marnie when I came to these realizations. I encourage you to write your own message to your beloved. I encourage you to feel it fully, and to affirm its truth.

"I hope that I am absolutely filling you with love right now, Marnie. I hope that I am filling you with joy by affirming how much you mattered to me and by recognizing how intensely I love you. I hope that I am making you absolutely glow by expressing my intense love for you now. I want to do that now. I want to do that forever. I look forward to spending eternity with you. You are my heart.

After your body died it was so easy to look back at all the regrets, at all the ways I didn't love you as perfectly as I wish I had. I know I really loved you, but there is so much that I wish I had done then, with the depth, the consistency, the subtlety, and the intensity of the love that I feel for you now.

But I believe now in the reality of your living soul. I believe in the reality of our living connection. And I believe in the reality of our coming rejoining. Feeling these beliefs makes me smile and makes me cry.

I will be with you again. And I will be carrying with me all the knowledge and all the depth and intensity of feeling that was born from the painful ashes of your physical death. I so look forward to it Marnie.

It is in the joining, in the rejoining of our souls, that absolute fulfillment will be achieved for me. The death of your body has become a gift because I know that your soul is real, because God is real. You are my heart Marnie.

Heaven is a state of pure joy and pure love in simply being. Heaven for me will come in rejoining you, Marnie."

Can we even remotely plumb the depths of God with our limited human consciousness? Can we fully plumb the depths of another human being who is a living dimension of God?

No. I don't think so. We can go deeper and deeper into another, but their limits are infinite. The potential depth of our knowledge of another is limitless. The process of loving and learning is never-ending. Marnie and I will share a never-ending love story together. You will share a never-ending love story with your beloved.

We are each unique dimensions of God. God is our essence. I say to Marnie, "We are one in love, and one in God. God is not something separate from us. You are not something separate from me, Marnie. I love you. In our love, you and I are one. You and I in our love, are one with God."

All that I have written about God and Marnie and me is true for you and your relationship with your beloved. Both you and your beloved are indeed unique dimensions of God. You will carry your living souls forward throughout eternity. Though that concept is still mind boggling to me, it gives me real hope. I hope it does for you too. I believe that our destinies and the destiny of our relationships with our loved ones are each meant to be a never-ending story of love and joy -- together.

    In God and the living soul, your tears can be transformed from tears of sadness to tears of joy. Heaven is a state of pure joy and pure love in just being. In your heaven, you will be rejoined with your beloved.

And I'd choose you;
in a hundred lifetimes,
in a hundred worlds,
in any version of reality,
I'd find you and
I'd choose you.

-THE CHAOS OF STARS

Chapter 29: Living now with Marnie's Soul

Marnie is woven into the very fabric of my being. I can't think without thinking of her. I can't feel without feeling her. Nor do I want to. I want to feel her presence constantly. I think of her in every place that I go and in everything that I do. We are truly one, Marnie and I.

As I expressed it to her on a morning walk: "Oneness with you is a fundamental part of my being, Marnie. It is a part of my self-concept. It is a part of who I am. I am one with you, Marnie. I couldn't leave you behind. I couldn't push you into memory. I couldn't move on from you. I couldn't let the death of your body break us apart. We are one. That is our essence."

With that being said, living now exclusively with Marnie's soul requires an ongoing balancing of the feelings of loss with the belief in her presence. My world is shaped by my thoughts and my conversations with Marnie. Interacting with Marnie's soul is the primary dimension of my life now. In doing so I am bringing greater and greater joy back into my life. Here are some of my conversations with Marnie that reflect that interaction:

"When you were alive Marnie, physically alive, I was happy just being. I felt at peace simply being in your presence. I carried inside me a basic feeling of happiness. All I needed was to have you in my life.

Now that you're not here physically, I have to discipline and focus my thinking to feel that sense of peace and happiness. My morning, nighttime, and sunset walks are essential. It is through these that I maintain my connection with you -- that I feel it. Being outdoors in nature helps immensely.

The rest of the time I exercise, I write, and I spend time with the children. The exercise keeps my mood up. The writing and the children give my life purpose. I have to maintain a balance among all these things to keep feeling that sense of peace that came so naturally when you were here with me physically. When I don't keep things in balance, I sink into sadness.

Sometimes it feels like hard work, maintaining that balance, but its's worth it. I love you, girl. I really do miss you. And I need to keep being with you.

I've come to realize that it's when I get lost in the memories of special things we shared together, the special things that I feel I'll never be able to do with you again in this lifetime that I get deeply sad. I can get lost in that sadness. Thinking of you only in memory moves me into sadness. Sadness is the last thing I want.

Joy comes in feeling and expressing my love for you now, and seeking out the ways that I can love with you in me in this lifetime. And joy comes when I look forward to what I can share with you in the next lifetime, when I look forward to what we are going to do together in that lifetime. Those are the most intense sources of joy for me.

But I've also noticed something else. It's the balance between missing you and actively loving you that determines whether it's a good day or a bad day for me. Every day I love you, darling. And every day I miss you. But when I'm missing you intensely, if I let it dissolve me into tears, then I'm transformed back into feeling my love for you. And the bad day becomes a good day. It's only when I'm disconnected from my intense feelings that I'm truly unhappy. I have to fully feel the sadness to find my way back to joy – to find my way back to you.

More than anything now, I'm trying to live my life with the perspective that I gained from the death of your body, Marnie. I realize how profoundly I was blessed by having you in my life. I realize how profoundly important it is to treasure every moment. I realize now what really matters."

Those are some of the thoughts that I shared with Marnie. I try to consciously carry the realizations that I described to her with me every day in everything I do now. For now at least, my life is pretty simple. It's exactly what I described to Marnie. I walk and talk with her. I write and spend time with our children and grandchildren. I exercise, and I pray.

But there are things I've learned in the course of doing those things that I think might be valuable to share with you.

First, I try to take every memory that brings grief into my heart and transform it in my mind into a vision of what we will share in the next chapter of our never-ending love story. So grieving memories become a part of healing, a part of loving Marnie now by sharing with her, and a beautiful vision of what is to come.

A second thing that I do is to look closely at what the lessons are that I need to learn before I rejoin Marnie in the next lifetime. What is the growth that I really need to accomplish to be able to rejoin with Marnie on her level? What are the lessons I need to learn from suffering the physical loss of someone so precious to me? In thinking about this I said to Marnie:

"In our life together, Marnie I did too much 'doing' without maintaining full consciousness of us 'doing together'. I too often lost conscious awareness of you and me in our relationship, sharing together in the doing. Now with the perspective I've gained from the death of your body, I realize that the awareness of our relationship, of our doing together is far more important than just the doing. I look forward to 'doing together' in the next chapter of our never-ending love story.

Love and relationship are what truly matter. Ultimately, love and relationship are all that matter. Seeing now from the perspective of death, I realize that as I was self-centered, I was off track. As I was other-centered, love-centered, I was on track. What really matters is the soul, not the body. The important thing is to care for the body in a way that nourishes the soul, not to just care for the body for its own sake. "I will remember that when I'm with you again, Marnie."

Patience, humility, and forgiveness are fundamental qualities that I need to develop and strengthen before I'll be ready to fully rejoin Marnie in the next phase of our life together. Patience in particular is huge for me. I've always needed to have things "now". Much of the hurt I caused Marnie in our physical life together grew out of my immaturity and impatience in wanting my desires filled "now". So patience is a virtue that I'm being forced to learn "now." To stay alive I have to develop the patience to keep living and loving on this earth while I wait to rejoin Marnie. Patience needs to be a virtue that I accept and embrace so that I can carry it with me into the next chapter of my life together with Marnie.

A third thing I've looked at are the flaws in me that I really need to address so that I can rejoin Marnie without carrying any negative baggage with me. Addressing them also makes me a better human being now in this physical lifetime.

My defensiveness, my need to justify myself, my need to make people see things from my point of view, my obsessive worry about what other people think of me, and the fundamental feelings of inadequacy that tie all those things together – those, I think, are the primary flaws I need to address. Those are traits that I need to change.

I don't want to carry any of that stuff with me into the next lifetime. I don't want to carry anything with me that will limit the quality of the love that I can give to Marnie. I want to root those things out of me in this lifetime. It will benefit me both in this lifetime and in the next.

I have a real tendency to be obsessed about what people say to me. I'm particularly obsessive when I feel like someone has criticized me unfairly in some way. I've carried that trait with me from childhood, and I still affected by it. That needs to change.

I want to let go of my self-importance. My real importance comes from being a child of God. My real importance comes from being Marnie's forever husband. It's in being loved and in loving that I have real worth.

A fourth thing that I do is that every day I describe to Marnie a vision of a "Journey of Love and Joy" that I want to share with her when we rejoin. I share this vision every day at sunset. I describe each of the special places that we kissed at sunset in our physical lifetime together. I describe each of the special things that we did at those places. I describe exactly how I'd like to do and feel those things in sharing them even better on our "Journey of Love and Joy" in the next life. I regularly add new parts to that vision – new places, new experiences in old places, new adventures to share together.

I see, feel, and describe the journey that I want to share with her. I feel it and share it with intense emotion. I almost always weep with the intensity of the feeling I experience in that vision. I do it as an act of love for Marnie now. And I do it as my way of perhaps helping to create a special future in our personal heaven together.

I believe that these are all things that you can share with your beloved as well.

- Transform every memory of sadness into a vision of shared joy.

- Look closely and in detail at the lessons you can learn about yourself from the passing of your beloved into the next lifetime.

- Look closely at the flaws you need to address, and do your very best to address them in this lifetime.

- Create a special vision of what you'd like to share with your beloved your next lifetime together. Let it bring both of you joy now.

I talked with Marnie about our life together now and about my visions for our shared life to come in the next chapter of our never-ending love story. Here is part of that discussion:

"I want to have a real, ongoing relationship with you now, Marnie, while only your soul is present to me. That means I want to know about your world, Marnie, not just talk about mine. But ultimately I don't (and probably can't) know about the afterlife until I die and experience it for myself. I can't know about your world, but I can wonder about it. I have so many questions.

Can we relive things in heaven? Can we do things all over again without carrying the negative baggage that diminished it, that stopped it from being all that it could have been in our physical life together? If we are not limited by time and space and place in eternity, perhaps we can really do that -- go out and live it, live it with all the joy and richness and fullness that we had in our physical lifetime together and bring so much more wisdom and perspective to it the second time around.

I want to be able to go out and play with you Marnie. Will we be able to go out and play together again? I want to be able to climb with you and run with you and wrestle with you and tickle you and laugh together. Can we play together in the afterlife? I want to roll down hills together and kiss you joyfully. I can do that in my mind's eye now. We did that on this physical earth. I want that to be part of our heaven together too. I certainly know what I hope for.

You know I've thought about the fact that thought is creative. So I wondered if in the next life, perhaps the fact that thought is creative can go even further, without limits. Perhaps in our next life together, the thoughts, the visions, all the things that I'd like to share with you can become real. We could create our new reality directly, together.

We could be together on a sailboat out in the ocean. I could gaze on your beauty, watch you create things, and make love with you. And that's just one possibility. I feel truly excited thinking about future lives and future possibilities together -- creating them from our thoughts and visions, and from our love.

Maybe we can create and live multiple lifetimes together, while retaining our consciousness and retaining our awareness of one another. We will always recognize one another's souls. We are bound together in loving oneness in our souls. We can continue to grow, together. We need not lose track of one another, of us, of ourselves, and of our bond as we move in and out of future lifetimes.

And I delight in the idea of really cherishing each moment, every second of the new lifetimes that we create together. Cherishing each and every moment is a gift that has come out of our separation now. I feel profoundly how precious every moment was that we had together before your physical death."

Let yourself get lost in those kinds of visions of the afterlife. Create them. Revel in them. The more clearly you can see and feel them, the more power you give to them. The more likely they are to become reality. And in the process you are showing your beloved how much you care. You are bringing them joy now in weaving dreams about your future together.

I want to re-emphasize the importance of prayer in my daily rituals. For me, prayer has become essential. I begin every morning walk with a prayer for faith. I ask God for a deepening of my faith. I ask that I feel that faith through feeling Marnie's presence. I pray for absolute certainty about the reality of her presence. I ask that I feel her presence deep in my heart and soul. It is in feeling Marnie's presence that my faith in God is confirmed. Then I move on into discussing my day, my thoughts, and my feelings with Marnie.

And my nighttime walk is fundamentally a prayer walk. The walk can begin with me sharing thoughts and feelings with Marnie. It can involve looking back through the day and trying to understand all that I thought and felt. But eventually I shift into prayer. I described much of that prayer in chapter 16. What I described there is the foundation for my prayer every night. But every night it varies. I speak to both God and Marnie from my heart. Sometimes it is quite elaborate. Sometimes it is simple. But as I pray from my heart, my day is transformed. My day is fulfilled. My nighttime prayer is an absolutely essential dimension of my happiness and healing.

Then I come home and read to Marnie. When the reading is done, I tell Marnie how much I love her. And I tell her to have a wonderful night and go wherever she needs to go and do whatever she needs to do as I sleep. ("Good night, darling.")

That's a pretty complete picture of how I'm living my life these days. There's one little side point that I haven't mentioned. It's something that I don't fully understand, but it's something I've found through experience to be true. I connect with Marnie far better when I look up rather than looking down as I walk or bike.

When I look down, I tend to get lost inside myself. I can easily get lost in feelings of negativity and sadness. When I look up, I tend to feel Marnie's presence. I share with her much more fully and comfortably.

I really don't know why these things are true for me. I just know that they are. So I suggest that you be aware of those differences for yourself. And if they are real for you too, look up.

"In my life now, I love more. I love for you, Marnie. I love with you in me, Marnie. I love as you. I love through you. And the more I do that, the more I find that I'm loving for me too. And I believe that in loving you, Marnie, I'm loving God.

Being able to wait is a sign of true *love* & *patience*. Anyone can say "*I love you*," but not everyone can wait & prove that it's *True*.

Chapter 30: A Miracle

I was initially reluctant to write this chapter. It reflects an experience that was so foreign to me, so beyond my level of comprehension that it left me in a state of disoriented confusion. Both of my son's, however, encouraged me to write it. It is an absolutely real occurrence. I am still stunned by it. I have a hard time accepting it as real, even though I can find no way of explaining it away.

I was afraid that the description of this experience might seem so out of the realm of realistic possibility to you, that it might cause you to question the validity of the rest of what I have written. However, you've already read almost everything I've had to offer. I hope and believe that you've already made a positive judgement about its worth to you in your life. So what follows is my experience….

Every day after Marnie's body died, I wore two lockets on a silver chain around my neck. One is a smaller golden locket that Marnie wore when she was 16. She kept my picture in it. The second is a larger silver locket that our son, Jeremy gave to Marnie on our 25th wedding anniversary. It had the name, "Cantkiya" engraved on the back.

After the death of Marnie's body, I began wearing those lockets every day. I wanted to carry her close to my heart. In the smaller locket, I have a picture of Marnie on one side and a picture of me on the other so that when you close the locket we are pressed together. In the larger locket, I have our wedding picture on one side and a picture of Marnie and me with our grandchildren on the other side. I've worn those lockets every day without fail.

This past December (2017) when my son, Ben, his wife, Nellie, and my grandchildren were with me in Florida we went to Siesta beach in Sarasota. The sand is deep, white, and sugary.

The waves are gentle, and the water is warm. (At least it feels warm to those of us from Montana.) We played at the beach all day. I went for a 4 mile run along the water in the course of the afternoon. When I run, I move the lockets to my back where I'm less bothered by their bouncing.

When we were leaving the beach in the late afternoon, as we left the sand and approached the parking lot, I reached up to touch my lockets as I often do. I only had one. The silver locket was gone. I was deeply upset and saddened. I cried. My son Ben offered to run back to the spot where we had spent the day. That was a quarter to a half mile back through the deep sand. And I had run the beach that day. I had also wandered all over the beach with my grandson looking at the sand sculptures that various people had made. I didn't think there would be any way Ben could possibly find a locket the size of a quarter in deep sand along such a long stretch of beach. And sunset was approaching. I said no.

I grieved the loss of something so precious to me. I cursed my stupidity for not noticing it when it fell off the necklace. I'd had problems with the clasp on that locket before. I felt stupid for not having replaced it. But there was nothing I could do. So I went to a private place where I could watch the sunset and talk with Marnie. I had to let it go and move on.

Ben and Nellie and the children went back to Montana the first week of January, and I spent the next three months alone in different state parks, talking with Marnie, talking with God, and writing this book. Every day throughout that time I maintained my rituals. I walked and talked with Marnie and did a short prayer to God asking for faith every morning. I walked and talked with Marnie at every sunset. I walked and talked with God and with Marnie every night.

I have 8 different laminated pictures of Marnie that fit into my pockets. I carry one with me in either my shirt, or my pants, or my jacket everywhere I go. I take them out and press them to my heart when I need an infusion of Marnie's love and strength. I know every one of those pictures intimately. I know which pictures are in which pockets of each item of clothing. When I wash clothes or change what I'm wearing, I move the pictures. I'm always aware of them. I'm compulsive when it comes to Marnie's pictures.

This past March (2018) I was camped at Buccaneer State Park along the Mississippi coast. My faith in Marnie's living presence had been growing progressively stronger in my mind and heart. Every day I had been asking God for that. Every day I had been thanking Him for strengthening my faith. On a morning walk and talk with Marnie I told her how much it means to me to be able to feel her presence. I told her how I felt my belief was growing progressively stronger, but I teasingly said to her, "It sure would be nice if you could somehow give me a really blatant sign that I absolutely couldn't ignore or write off as coincidence to demonstrate to me your living, conscious presence."

Later that day a cold front blew in from the north. I think that was about the same time a nor'easter was hitting the east coast. The temperature along the Mississippi coast dropped into the upper 40's that night. So for my nighttime prayer walk I put on a sweatshirt and got my polar fleece jacket out of the closet of our travel trailer. I hadn't worn that jacket for about two weeks because the weather had been warm and it was unnecessary. However, I had worn it several times when the nights were cold as I was traveling north through Florida in late January and in February. I knew exactly which picture of Marnie was in the inside, left hand pocket of that jacket. It had been there every time I wore the jacket as I traveled north. The left hand, inside pocket is where I always keep the pictures of Marnie so I can easily press them to my heart.

When I felt for the picture this time, it wasn't there. I reached into the pocket. It wasn't there. I checked the right hand inside pocket. I checked both of the outside jacket pockets. There was no picture. I went through the pockets of every shirt and every jacket that I own. That picture was missing. I checked the floor of the closet. I checked every conceivable place in the trailer where I could have possibly put a picture. It was gone. I had 7 pictures of Marnie. The eighth was gone. I knew which picture of Marnie that eighth picture was. I laid out the other seven pictures on the table in the trailer. That picture, which I had been sure had been in the inside left hand pocket of that jacket was gone.

    I went back to the polar fleece jacket and felt for the picture again. It wasn't there. But I felt something that felt like a rock in the bottom of that pocket. I reached in and took out the silver locket with our wedding picture and the picture of us with our grandchildren still in it. The locket was badly tarnished. The clasp was missing. It was as if the locket had been laying outside for a long time. But even through the tarnish, I could read the name, Cantkiya engraved on the back. Cantkiya – to make her my heart.

    I wept, disbelieving. A trade had been made – Marnie's picture for the locket. The picture I can replace. The locket was irreplaceable.

    I had asked Marnie that day for a sign I absolutely couldn't ignore. I got one I couldn't believe. But I hold on to that locket whenever I doubt. It is absolute confirmation of Marnie's presence.

Chapter 31: A Final Perspective – Looking Back

I thought I was done writing this book until I came to Galveston, Texas. It was one of our special places. Marnie and I had been coming here since 1985 when our son, Ben was only two years old. Galveston holds a treasure trove of memories (of us) for me. It is a place that Marnie really wanted to share with our grandchildren. Bringing them here for spring break would have fulfilled another one of her dreams.

So I made reservations to stay here some 8 months in advance when I thought Ben and his family would fly down and join me for their spring break. I never thought I would come here alone. But circumstances arose that prevented Ben and Nellie and the children from coming. I ended up going to Galveston alone.

I felt like I didn't belong. Memories of Marnie were everywhere. Everywhere I went, everything I did, triggered a memory. I wasn't supposed to be there alone, without Marnie. I hurt profoundly. I felt sick inside. I cried and cried and cried and cried for the first two days. I missed Marnie intensely. It felt like grieving was beginning all over again for me. Though I told myself I had the psychological tools to eventually make it through, I felt like I was really failing Marnie to be so sad if I truly believed in her presence. I again had to face the question, "How can I be so profoundly sad if I truly believe in Marnie's living presence?"

Then the insights came. They led me forward and they led me back. They allowed me to feel comfort and healing in the midst of my sadness and grieving. I knew I needed to write just one more chapter. Perhaps for me, this is the most important chapter.

I never know when insights are going to come. They aren't logical extensions of thoughts I've been thinking. They just appear in my mind, and they end up making so much sense to me. I'm surprised by them really. I realize they are a gift that Marnie (or God) has given to me. And I have to respect them as I wish I had respected the intuitive awarenesses I had before Marnie's body died. They lead me on to far more thinking. They led me on to this chapter. I hope it holds as much meaning for you as it does for me.

    I was out on a bike ride in Galveston trying to climb out of my sadness and feel my connection with Marnie. Suddenly a clear thought came into my mind, "It's OK. You're not failing me. You haven't been failing me." It was Marnie speaking to me in my mind.

    I had been feeling like I was failing Marnie when I miss her so much even though she's still real, even though she's still with me and watching over me. But with that message from Marnie my thinking was transformed.

    I was able to say to Marnie, "It's like you're on a trip isn't it? You're not gone. You're just in a different place. It's like when you were away at school in California, early in our relationship, and I was still working back in Boulder (Colorado). You were still real, but you were in a different place. I missed you. We would talk for hours together on the phone. I spent as much money on phone bills as I did on rent back then. I couldn't see you. I couldn't touch you. I couldn't hold you. I could only hear your voice. I really missed you. But of course I knew you were real.

Now you're on another trip. I can still talk to you. But it's like we're talking over the computer now. My camera and microphone are working. So you can hear me and see me. But your camera and microphone don't function where you are. So I can't see you or hear you as you can see and hear me. And I still can't touch you. I can't hold you. I can't kiss you. So of course I miss you. That's not a failing. That's just real. It doesn't in any way negate your reality. I just plain miss you and it hurts. It hurts deeply. I miss you, just as I did when you were away in California. But now I can't even hear you. So the missing you is even more intense.

And I don't know how long we'll be apart. I'm on a job here and I can't come home yet. I can't come home (to your arms) until the work is completed. And I know it is work that you want me to complete. But I still miss you profoundly even though I know you're still real. You can be totally real, and I can still miss you. I'm not a failure for missing you. I love you.

It's taken me a long time to catch on, Marnie. You're still real, and it makes sense that I miss you. That makes it even more special when you wrap me in your love and I feel your presence. It soothes me. And I can feel joy, just being in your presence.

I'm not sure where this insight came from. I think it was born out of my feeling such deep sadness being here in Galveston without you. It's just like it appeared in my mind. You sent it to soothe me. Thank my sweet. I love you so much."

Having that first insight led me to another. I can express it best in the words I said to Marnie,

"You're real aren't you sweetheart. You've been trying to tell me you're real since the moment your body died. I don't know why

I've had so much trouble listening and believing. I don't know why I do so much questioning. But from the bunny to the locket and everywhere in between, you've let me know that you're real, that you're here, and that you love me...."

I need to back up in time to explain.

I don't know if you can see the words clearly in the above photo. It's a poem by Anne Bradstreet. The words are beautiful. (I will include them at the end of this chapter.) I don't remember where I found that poem or how I found it, but I found it the week after Marnie's body died.

The magic is in the line drawing of the bunny in the middle of the poem. The afternoon after I discovered the poem, a bunny, the one pictured in the photograph to the left of the poem, appeared in our back yard. I had seldom if ever seen a bunny in our yard. I took his picture because I was so taken by the fact that he appeared right after I had discovered that poem with its bunny.

The next morning I saved the picture of the poem and the picture of the bunny on my computer. Then I began looking at pictures of Marnie. We have a large deck with glass doors that open out onto that deck from what Marnie and I called our work room. It's where we did all of our sewing for our puppet making together. It's where I do my computer work. My computer desk is directly beside the glass doors.

As I was looking at the photos of Marnie and missing her intensely, that same bunny came up the stairs of the deck, ran across it, and literally leaped up against the glass doors directly beside me. Then he ran back across the deck and back out into our yard.

That memory came back to me vividly in my new insight from Marnie. She has been showing me in every way that she can, since the day that her body died, that she is real. She is still here. She is watching over me. She loves me. And she will do everything that she possibly can to help me make it through until we can be rejoined in eternity.

Since having those two insights, magic for me has been happening all over again. Birds show up at just the right time. Birds call at just the right moment. A single lightening bug flew to me and over me. It's been a restatement, a loud and clear restatement that Marnie's here. I still miss her so very, very much. It makes it hard to listen to the messages. But as I write these words, there are now at least 100 birds (starlings) feeding in the grass directly outside my window. I don't know where they came from. I don't know when they arrived. But they are here and they are a confirmation of the reality of what I have to say.

The insights prompted me to go back and look at my journal from the week that Marnie died. I know that I've shared much with you about the seemingly magical nature experiences I've had in my travels over the last two years which seemed to confirm Marnie's living presence. But now I've gone back to the first week after the death of Marnie's body and discovered that Marnie has always been here with me. I just hurt too much to understand. She is with me still.

I had originally included the story of the locket only as a post script to this book. But the insights that were given to me in Galveston caused me to rearrange the chapters and to add this one. The incident with the locket was stunning to me. It was profoundly difficult for me to accept as real. It represented a fundamental transformation of physical reality. I didn't know if either I or you could accept that.

But I see it now as a part of a whole pattern of miraculous experiences that I can look at with the wisdom of hindsight and perspective and say, "These are a testament to the reality of Marnie's living soul."

I hope they will touch your heart. I hope they will help confirm for you the reality of a living, eternal soul that is our essence. That eternal soul is the essence of your beloved. Your beloved is here. Your beloved is real. Your beloved is watching over you and loving you.

What follows this paragraph are some of the signs that I can now say confirmed the reality of Marnie's living presence and her active love for me. I'm simply going to list them. Sign after sign. They all came in the first month after Marnie's body died. I guess I was a slow learner. It's only now, almost two years later that everything seems so much clearer to me. I think I was in so much pain that first month that it drowned out the messages of presence. Or at least it prevented those messages from sinking in and truly soothing me. Or perhaps it was those messages that soothed me enough to keep me alive for that first month.

Here are the messages, the miracles. I had dreams about Marnie:

- I saw an image of a fabric knot. (Marnie was a fiber artist.) And I heard the words, "We're tied together you and I. So of course I'm here with you."

- I was weeping and I saw an image of Marnie trying to tear a veil and climb through to get to me. Her tears were visibly falling as she said, "Oh sweetie, I'm right here and you're okay."

- I had an image of Marnie wrestling, saying the words, "It's the fight of a lifetime against you to get you to believe."

- I heard her say directly, "It's OK man. I'm with you. We're just beginning…of course I'll recognize you."

- I heard Marnie say, "My breast hurt like hell. Even my fingernails hurt. My body had to go." (The words were precisely, "My body had to go." Not "I had to go".)

In addition to the dreams I had a massive number of experiences in nature the first few months after Marnie's body died that I can now clearly say demonstrated the living presence of Marnie's soul.

The bunny who appeared in our yard the very day I discovered Anne Bradstreet's poem and who jumped against the glass as I thought of Marnie and looked at her pictures seemed to have gone away from our house. But several days later, I was hurting deeply. I was sobbing. I said to Marnie, "I don't know if I can go on." At that moment, when I looked up, the bunny was back, right there outside my window.

After biking 22 miles up into the mountains, on a dirt road leading to a pass between Montana and Idaho, a badger ran down the mountainside and stopped directly in my path, facing me. I stopped. I looked for a long time at the badger who just stood there facing me, unmoving. Then I looked around to get my bearings. I saw that I was precisely at the spot where Marnie and I had stopped, laid out a blanket in the grass in a spot hidden from the road, and made love when we were on a long bike ride together several years before.

In the weeks following her death, when I was hurting and needing her, I'd go outside and walk and talk with Marnie. Magical images would seem to take shape in the clouds. I'd see what appeared to me to clearly be angels. I'd see magical animals, often in pairs that would remind me of her. Marnie was an artist. It made sense that the sky would be her palette.

And these words came to me in a dream, "When shadows pass over you and make you frightened, look up and see the palette, notice Gavin" (our youngest grandson).

Owls, king fishers, crows, dippers, eagles, and a pair of moose all appeared when I was out walking, hurting deeply, and asking for help. Often they would come in pairs.

As I drove home one night weeping and missing Marnie, a blonde black bear walked out onto the road directly in front of me, then ran at full speed for a quarter of a mile down the road. It was exactly like the experience of seeing a blonde black bear running up the mountain side when we were together in Truchas, New Mexico some 37 years earlier.

I swam across Painted Rocks Lake multiple times in the first month after Marnie's body died. I swam to honor her and to try and escape the pain of missing her. As I described earlier, I'm a fearful swimmer. The first time I swam, I was especially afraid to start. But when I did, a whole flock of swallows flew in low, directly over me, and stayed with me all the way across the lake and back. It was as if they were there to protect me as Marnie was when we swam together across the lake in this same spot.

Two months after Marnie's body died, in the week before our wedding anniversary, I spoke with Marnie as I walked. I said, "I need to know that you're here. I need more than a subtle sign. I need blatant. Could you send a dipper or something?" At that moment, a leaf floated down from the sky. I said, "A falling leaf is not a dipper!" A moment later, a dipper flew in landing in the water and leaving a wake behind him. He began feeding.

I walked on to the bridge and stood looking out over the river and wondered if I was imagining things that were really nothing more than coincidence. On my walk back home, when I approached the place where the dipper had landed, I said, "It would be more of a miracle if there were no dipper here." There was no dipper.

Coming home one night after my prayer walk in the wilderness with Marnie I was still feeling sad. I asked for a sign. I came in the house and turned on the television to escape the pain for a while. The show that came on was "America's Got Talent." The performance that began immediately was Linkin' Bridge singing "When I See You Again." I was emotionally floored. There couldn't have been a more touching, powerful sign for me than the lyrics of that song. (I will include some of the lyrics at the end of this chapter.)

I repeat again the words that Marnie said as she was wrestling in my dream, "It's the fight of a lifetime against you to get you to believe."

I'm looking back now, almost two years later, and I see a pattern that I can no longer ignore. It began with a bunny and progressed through dreams. It continued in the clouds and progressed through experience after experience in nature. It culminated in the miraculous appearance of Marnie's tarnished locket. I was so slow to catch on. I was so doubtful of myself. But the messages couldn't have been clearer or stronger – "I'm here. I'm with you. I will always be with you. We will be rejoined."

There has been one more layer of confirmation that has become real to me since I wrote the initial draft of this book. You know that I talk to Marnie directly. I've talked to Marnie since the first week after her body died. Sometimes I ask her questions. I've heard answers to my questions in my mind. But I've always questioned the validity of the answers to those questions. They were thoughts that came into my mind. I feared they were simply creations of my own desire.

Today when I talked with Marnie, I asked, "Do you really answer when I ask you questions? I always hear your answers in my mind, in my mind's voice. And the answers are so often what I want to hear. Do you really answer when I ask you questions?"

The reply I heard in my mind was, "Of course I talk with you in your mind. That's how I have access to you. You hear my replies to your questions as your thoughts because that's the avenue I have available to me to reply. It's the most direct way I can reply."

That was profoundly significant to me. I stopped, stunned. I cried. It opened up a whole new dimension of communication and with that, a strengthened feeling of connection and presence. No longer would everything have to be communicated to me through external signs. Our connection is deepened. Not only do I talk with Marnie every day, now, I listen to her replies. My life is enriched.

One final insight came to me the morning after I initially began writing this chapter. In my mind I saw an image of people sitting together smiling, talking, and saying, "Do you remember when...?" They were sharing memories – memories that brought them joy and laughter.

I realized that memories need no longer sink me into sadness. Instead of remembering and feeling the sadness that comes from thinking, "We'll never be able to do that again in this lifetime," I can now share that memory with Marnie. I can say, "Remember when we ...?" And it becomes a positive, joyful, shared, remembering experience – rejoicing in what we did together rather than grieving its loss.

And, as I said in chapter 29, I can also translate that memory into a vision of what we'll be able to do and share together in the next chapter of our never-ending love story. So I now have two options for transforming memory into joyful sharing.

That is part of healing.

Still, I will always miss holding Marnie, touching her, seeing her, kissing her. There is a part of me that will keep missing her for the rest of my physical life on this earth. Every morning begins with the sadness of realizing that Marnie is not here in her body to share the day with me.

So every morning I need to make the fundamental shift from dealing with physical reality (as if it _is_ reality) into spiritual reality. There God is real and Marnie is real and the soul is real. It's a fundamental shift in a level of consciousness that I have to make.

When I'm sitting stuck in physical consciousness, in physical reality, I'm lost in sadness. When I go out on my morning Marnie walk and make the shift into spiritual reality then I find peace and joy in my heart again. This physical world is real, but it is not all that is real. I have to shift to a higher level of consciousness, a higher level of vibration to move out of the sadness.

I need to get to the point each morning where I can be in physical reality and carry Marnie's spiritual reality with me simultaneously. That's when life will become truly rich again.

The full healing of my heart will come when I am rejoined with Marnie in our next lifetime together. For now though, there is an even deeper level of Marnie's presence available to me as I live in faith.

Grieving and healing are not mutually exclusive. They can happen simultaneously, and for me, they probably always will until I am rejoined with Marnie in the next chapter of our never-ending love story. The same will most likely be true for you and your beloved.

Finally, I think it is important to point out that as of the writing of this book it has been exactly 20 months since the death of Marnie's body. One of the first people I had read the initial draft of this manuscript commented on how, though she believed I had clearly demonstrated the reality of Marnie's ongoing, living presence, she (the reader) was troubled by how much sadness I seemed to still carry.

On one of my walks in a state park wilderness a met a woman sitting alone on a bench by a lake. I stopped and talked with her. She asked if I was here on vacation. I said no. I told her about

Marnie and the book I was writing. She told me that her husband had died 5 years ago. She said that the second year after his death was the hardest. People were more willing to accept her grieving the first year. But the pain didn't go away in one year. The pain and the grieving went on. But in the second year, other people had a hard time staying with her in that grieving process.

I'm still in that second year. Sadness does show through clearly in my writing. But so, I believe, does hope. So does healing. So does the rebirth of joy in my life. And that is because Marnie is fully alive in everything but her body. She is with me. She is with me now.

Over time, the sadness has been easing for me. I believe that with more time, the sadness and the pain of the loss of Marnie's body will continue to diminish. But because I keep Marnie actively alive in my life every day, the feeling of her presence does not and will not diminish. Our connection does not and will not weaken. My joy in loving her and loving with her grows stronger by the day. My connection to her soul continues to grow.

Keeping your beloved fully alive in your heart and in your consciousness brings with it a rebirth of joy. It makes the sadness more tolerable. The sadness will fade slowly into the past. Sadness comes from missing the presence of the physical body of your beloved. That will gradually weaken with time. Joy comes from feeling the presence of their soul. Joy is increasingly strengthened by your connection to their real essence, their real, lasting being.

I think in another year I may have written this book differently. I think it would reflect less sadness and more joy. But I think that writing now, while I'm still in the midst of healing, makes my story more intensely real, especially for those of you who are traveling along on your journey through grieving. My sadness is real, but so is my joy. And I can honestly say that my sadness is diminishing and my joy is growing.

I wish that for you as well. I wish you love, joy, healing, and ultimate fulfillment in rejoining.

I found an entry from my journal from the first month after the death of Marnie's body. It said, "Always remember, you don't have to be perfect to be perfect for one another." That is true for each of us. I was a slow learner throughout our relationship, but I have learned. Please be gentle with yourself.

And in looking through my journal, I discovered a page that had fallen out of one of Marnie's. The entry said, "The world is opening doors for us, guiding us towards our happiness in a way that benefits the world. Coincidences happen. Amazing things happen. Opportunities avail themselves to us to see our dreams come true. We don't let setbacks keep us from believing that God is taking care of us."

I don't believe that finding that entry was mere coincidence. Trust. Neither God nor your beloved will let you down.

How Could We Not Believe (I modified it slightly)

You were so beautiful, how could I not believe?
So beautiful, how could I not believe?
How could I not believe,
Having lived through times like these?
You were so beautiful, how could I not believe?

Ben Harper

Living in Love

If ever two were one, then surely we.
If ever man were loved by wife, then thee;
If ever wife was happy in a man,
Compare with me, ye woman, if you can.
I prize thy love more than whole mines of gold,
Or all the riches the east doth hold.
My love is such that rivers cannot quench,
Nor aught but love from thee, give recompense.
Thy love is such I can no way repay,
The heavens reward thee manifold, I pray.
Then while we live, in love let's so persevere
That when we live no more, we may live ever.

Anne Bradstreet

When I See You Again *(I modified it slightly)*

Why'd you have to leave so soon?
Why'd you have to go?
Why'd you have to leave me
When you know I need you so?
Cuz I don't really know how to tell you
Without feeling much worse,
I know you're in a better place,
But it's always gonna hurt.
Carry on
Give me all the strength I need,
To carry on.
I'll let the light guide my way,
Hold every memory as I go
And every road I take
Will always lead me home…
It's been a long day without you my love
And I'll tell you all about it
When I join you above.
We came a long way
From where we began.
Oh I'll tell you all about it
When I see you again.
When I see you again.

Charlie Puth

Chapter 32: Lessons From Beyond

After finishing the initial writing of this manuscript, thinking it was complete, I read the books "Lessons from the Light" by George Anderson, and "The Light between Us" by Laura Lynne Jackson. Both George Anderson and Laura Lynne Jackson are mediums. They are able to receive communications from souls in the afterlife. Laura Lynne Jackson is a "certified medium" who has been subjected to rigorous scientific testing for verification of her abilities. I would encourage you to read their books for yourself and come to your own conclusions about them.

I am not a medium. What I have presented to you in this book are my thoughts and my experiences. I have tried to open myself to you fully. I have tried to share my thinking and my emotions with you without censorship. My thinking and my feelings led me to some very specific conclusions that I hope I presented clearly. I offered the description of my journey to healing from the physical death of my beloved as a guide for you to consider in your journey of healing from the physical death of your beloved.

For me, my thinking was clear. I considered my conclusions to be true and valid. The path that I chose to follow made sense to me. But ultimately, it was grounded in faith. Everything I presented to you in this book is grounded in faith. I am living in my physical body on this earth still, while Marnie has moved on to what I believe to be a whole different dimension of being. Our eternal connection is grounded for me in faith. What I asked of you was to consider everything that I presented to you and decide if you too were willing to make a fundamental leap of faith to bring about your healing.

Faith is still required. Faith, in my view, is still the key to healing from my loss and yours. But in reading these two books I discovered what was for me, a dramatic level of confirmation that the path I have chosen to follow, the path that I have presented to you, is a valid pathway. It makes absolute sense.

Here is my understanding of some of the important truths communicated directly from souls in the afterlife, as described in these books:

You are not alone. Your beloved is alive. S/he is no more gone than if they were in another country. Death does not and cannot sever the bonds you have with your beloved. Death cannot sever bonds of love. Your beloved is with you all the time. Your beloved has not left you. Your beloved is never going to leave you. Your beloved will always love you. Your beloved is everywhere, all around you.

Our loved ones in the afterlife are without a doubt happy and at peace. They know for a fact that we will be reunited. Though they don't feel the pain of separation as we do, they recognize it in us and try to help us get through it in any way they can. Though they are separated from us on a physical plane, they are fully connected with us emotionally. Nothing separates us but the little time until our rejoining.

Through our thoughts, our actions, our love, and our understanding now we can help our loved ones on the other side continue to grow. Our capacity to love and forgive, our capacity to accept the fallibilities in them and in ourselves is our greatest strength. Every act of kindness and forgiveness is greatly consequential.

The loss we have suffered is only a loss of the physical. In their reality, nothing has been lost by the soul. We can communicate with the soul of our beloved by thinking of them, by praying to them, or by speaking out loud to them. The soul of your beloved hears everything that you tell them. They always know what you are doing. They love to be talked to. They can be with you whenever and as often as you need them. It is never a bother. You are not keeping them from their spiritual growth.

Souls in the hereafter communicate with us, often in subtle ways. It's important that we not dismiss those communications as coincidence. The universe is designed for us to be there for each other.

The books also went on to talk about what souls in the afterlife had to say about the lessons we need to learn from their physical deaths, and about how we need to live our lives on this earth until we can be rejoined with them again. Here are some of those lessons:

In our journey of grief on this earth, faith and hope are our roadmap. The only spiritualism that truly matters is faith in God and love in its purest form. Much of what we will experience on this earth from this point forward is an exercise in faith. But even as faith helps us believe that our beloved continues to live, we must still deal with missing their physical presence. We must still deal with the hole that they leave in our physical existence. The physical loss is a pain that will stay with us until we are rejoined with them.

Crying is probably the most beneficial thing we can do to deal with that loss. It washes our souls clean. We will never "get over" the physical loss of our beloved, but we can grow. We can transform our suffering into a gift. Death forces us out of ordinariness. The sorrow that comes with death helps us put our priorities into perspective.

How we live from this point forward is the most powerful gift we can give to our beloved. It is the most powerful testimony we can give on their behalf. It is through the perspective that comes with the death of their body, that we learn true compassion for others and develop a full appreciation of life and living. We are on this earth to grow in love and to help others do the same.

After the death of our beloved, we each must answer one fundamental question: What is the growth I must accomplish by suffering the loss of someone so meaningful to me? Finding the answer to that question will require spiritual growth. It is growth that we will have to do alone. Our beloved can't help us with it. But it is growth that will help us achieve full rejoining with them.

Anything that we truly love will be waiting for us in the hereafter. Our task is to go forward toward the light (of God) in peace, love, faith, and hope. When you truly love someone, you love them forever.

Sharing our pain and giving and receiving love is how we heal our grief. The greatest gift we possess is the infinite capacity to love and it is in loving that we heal.

That's a small sampling of direct communications from souls in the afterlife. For me, it was a profound confirmation of what I had come to believe in my own mind and heart and tried to share with you in this book. I hope these communications from souls in the afterlife will bring you an increase in faith and hope, as they did for me.

We will be rejoined with our beloved....

*"To the world you may be only one person,
But to one person, you may be the world."*

Afterword

It's so inspiring to hear the stories of survivors. The stories of those who against all odds faced a disease like cancer, fought their way through it, and recovered. They teach us to never give up. They teach us that no matter how impossible the odds, we can fight our way through and come out the other side alive, with a new appreciation for life and a new perspective on what really matters.

Marnie fought with all her heart and soul. I fought alongside her with all my heart and soul. We fought for 4 years and never gave up. We didn't win the fight (in this lifetime). But we did not fail.

There are many, far too many, who die. There are many who fight with everything they have in them and never give up, and still die. They did not fail. We did not fail them. The inspiring stories make me weep. I so wish I was telling one of those inspiring stories about beating cancer in this lifetime. It can feel absolutely crushing to not be telling one of those stories.

But I am here to tell you that we too are survivors. In the perspective of eternity, we did not lose the battle. If we don't give up, if we continue to live love and work to keep our relationship with our beloved alive, we are survivors. Our stories are inspiring. We are the survivors who are here to inspire all of those who also lost their beloved in this physical lifetime.

When you first get it, the diagnosis of cancer can feel like a death sentence. But you need not accept it.

Actual, physical death from cancer feels like the ultimate, irrefutable, undeniable death certificate. But we need not accept that either. We can reject it. We can fight to overcome it. We can discover the eternal life of the soul in and through God. We can achieve ultimate victory and be an inspiration to all the others who have lost someone special. (And ultimately, that will be everyone who ever lives on this earth.)

If you keep your love and your relationship with your beloved alive, you become a model for everyone who lives on this earth. And you live with an appreciation for life and a profoundly new perspective on what really matters that transforms your life.

You become an inspiration. Love glows in you and flows through you. God glows in you and flows through you. There is nothing more important. There is nothing more inspiring.

I believe this to be true about Marnie and me, about you and your beloved:

We are bonded together in God. We are bonded together in love,

Heart to Heart,
Unbreakable Bond
Forever Connected.

Bill Winn

It is my hope that the photo that follows is a vision of Marnie and me in resurrected bodies in the next chapter of our never-ending love story….

www.ingramcontent.com/pod-product-compliance
Lightning Source LLC
Chambersburg PA
CBHW020736160426

43192CB00006B/215